W9-CKB-046

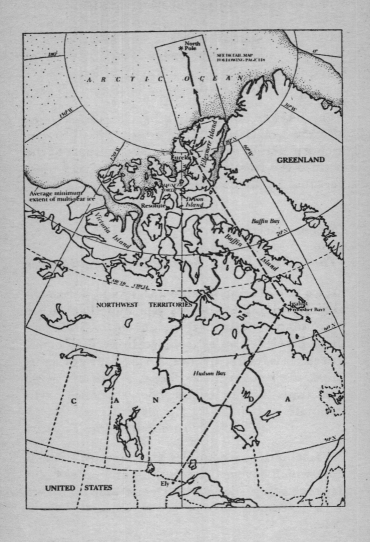

North
*Pole

SEE DETAIL MAP
FOLLOWING PAGE 118

A R C T I C   O C E A N

GREENLAND

Eureka

Ellesmere Island

Resolute

Devon
Island

Average minimum
extent of multi-year ice

Baffin Bay

Victoria Island

Baffin
Island

ARCTIC CIRCLE

NORTHWEST   TERRITORIES

Iqaluit
Frobisher Bay

Hudson Bay

C   A   N   A   D   A

UNITED   STATES

Ely

NORTH TO THE POLE

WILL STEGER WITH PAUL SCHURKE

IVY BOOKS • NEW YORK

Ivy Books
Published by Ballantine Books
Copyright © 1987 by Will Steger and Paul Schurke
Maps copyright © 1987 by David Lindroth

Library of Congress Catalog Card Number: 87-40197

ISBN 0-8041-0407-7

This edition published by arrangement with Times Books, a division
of Random House, Inc.

Manufactured in the United States of America

First Ballantine Books Edition: January 1989

THIS BOOK IS DEDICATED TO THE SPIRIT
OF MATTHEW HENSON,
THE GREATEST UNSUNG HERO IN THE
HISTORY OF ARCTIC EXPLORATION.

ACKNOWLEDGMENTS

The spirit of our endeavor was the collective spirit of the many people who contributed their thoughts, prayers, time, talents, and material assistance to it. We are deeply indebted to you all for your support, and are honored to have shared this dream with you:

Bill and Margaret Steger, parents who nurtured a free spirit in their children with love and encouragement.

Roger and Lois Schurke, who instilled in their children the gift of inquisitive minds.

Susan Hendrickson-Schurke, the third leg of the tripod, who brought stability to our planning process and who served countless hours as the expedition seamstress.

Our support staff, the unsung heroes who lived, worked, fretted, rejoiced, schemed, and dreamed with us for many months: Gaile and Indre Antanaitis, Mary O'Donnell, Darlene Quinn, Chuck Benda, Jon Petra, and Jim Gasperini.

The business staff and volunteers of our Minnesota Support Campaign, spearheaded by Senator Dave Durenberger, who worked diligently to fill our "wish lists" of expedition needs: Jean and Milt Larson, Dick and Debbie Bancroft, Bob Firth, Bill Monet, Donna DiMenna, Terry Lynne Nelson, Sanny Fredericks, Bill Heldt, Judy Stern, Carolyn Larson, Patti Steger, and many others.

The people of Canada's north, whose knowledge and traditions were an integral part of this project.

The sponsors who took the big leap of faith with us, in particular Ken MacRury, Government of the Northwest Territories; Wayne Shufelt, Du Pont Fiberfil; Don Harling, Science Diet Dog Food.

The journalists through whom our story was accurately and sensitively shared with millions of people, in particular Jason Davis, Sharon Schmickle, Sam Cook, Don Fridel, Mike Zerby, and our friends at *National Geographic*.

The millions of followers who took part in this journey vicariously and whose thoughts and prayers gave us the extra edge we needed to reach the top.

Thank you. We felt all of you standing by us every step of the way.

CONTENTS

PROLOGUE   1

THE ODYSSEY BEGINS   7

THE FIRST WEEK
WE MEET THE ADVERSARY   35

THE SECOND WEEK
CROSSING THE SHEAR ZONE   99

THE THIRD WEEK
A STORM STRIKES   139

THE FOURTH WEEK
OUR FIRST FAREWELL   163

THE FIFTH WEEK
THE BIZARRE ENCOUNTER   191

THE SIXTH WEEK
DESPERATION CAMP   219

THE SEVENTH WEEK
THE FINAL DASH   241

THE EIGHTH WEEK
THE POLE   253

EPILOGUE   279

APPENDICES

APPENDIX A: The Team Eighteen Months Later   289

APPENDIX B: Daily Log   292

APPENDIX C: Typical Daily Rations   294

APPENDIX D: Our Dogs—The Real Heroes of the
                 Journey   295

APPENDIX E: Equipment Used on the Expedition   297

APPENDIX F: Psychological Profile of the Steger
                 Team   299

APPENDIX G: Medical Profile of the Steger Team   303

PROLOGUE

Our bodies, weary and bent from endless pushing on 1,000-pound sled loads, bolted upright. The dogs, too, snapped to attention, poised in alarm at the muted rumblings coming from a nearby twenty-foot mound of rubble ice. On March 15, 1986, Day 8 of our dogsled journey across the Arctic Ocean to the North Pole, the deep silence of the polar sea was broken. The moment we had dreaded through years of planning and preparing for this epic adventure was upon us.

In a momentary burst that roared to a crescendo like an avalanche, the ice had begun to shift. Huge, city-block-sized plates of firm, older sea ice, called pans, which cover the ocean in a quiltwork pattern, were being squeezed together by titanic forces in the deep black waters beneath. It was like an earthquake at sea. As the eight of us watched from our refuge in the center of the pan, jumping in place and windmilling our arms to bring warmth to limbs numbed by −60-degree temperatures,* the ridge of cobalt blue blocks that bordered our pan like a hedgerow was thrust skyward to a height of forty feet. The ten-foot-thick ice beneath our feet groaned under the stress and began to throb like a giant heartbeat. Our five teams of dogs milled about nervously, some cowering alongside the sleds.

Some fifty miles out to sea, one-tenth of the distance to our goal, we had reached the zone where powerful ocean currents beneath the ice gain leverage over the intense cold that holds the ocean surface near the shores of Canada's high Arctic islands in frigid suspension. Dubbed the "shear zone" by early polar explorers, this transition zone between land-fast ice and moving pack ice had been found by many of them in certain years to be laced with gaps of open water, called leads, that can meander like a stygian river for hundreds of miles across one's route. Some early expeditions, including one of Admiral Robert Peary's turn-

*Temperatures throughout the book are calibrated in Fahrenheit.

of-the-century attempts to reach the Pole, were critically delayed as the explorers waited for mile-wide gaps of black, fog-enshrouded water to close or refreeze.

Standing transfixed in apprehension and wonder, Paul Schurke and I, the leaders of this seven-man, one-woman expedition, pondered what fate the fickle polar sea would deal us. Our goal, in a deliberate throwback to Peary's days, was to reach the Pole solely by our own power and perseverance and that of our forty-nine sled dogs. Having embarked from Canada's northernmost shore with five sleds carrying 7,000 pounds of food and gear for the estimated sixty-day journey, we were determined not to rely on aircraft to hopscotch us over difficult stretches or bring in additional help or supplies when the going got tough. Unlike all other surface journeys to the Pole since 1909, the year when Peary's crew claimed to be the first to reach the top of the world, ours would be entirely self-reliant, pitting people and sled dogs against some of the most hostile and desolate surroundings on earth.

More than anything, this expedition was to be a giant exercise in faith: faith in the indomitable power of the human spirit, faith in the skills, knowledge, and resourcefulness my teammates and I had accumulated through years of wilderness travel, and faith in the fortitude of our Siberian huskies and Canadian Eskimo dogs. The kind of faith that moved mountains would, we believed, move our sleds and us over an ocean of shifting ice.

Though we stood to make history by accomplishing the first confirmed "unsupported" or "unresupplied" trek to the North Pole, it was this exercise in faith that gave Paul and me the real power to pursue our dream. Starting a few years ago with empty pockets and a lot of grit, the two of us had scratched together a half-million dollars' worth of sponsored funds, materials, and equipment, working from our wilderness base camp near the Canadian-border town of Ely, Minnesota. From among our acquaintances and through recommendations, we selected six other team members: carpenter and dog driver Bob Mantell, thirty-two, a trusted traveling companion from earlier expeditions; New Zealander Robert McKerrow, thirty-seven, a wilderness-skills instructor with Antarctic experience; Canadian cross-country skiing medalist Richard Weber, twenty-six; Alaskan Geoff Carroll, thirty-five, an Arctic wildlife biologist; Minnesotan Ann Bancroft, thirty, a physical education teacher and mountain climber; and Brent Boddy, thirty-one, a veteran dog driver and resident of Frobisher Bay, an Eskimo village on Canada's Baffin Island.

For the previous six months the eight of us and our seven-member support staff had been together—for four months in Ely and two in Frobisher Bay—conditioning ourselves, training dogs, building sleds, tailoring clothing, packaging rations, and making numerous short forays or "dress rehearsals." The training had been intense and thorough. But it was barely adequate preparation for the ordeal that we were now undergoing. These first days on the trail were an immersion in a journey that would prove to be a far greater physical epic than any of us had ever imagined. For testing sheer fortitude, it would have no equal among the many endeavors my team members and I had previously undertaken. We would be obliged to operate at full capacity—mentally, emotionally, and physically—during every waking hour for two months. Cold, hunger, fatigue, and despair would haunt us almost daily. We would fight our way inch by inch over ramparts of ice, sometimes pushing, pulling, and prying for hours on end, yet gaining only a few hundred yards.

It would be a journey in which we would learn as much about ourselves as about the vagaries of the polar sea. Occasional bouts of self-doubt, the whispers from inside that say, "You can't make it," would drain our energy as surely as would the rigors of the cold and the sea ice. Yet in blind faith we'd carry on. The brutal conditions would eventually claim the health of two of our team members, who would have to be evacuated with injuries. And they would claim the life of one of our sled dogs, the animals with whom our well-being became ever more closely intertwined as the journey progressed. We found ourselves alternately cursing at and crying for these dogs, whose power was desperately needed to move our lifeline of food and fuel, yet who suffered from the deep cold and total fatigue as much as we did.

As a team, our strength lay in our single-minded focus and the diversity of our skills. But the bonds between us would be severely strained. Camaraderie would wear thin as we spent each night in the same tight, frosty quarters, huddled together for warmth. As food stores became depleted, diversity of opinion over strategy would seriously erode group unity. Fears of an open clash would prey on our minds. And then would come that magic moment when it suddenly dawned clear in all of us that we'd make it, and the joy of victory would sweep us forward. Marching along like kids on parade, we knew we would soon stand at the point around which the planet spins.

THE
ODYSSEY
BEGINS

AN AWESOME ASSEMBLY

"DOGS UNDER OUR SEATS, DOGS IN THE AISLES.
DOGS EVERYWHERE!"

FROBISHER BAY, NORTHWEST TERRITORIES—Our odyssey
into the high Arctic had begun March 1, 1986. Early that morning, the frigid predawn stillness of Frobisher Bay, an Eskimo
village on Baffin Island in Canada's eastern Arctic, was abruptly
broken by the roar of a plane sweeping in for a landing. We had
chartered this Hawker-Siddeley 748 cargo plane to carry our
expedition 1,200 miles due north to Ellesmere Island, from
where we would venture out onto the polar sea. This day represented the culmination of three years of planning, preparing, and
training. Our assembly of people, dogs, equipment, and supplies
would be funneled into an air freighter, severing ties with our
support base. This pivotal moment was one I had anticipated
apprehensively for months. I had envisioned our departure from
Frobisher Bay as a bittersweet affair, filled with prolonged goodbyes. An orderly progression of supplies, equipment, and dogs
would file into the plane and we'd lift off. Reality to the contrary,
the episode that followed was one I find almost too traumatic to
remember. We were about to get a glimpse of the magnitude of
the project we had taken on. Life's lesson never to rely on pre-
conceptions was once again to be painfully taught us.

The pilots of the plane scheduled to fly our expedition northward hurried from the predawn stillness into a bunkhouse to
catch a few hours sleep before our flight. Most of our team and
support staff had been up nearly all night loading, packing,
organizing, and bracing themselves for an emotionally wrenching farewell. Bob McKerrow had awakened with the sound of

9

the plane and was stirring people from their sleep. He found Bob
Mantell draped over his sled, snoring away, still clutching the
lashings he had been tightening during the night. Paul and his
wife, Susan, who had turned off the sewing machine on which
she had just made final adjustments to gear, were spending a last
quiet moment together with their infant daughter, Bria.

Our support staff, Mary, Indre, Gaile, and Jim, were preparing the "last supper," actually a pancake breakfast, in the cook-
house. McKerrow made a final phone call across the world to
say goodbye to his wife, Joan, and five young daughters in New
Zealand. One by one, Anita, Tania, Ruia, Kira, and Aroha
shared a final fleeting connection with Dad. But the satellite
phone link between their semitropical environment and the Arctic did little to increase their comprehension of the journey he
was about to undertake. Brent arrived from his house in town
and began shuttling more truckloads of supplies to the airport.
By 7:00 A.M. our entire expedition, minus team members and
dogs, was assembled in one pile for the first time on the airport
runway alongside the 748. The workhorse of the Arctic, this
plane has an official capacity of 11,000 pounds. Unofficially, it
will take a third again as much, depending on the length of the
flight and the pilot's discretion.

I arrived with the last load, surveyed the monstrous pile, and
then peered inside the cargo hold of the plane. My heart skipped
a beat. It was definitely a very serious case of trying to cram a
size-twelve foot into a size-eight shoe. I called Paul. "We have
a very serious space problem down here," I said. He read the
anxiety in my voice. "I'll be right there," he replied.

During our preparations in Ely, we had filled numerous
sketchpads with notations and mathematics attesting to a load
calculated to be comfortably within our chartered aircraft's
11,000-pound limit. Conversations with flight crews in Frobisher
had reassured us that the immense volume of our five sleds
would fit, as long as the upstanders and bags were removed.
People, dogs, food, and equipment could certainly be shoe-
horned in somewhere, we figured. But the expedition on paper
differed dramatically from the one on the runway.

The weight and volume of our expedition package had taken
a quantum leap in January when we decided, after considerable
debate, that we would need a fifth dog team and sled. Our goal
had been to keep initial sled payload weights to around 1,000
pounds each. An additional sled and dog team, plus the food to
sustain them, contributed 1,000 pounds to the load, but would

reduce the initial payload weight per sled by a few hundred pounds. What with the bits and pieces of equipment that were added piecemeal to packs during the Frobisher training, we were now looking at a planeload whose weight far exceeded estimates. Blind optimism had kept us thinking it would somehow all fit. We had made a big mistake by not doing a full dress rehearsal in Frobisher, loading up all five sleds as they would be on the sea ice, weighing them in, and comparing their volume with the cargo space in the plane. We now paid the price for this oversight.

As Paul and I pondered the situation, the four journalists who would accompany us on the flight arrived, loaded with bags of cameras and clothing. All we could do was start loading and hope for the best. At 9:00 A.M., while we were loading the third sled, forklifts came rolling out from the hangar, headed for the plane. The flight crew had grown very anxious about the sheer mass of material being hoisted into the plane, and had called for a weigh-in. Everything still on the runway was hauled to a massive scale in the hangar, while baggage handlers crawled over the gear already on board, "guesstimating" the weights. Adding in the projected weight for fifty dogs and twelve people, their estimate put our total load at 15,000 pounds, two tons over the plane's limit. In shocked disbelief, Paul and I questioned their computations. We knew the expedition had bulged a bit in the preceding weeks, but couldn't believe we had so grossly exceeded our projections. Our anxiety led to suspicions, which later proved unfounded, that the charter service was trying to stick us with a second 748 charter flight, so that they could rake in another $21,000. We, too, "guesstimated" the load on board and noted the figures on the scale in the hangar. Our computations put us at around 2,000 pounds overweight. That, too, was a considerable amount, but, we consoled ourselves, would fit in a Twin Otter, a smaller plane that would cost $12,000 to charter. We later learned that the airline's weight estimate was the closer one. In any case, we were suddenly faced with a serious cost overrun. With blind faith we felt that somehow our business coordinator, Jean Larson, and her volunteer support staff back home would find a way to raise that amount.

Relations remained tense but cordial between us and the flight crew as we debated the weight figures. During the shuttling process, piles of gear and supplies had been spread out in various locations. The arguments centered on which piles had been accurately figured into the weight estimates and which hadn't. Utter confusion reigned. Before the dispute was finally settled, we unloaded, weighed, and reloaded the entire expedition three times. Meanwhile, Paul and I raced back and forth between the hangar, the plane, and the charter office, hammering out solutions and trying to keep tabs on the flow of our precious supplies.

The amount of stress we were under was mind-boggling. We were running substantially over budget, dealing with irritated people, and watching gear that had been carefully organized in units get shuffled about like cards in a deck. And all that stress was being loaded on frazzled minds and bodies that had not gotten a decent night's rest during our six weeks of training in Frobisher.

Our media crew, observing the chaos on the runway, saw a dramatic news story brewing. Cameras, microphones, and notebooks were in action all around us. Fortunately, the crew was sympathetic and they allowed us a fund-raising plug as part of their story. But their fervent inquiries just added to our frustration. After much negotiating, the charter service said they would accept our load if we trimmed 3,400 pounds from it. We jettisoned 400 pounds of dog food and found that the remaining 3,000 pounds could be shipped by a commercial flight scheduled to leave a few days later for Resolute, an Eskimo village roughly halfway between Frobisher and our departure point on Ellesmere Island. From there it would have to be shuttled in two Twin Otter loads to Ellesmere. This plan would keep the unexpected debt load to just under $10,000. But the real cost, which filled us with anxiety, was the risk we faced by leaving precious expedition supplies, including several cases of food, two sleds, and our canoe, to the vagaries of airline schedules and baggage handlers who had no idea that our load was worth its weight in diamonds. If a single case of supplies was misplaced en route, the expedition's chances for success or, worse yet, our health and safety, might be jeopardized.

At 3:00 P.M. the pilots announced that because of diminishing visibility we would have to finish packing in half an hour or the flight would be canceled. We threw on the rest of the gear in a frenzy. Dogs were loaded through both doors, each dog tethered by a short line to clips on the floors or walls of the plane, or perched on sleds and drums of fuel. After every inch of surface space in the hold was covered by the shadow of a dog, we still had ten left to load. Mantell surreptitiously began stuffing them around and under the seats of the passenger quarters. That, we knew, was a no-no. Fortunately, the flight crew kindly let the rules slide, though as a precaution they lined the floor with a layer of plastic and an inch of cat litter.

Regulations required that one flight attendant be stationed in the passenger section during the flight. That job was filled by a young woman from Ottawa who had cheerfully told us earlier that day that she had requested the flight because it sounded exciting. When she climbed on board and looked across a sea of dogs, she broke into tears and sought refuge in the bathroom to muffle her crying. Her apprehension was understandable. McKerrow poetically captured the scene in his journal: "Five dogs were put in the seating area which had but twelve seats for eight team and four media crew members. Dogs under our feet, dogs in the aisles. Dogs everywhere!"

As final items were loaded, Ann noticed that Hank, one of my dogs, was missing. The pilots, watching the weather darken, were growing anxious. "Finish loading in fifteen minutes," they shouted, "or the flight is canceled." Ann caught a ride in a truck idling nearby, and frantically began searching the town for Hank. He had apparently slipped his chain and was nowhere to be found. So she grabbed Slidre from the kennel at Brent's house to take his place. She arrived at the plane as the pilots were beginning to fire up the engines, and hoisted Slidre up into the hold, but we could find absolutely no place to put him. One dog would have to be bumped. Mantell offered to leave behind his dog Jean, who had a slight injury on a foot pad. Thus we embarked for the Pole with the awkward number of forty-nine dogs.

The final farewell was over in a flash. After a blur of hugs, tears, and goodbyes, the plane door closed. A small group of villagers had also gathered to see us off. Paul and I gave a final bear hug to Ken MacRury, the regional government director whose imagination had been piqued by our dream and who had so generously assisted us with our training in Frobisher. The last hug was for Susan, who had Bria snugly protected from the wind and cold in the papoose-style hood of her Eskimo parka. Paul and I boarded the plane and, through the porthole windows, waved farewell for the last time.

Feeling very nervous, we took special care in tightening our seat belts, taking some solace from the fact that Bradley Air pilots are, by reputation, among the best in the world. As the plane taxied for takeoff, the tensions I was shouldering suddenly poured out in tears. I cried out of fear for the flight, out of relief of finally being under way, and out of heavy sadness for the separation from loved ones left behind on the runway. The moment of truth was upon us. Years of dreams and efforts had been funneled into this moment.

When I looked out the window again, Frobisher Bay was drifting off into the distance as a memory. Joyous relief swept over me. The day's monumental hassles were behind us now. Having placed part of our expedition in the hands of cargo people still left an edge of discomfort, but it was simply one of the many steps in launching this expedition in which we had to operate on blind faith.

The team members sitting around me were pensive, chins resting on hands folded in prayer. But the flight was smooth and we slowly relaxed and began chatting among ourselves as the flight attendant, who had regained her composure shortly after takeoff, passed out sandwiches and fruit. Though no one dared break the reverie by broaching the topic, our minds were all fixed on the North Pole. Despite the chaos of the day, our determination was as strong as ever. As I looked around, the scene of our team members and dogs huddled tightly together, flying north into the Arctic night, filled me with a sense of strength and confidence. Brent, straddling a sled in the cargo hold, was having little trouble keeping peace among the dogs. Only an occasional muffled growl could be heard. I was proud of "our boys." In their overheated panting, one could sense that they too were excited about the magnitude of the event. From previous expeditions, they had learned to sense when a big adventure was in the making and were now as anxious as we were, I was sure, to hit the trail.

After stopping briefly at the northern Baffin village of Pond Inlet to refuel, we carried on to finish the six-hour flight to Eureka, the layover point from which we would shuttle gear to northern Ellesmere by ski plane. At 9:30 P.M. the thick darkness outside our windows was broken by the red and green lights that marked the runway of Eureka. A weather station established in the 1960s by the Canadian government, Eureka houses some ten year-round staff with additional space for visitors to the high Arctic. Mantell and I had arrived here once before, by dogsled in 1982, as part of our eighteen-month trek across the Arctic. The station, a neat collection of two dozen shiny tin buildings, is located at eighty degrees north on Slidre Fiord, along the western edge of Ellesmere Island. My dog Slidre had been given to me by the staff during our stopover here four years ago. I pondered the ironic circumstances under which Slidre was now revisiting his birthplace.

We circled, landed, and taxied to a stop alongside a group of trucks. Their headlights were trained on the plane doors, which the flight crew now found to be frozen shut. As they pushed and pried, our dogs grew edgy and we sweltered in our Arctic clothing. Finally they cracked it open and we bailed out into the −45-degree night. Station chief Dennis Stossel welcomed us graciously to this little oasis. The pilots cut the engines and joined the relay gang that was removing dogs and gear from the plane. They worked feverishly, knowing that if the plane batteries cooled, the big twin engines would be unable to start. In forty-five minutes, all was unloaded. The engines roared to life again, and the plane disappeared south into the ink-black night.

I took a moment to walk away from the glow of the runway lights and gaze at the North Star. It glimmered nearly straight overhead, 80 degrees from the horizon, 10 degrees from the zenith. We were but 720 miles from the North Pole. The umbilical cord to friends, family, and support staff had been severed. We were committed now. There would be no turning back until we reached our goal; the only direction home was north. Though the day's events had sunk us deeply into debt, worries were not on my mind. The penetrating cold had sparked my spirit. Vitality welled up in my worn body. I looked up again at the North Star, twinkling against the dancing green curtains of the aurora, and smiled.

Ever since I was a child, I had dreamed about the remote places of the world, like the one the North Star leads to. I believe I was a born explorer. Though I was the second oldest of nine children, I ventured out more often on my own or with my neighborhood gang than I did with my siblings. Growing up in the suburbs of Minneapolis, I was always drawn to the tiny woodlot refuges surrounded by burgeoning blocks of homes. Colors, sounds, birds, and flowers mark my earliest memories. My father, a materials engineer who developed and marketed his own water filtering system, was a strong believer in giving his children the freedom to explore, to follow their curiosity. He and my mother rarely held us back. They also taught us that we could reach our goals if we were willing to work very hard for them.

Like most adolescents, I was big on sandlot sports, football and baseball. But when I was nine, my interests began to diverge from those of my friends. While they joined school and city park teams, I was drawn ever more steadily toward the outdoors and adventure. Destiny was calling when I traded my hockey skates for a stack of old *National Geographic*s from a neighbor down the street. I remember how excited I was as I pulled my sled home stacked high with dusty yellow journals. That magazine became my major source of inspiration. A 1958 feature on a Yukon River journey led me to kayak through Alaska when I was eighteen. Another story, on the Sierra Nevada, inspired me to spend my savings on manila rope at the hardware store and head out to climb the mountains of the far West. My other key source of imaginative vision was *The Adventures of Huckleberry Finn*. When I first got hooked on it, I carted the heavy volume around for a month, reading a page at a time at my locker at school, during class breaks, or before altar-boy practice.

My fascination with the north first registered the night I had my first baby-sitting responsibilities at home. When my folks came home at midnight, they took me outside to share an unforgettable scene with them. The northern lights, Aurora Borealis, were in full regalia, shimmering in myriad pastel shades. This was in the days before the Sputnik satellites had shed light on their origins. No one knew for sure what caused northern lights. My dad shared the mystery with me, conjecturing that they might be radio signals from another planet, or perhaps reflections of sunlight off the Arctic Ocean. The idea of a link between these dancing lights and the polar ice cap caught my attention. Something clicked. I was drawn north.

I studied geology at St. Thomas, a Catholic college in St. Paul, Minnesota, and spent my summers in the north—the Yukon and Alaska. With a friend or two, I'd kayak, canoe, and hike the land, setting aside enough time to earn each year's tuition through high-paying "bush" jobs—fighting fires, surveying, or loading river barges. Having strong misgivings about the Vietnam War, I secured a draft deferment by getting a master's degree in education and teaching high school science for three years.

At twenty-five years of age, I felt I had gained what urban life had to offer me, and moved north to a remote, forty-acre tract of land I had purchased for $1,000 six years earlier. There, on a tiny lake near the Boundary Waters Canoe Area in northern Minnesota, nearly two miles from the nearest road, I carved out a home from the trees and rocks, learning woodworking and masonry by trial and error, and built a log cabin, workshop, sauna, and root cellar. Like so many other people in the 1970s, the "back to the land" movement had captured my imagination.

When my savings ran out—money earned from driving cabs and working at assembly-line jobs during my last years in the city—I led wilderness trips for the nearby Voyageur Outward Bound School. In helping them establish a winter camping program, I found that travel and camping in the cold gave me a sense of robust health and vigor that I had never experienced before. I was hooked. In 1973, I leased a team of dogs from a friend and opened my own winter business, Lynx Track Winter Skills School. During the next ten years, my various staff people and I would lead dozens of winter courses for varied groups—colleges, grade schools, chemically dependent teenagers, disabled persons, children—introducing them to dogsledding, snowshoeing, skiing, building snow shelters, and winter camping in five- to fifteen-day trips. The school was a source of income, a source of freedom from traditional employment, and a means of developing a dog team so that I would have the mobility for venturing north into the Arctic winter.

A HIGH ARCTIC INTERLUDE

"IN THE ARCTIC THERE IS NO HURRY."

EUREKA, NORTHWEST TERRITORIES—We awoke late the next morning, and our striking surroundings were unveiled in the fleeting daylight of the Arctic winter. Perched along barren slopes that sweep up from Slidre Fiord, Eureka has special charm. The distant, snow-covered hills blended gently with a frozen sea in a breathtaking panorama. Adding to the unique vista was a huge lone iceberg, grounded just offshore and protruding like a miniature, baby-blue Matterhorn some 100 feet above the shimmering sea.

The dozen shiny tin prefabricated buildings are sturdily braced against extreme wind and cold. Thickly insulated pipes strung through steel trestles pump heat and power from the engine house to the barracks and work buildings. Smaller sheds dotting the premises shelter instruments to track weather systems that sweep south from the Arctic in winter and impact on much of North America.

We were stopping over in Eureka merely to change planes.
Because the 748 was too large to land on the ice shelf along
Ellesmere's northern coast, Bradley Air would be shuttling us
there in several loads by Twin Otter ski planes—smaller, one-
ton-capacity craft whose powerful engines allow them to take off
on very short airstrips. These planes were based in Resolute, 400
miles southeast of Eureka, on Cornwallis Island. But when we
awoke late the next morning, we learned that Resolute was
gripped by a snowstorm. Thus our departure would be delayed.

We busied ourselves by sifting through personal gear, which
we spread out on bunks in the tiny, cloistered rooms of an unused
barracks. Early that afternoon we played an expedition version
of "show and tell," looking over each other's display of gear to
make certain there were no unnecessary duplications in equipment. We shed a few pounds in the process. For example, some
of us opted to double up on toothpaste and some of the younger,
less experienced team members jettisoned clothing that they
learned from older team members was of questionable value. In
Frobisher, Paul and I had allocated an eighteen-inch-by-three-
foot duffel bag to each team member. Our personal "worlds"
would amount to whatever we could fit into them. The only
frivolous items we allowed were a few party favors for the Pole,
and mementos of little weight and volume. My party kit, for
example, consisted of four Mickey Mouse balloons, a pair of
rhinestone-studded sunglasses, and a lavender sequined hat.
There were only a few books along. McKerrow, our resident
evangelist, had a tiny New Testament, and Ann had Viktor
Frankl's *Man's Search for Meaning*—minus its cover, to save
weight.

We spent some time relaxing in the station lounge that afternoon, finding ourselves straddling two worlds—anxious to hit
the sea ice but hesitant to let go of the warm beds, showers, and
sumptuous meals to which we had access. "We lounge around
the comfortable facilities at Eureka in overheated buildings," I
wrote in my journal, "eating pastries, and watching TV as the
bitter winds blow by frosted windows. My restlessness is dulled
by the luxury of excess time, the first I have had in six months.
Mesmerized by the conveniences, it's hard to conceive life as it
will be on the sea ice at −60. We quietly wait, sipping tea over
light conversation and pastries. Billiard balls crack, silly game
shows blare on the large-screen TV. Outside the frosted windows, the wind drives snow parallel to the ground."

We were anxious about the delay because every day spent

sitting in Eureka meant one less day to reach the Pole before the advancing Arctic spring weakened the sea ice. But we kept reminding ourselves that in the Arctic there is no hurry. "Here you adapt around the conditions," I wrote, "for the Arctic will never adapt to you. The Arctic is the ruling force up here, and when you learn this, it is the great relief, for you can relax and simply take each moment as it comes."

It was one of the first days Paul and I had been able to relax in more than three years. We had been operating at a frenetic pace ever since I'd asked him to join me on this project, three years after he'd become involved with my winter program, Lynx Track. Tall and slender, with Nordic blue eyes and blond hair, he shared with me the drive, spirit of adventure, and willingness to tackle huge projects and hard work that I knew would be a prerequisite for reaching the Pole. Expedition business manager was his chief role among many during the planning years. A proficient wordsmith, he felt as much at home behind the word processor, cranking out sponsorship proposals, as he did on the trail, driving a team of dogs. Born and raised in Minneapolis, the fourth in a family of six, he also had shown a keen interest in adventure at an early age. His first major sojourn, a survival camping trip at thirteen, found him eating "minnow hash" along the shores of a wild river in northern Wisconsin while he stared at a canoe wrapped neatly around a rock at the brink of a falls.

Undaunted, he went on to become involved in many outdoor education programs, and after graduating in 1977 from St. John's University, a Catholic liberal arts college in central Minnesota, he and a friend, Greg Lais, founded Wilderness Inquiry II, a nonprofit program that opens wilderness adventure opportunities to persons who are deaf, blind, or paralyzed. The program was designed to stretch people's horizons and to be a social experiment. Its key feature is that each group is integrated so that a wide range of ages, backgrounds, levels of experience, and physical abilities are represented on every trip. The challenge of the wilderness then becomes the common denominator, serving to help people overcome stereotypical attitudes about physical differences. The experiment worked. The program grew rapidly and, in 1987, it entered its tenth year offering several dozen trips all over the continent. From his experiences with it, Paul gained his favorite maxim: "It's not the size of your resources or abilities that counts, it's the size of your dreams." And he gained a life partner, Susan Hendrickson, a diminutive and spunky recreation therapist whom he met along the canoe trail.

Through Wilderness Inquiry II, he also met me. In 1980 he and Susan, now a trip leader, were looking for a winter outlet, a counterpart to canoeing that would make the winter wilderness accessible. Dogsleds seemed an option. They contracted with Lynx Track to offer a pilot trip. Riding in "zip ships," short sleds pulled by two dogs, the disabled participants were able to gain independent mobility in the winter woods. Wilderness Inquiry's winter program was launched, as was my partnership with Paul. A year later, Paul and Susan left their home and jobs in Minneapolis—he was working as a magazine editor—to live in my cabin for a winter and run Lynx Track while I embarked on my third Arctic dogsled expedition.

Ely became their home, and in August 1985, in the midst of expedition planning, their daughter Bria was born. As the expedition clothing designer and seamstress, Susan now did double duty. With Bria in a cradle alongside the sewing machine in their tiny three-room house, she produced much of the clothing for the team members, the harnesses and booties for our dogs, and bags and tarps for the sleds. Working as hard and long on the project as Paul and I, she formed the third leg of the tripod that held the dream up as it took shape. The strength of their family unit added stability to the project. Playing with Bria became a favorite distraction for all of the team members during our months of training. Now, with the expedition about to be launched, Susan was staying with her parents in Red Wing, Minnesota, a quiet Mississippi River town, helping our business manager, Jean Larson, tackle the mounting debt.

In Eureka late that afternoon, a Twin Otter arrived that had slipped out of Resolute during a lull in the storm. It was carrying a three-man British expedition team that was also on its way to northern Ellesmere and had stopped in Eureka for the night to refuel. The group was headed by Ranulph Fiennes, a well-seasoned English adventurer whom I had met several years before when he passed through Minnesota on a lecture tour. A fledgling polar adventurer at the time, I won a drawing after his talk for an autographed copy of his book *To the Ends of the Earth, the Transglobe Expedition: The First Pole-to-Pole Circumnavigation of the Globe.* He and several companions, including the two who were with him now, had circled the globe north to south via jeep, ship, snowmobile, and rubber boat between 1979 and 1982. Ran claimed they were spending three months studying pack ice along the Ellesmere coast. Rumor had it that they were attempting a dash to the Pole, manhauling their supplies. In fact Richard had spotted special sleds in their plane. We wondered what the real story was.

By the next morning the storm in Resolute had moved on to Eureka and the planes were grounded once again. Most of our crew spent the morning at the airstrip on a special mission— trying to retrieve a loose dog. While unloading the plane the night we arrived, one of the half-wild renegades on Geoff's team of Eskimo dogs had slipped my grip and scampered off into the darkness. He was part of the team we had added to the expedition during our last week in Frobisher when we suddenly sensed that we would be severely underpowered with only four teams. Unfortunately, these dogs, which we had leased from the northern Hudson Bay village of Igloolik, were completely unsocialized and became totally freaked out when we tried to pet them. But they could pull a sled, and at this point that was all that counted. We hoped that in the coming weeks we would begin to gain their trust. Alas, the loose dog was the ringleader and the most skittish in the bunch, a dog Geoff had dubbed Mitt Grabber, since his favorite antic was to pull a mitten off the hand of an unwary bystander and take off with it. Efforts to capture him that morning involved lassoes, trip lines, and human chains, but nothing worked.

We held another team meeting that afternoon. Our frenzied rush in Frobisher had not allowed opportunities for extended group discussion, and several issues had surfaced during our idle hours in Eureka that merited much debate. Chief among these were the ground rules for our journey. Simply stated, our goal was to accomplish the first confirmed "unsupported" journey to the North Pole. That was the simplest, most concise definition of our goal that Paul and I could come up with. But the term "unsupported," being somewhat nebulous, led to confusion among the media and the public. Much to our chagrin, some reporters during our first year of preparations took it to mean that we would be attempting the journey without financial support. Faced with monstrous expenses and frantically seeking sponsors, we found that particular media coverage counterproductive.

Thus, Paul and I embarked on a slow, steady process of educating the public about the magnitude and historical significance of our project. Through interviews, lectures, and displays, we worked hard to help people understand that ours was to be a deliberate throwback to the days of the early explorers. Unlike the space program or the flight of the *Voyager* spacecraft, our journey would not be bound by the limits of technology. To the contrary, we were limiting the technology we would employ to reach the Pole. We would travel as one self-contained unit from the northern shores of North America to the top, receiving no additional provisions en route. Once we embarked for the Pole, we would be entirely reliant upon our own fortitude and resourcefulness.

Our journey had more in common with ones undertaken during the great age of exploration around the turn of the century than with more recent ones. The greatest difference between ours and earlier ones was that we had radio communication and access to airlifts. That allowed us one other crucial option the early explorers didn't have: the ability to airlift out sled dogs that would no longer be needed when our loads lightened. The standard unquestioned procedure for polar explorers before the age of aircraft was to feed weaker dogs to stronger ones as the journey progressed. For us, that was not a viable option. Our dogs were too precious. Therefore, we planned to have excess dogs airlifted out on one or more occasions, depending on conditions, during our journey.

Having a radio and plans for airlifts meant our access to the outside world would not be completely cut off. This was the rub that opened countless questions among the team. Should we allow ourselves to accept weather reports on the radio that might aid our travel strategy? Should we carry an emergency electronic navigation system in case the sun was obscured for long periods? Should we accept messages from friends and loved ones by radio? Or should we rule these out as being support from outside, if only emotional support? Should we ask the pilots on the airlifts to report to us about the ice conditions that lay ahead on our route? Should we grant interviews to reporters who joined these flights, or accept unexposed movie film or blank cassette tapes from them? Should we send letters, tapes, or exposed film out with them?

We looked at the issue of what constituted "support" from countless angles. For example, Richard, taking it to extremes, suggested that using snow to build igloos might be construed to represent support since it was a material we had not brought with us. If we happened upon a seal or a polar bear, should we allow ourselves the luxury of some fresh meat? Huddled there in the narrow hallway of our barracks, at the eleventh hour, we finally nailed down a watertight game plan. " 'Unsupported' means we will not accept anything," I said, summarizing the consensus we had come to, "not so much as a stick of gum, nothing from any airplane. Furthermore, we will allow planes to carry out excess dogs, film, guns, other valuable equipment that is no longer needed, garbage, and, as we agreed, a few letters. Basically, the rules we have set are that we cannot receive anything but we can send things out, such as excess gear, rather than disposing of it on the ice." We did agree to carry a small electronic navigation unit, but we would use it only in an emergency.

Then we tackled another sticky issue that had festered for months and would prove to be a source of contention among us all the way to the Pole. We had calculated the journey to take between fifty and sixty days, and we would carry provisions to sustain eight people for that long. But we knew that if the sea ice proved to be especially bad, it might take much longer than that to reach the Pole. In that event, some team members might have to be airlifted out so that rations could be stretched to allow a few to carry on. Paul and I had pointed out this possibility many months before. The team, understandably, had a hard time reconciling it. It would require a tremendous self-sacrifice to turn back partway to the Pole so that a few others could carry on.

Complicating the issue was the fact that airlifting people out to stretch the remaining rations might represent to some observers, as Richard put it, "reverse resupply"—that is, since we would have fewer mouths to feed, the few who carried on would more or less be receiving additional supplies. Our peer group, other explorers, and exploration support groups such as the National Geographic Society, might frown upon that and question our claims to a "first." Ran Fiennes, who had joined our meeting, concurred with this notion. "To be truly unsupported," he said, "it would only be acceptable to send team members back in the event of illness or injury." We accepted this advice, but nonetheless agreed that sending some team members back as a last-ditch measure so a few could make it was far preferable to having none of us reach the Pole.

Ran raised another issue that every expedition team should reckon with before embarking on a dangerous journey, reminding us that we were indeed laying our lives on the line. A serious tent fire, a sledding accident, an encounter with a polar bear, a plunge through a crevasse in the ice—many dangers existed that might cause a fatal injury or instant death. We all knew and accepted that, and had discussed it at length during our training. But, Ran asked, what contingency plans had we made for dealing with a dead body on the sea ice? Among the myriad issues Paul and I had raised with the team over the past seven months, this one had slipped through the cracks.

I had wrestled with the issue once before as a result of a tragic expedition accident. In 1965, on a mountain-climbing trip in Peru, two members of our crew fell to their deaths. We recovered one body but, perched at high altitude on steep mountain walls, had no means for carrying it out. Thus we had to bury it in a crevasse on a glacier and wrestle later with the anguish that the accident and the subsequent disposition of the body might cause to our team member's family and friends.

In the event of such a tragedy, should we call an end to the project? Should we carry on? What were we to do with the body? Should we call in an airplane to evacuate the body, or simply have a burial at sea? To have to make these decisions after a tragedy on the sea ice would make for a horrible scene. It was imperative that all of us state our preferences concerning the disposition of our bodies if we died on the journey.

At issue were the complicated logistics and huge expense of sending a body out, the grief of families having to deal with a body being shipped partway round the world, and legalities concerning cause of death. After a brief discussion, our unanimous, unquestioned decision was that no bodies were to be shipped out. We would document the cause of death through records and photographs, and then have a burial at sea. Paul and I asked that all of us state our feelings on these matters so that a written record of them could be sent to family members back home. Sharon Schmickle, the *Minneapolis Star and Tribune* correspondent who was covering our journey, took notes. She looked somewhat bewildered at being invited to witness such a somber event, but found that the statements, which were our last wills and testaments in a way, were sprinkled with levity.

I spoke first: "When we head out on that sea ice, I am fulfilling one of my ultimate dreams. . . . If I am killed, don't cry over my body, because I am doing what I want to do. . . . Tie something heavy around my foot—not something valuable, of course—and drop me through a hole in the ice. Dead or alive, I'm not going before the Pole is reached."

Brent spoke next: "I am willing to donate all of my organs and my flesh to my dogs."

McKerrow interjected with a grin, "How about your sledding partner?" He was referring to himself.

"I don't know about that," Brent responded. "I guess I'll donate him, too."

"What happens if your dogs don't accept your body?" I chided.

Geoff, in his usual matter-of-fact style, said, "Either feed me to the dogs, toss me in a lead, or lay me on the ice, whatever is easiest." Ann, Richard, and Mantell all nodded in agreement with these feelings.

Paul, adding more levity, quipped, "Donate my body to the Norwegian women's team," referring to a group that had embarked the day before on a ski trek to the Pole from the Norwegian coast.

For the record, Paul then prepared a written statement that all of us signed: "Being of sound mind and body I willfully request that, if I die on the North Pole journey, my remains be dealt with by my team members in the most expedient manner possible."

Case closed. Well, almost. Throughout our training we had frequently discussed the distinct possibility that we might lose one or more dogs on this trip, through fights, accidents, or illness. We were determined to bring them all back home alive and healthy, but the odds were that the vagaries of trail life would take their toll. We knew that at some point in our journey, we might be forced to face the loss of a dog. We had braced ourselves for this eventuality, but that afternoon a painful new twist was added. The staff at Eureka had given us notice that if the two dogs from Geoff's team that were running loose around the airstrip could not be captured, they would have to be disposed of. It wasn't that they disliked our dogs. Rather, they feared that loose dogs might, for example, raise havoc with the local wild animals by introducing foreign diseases or parasites.

Our hearts sank at the thought of killing the dogs. But the station staff was right; it would be utterly irresponsible to leave them running loose. If it had to be done, we would accept it as one of the hard, cold facts of expedition life. But what about the folks back home, we thought. How would they respond to headlines reading, **EXPEDITION TEAM MAKES FINAL PREPARATIONS; SHOOTS TWO DOGS**.

In this issue, as in many others, media impact had to be considered. The extensive coverage of our preparations had turned this expedition into a public event, and us into public figures. If we were forced to shoot the dogs, the impact on our project's image could be devastating. In Eureka, the press was always present and always welcome to attend our meetings. We argued and debated among ourselves in front of the reporters, and often asked them for their views on issues. For example, we often asked how they would report the nuances of our definition of the label "unsupported."

In a way, the press people were considered part of the expedition. Their coverage would ensure that the documentation of the journey was absolutely thorough. This, we felt, would stand as one of the project's unique features, and would reflect on the expedition's historical credibility. After all, lack of quality documentation is what has left Admiral Robert Peary's and Dr. Frederick Cook's claims of having reached the Pole some seventy-five years ago wide open for debate. We knew that the only way to keep from being mired in controversy was to be open and honest and make certain that we thoroughly documented every claim we made. That was the foundation of credibility, and the press would provide that.

On the other hand, the press was a burden. It placed heavy demands on our time, and its members who were accompanying us to our departure point relied on us to arrange for their lodging as well as some of their food and equipment for their visit to the high Arctic; we were now functioning as a top-of-the-world travel agency. Furthermore, we always faced the gnawing anxiety that they could report any mistakes or misfortunes that might reflect badly on our project.

During our stays in Frobisher and Eureka, press coverage had grown rapidly. Countless people were taking part vicariously in the tribulations, joys, and excitement of launching an expedition on the polar sea. By satellite telephone in Eureka, the crew accompanying us had play-by-play reports in the homes of our followers within twenty-four hours. And with a satellite telecast linkup from Resolute, Hubbard Broadcasting, owner of Twin Cities radio and TV station KSTP, would be providing live news stories from one of Canada's northernmost villages as we embarked for the Pole. An unprecedented feat, this would represent the first time news had been transmitted direct to viewers in the United States from so far north. How ironic it was, I thought, that the expedition being documented with the help of such high technology was designed in part as a deliberate throwback to the techniques of the early polar explorers.

On our third evening in Eureka, with the loose-dog issue weighing ever more heavily on our minds, Geoff headed a crew that redoubled their efforts to nab the runaways. Unfortunately, every imaginable type of trap proved futile. Then Geoff tried tranquilizing them by hiding sedatives from our first-aid kit in chunks of meat. A few hours after gobbling the bait, they wobbled a bit but showed no signs of slowing down. The next afternoon, in a last-ditch effort, he baited them with megadoses of the drug, nearly exhausting the supply we had for emergencies. The crew waited and watched. As darkness settled in, the dogs showed a few signs of weakening. With flashlights the crew closed in on the dogs once more, shepherding them between two storage sheds near the runway. The dogs were still wary, but their response had weakened. Inch by inch the crew crept toward them, closing in on the ranks in a tight circle. Then, on cue, Geoff and Brent took flying leaps toward the dogs and tackled them to the ground. Geoff's face brightened for the first time since we had landed in Eureka.

Earlier that day, the weather had broken. Ran's crew had taken off for Ward Hunt Island, and the supplies that we had shipped by commercial flight from Frobisher to Resolute—our solution to the weigh-in fiasco—had come in to Eureka on a Twin Otter. The stage was set for our shuttles to begin.

The next morning, March 5, Bradley Air announced that our first flight would leave at 10:00 A.M. Each shuttle could carry about 1,500 pounds. Thus we would ship our project northward another 200 miles in six groups over the next two days. Brent, Paul, Mantell, and I would leave on the first shuttle with one dog team, one sled, and one tent unit to prepare a base camp and survey the shoreline ice. As we were hurriedly packing the last of our personal gear, one of the weather station staff came running into our barracks to report that a pack of Arctic wolves were ravaging the equipment and supplies we had stacked on the runway to be loaded onto the Twin Otter. We couldn't believe that with but hours to go, we were faced with yet another crisis. We had known the pack was around. They had regularly been seen feeding on food scraps at the station dump. In fact, Eureka's main activity for tourists is to accompany the cook's helper out to the wolves' feeding grounds each morning to take pictures of them scrounging through garbage. But this time we weren't going out to take pictures of them. We were distraught—and furious. This could mean the end of the whole project.

Seven wolves were still tearing at carefully lashed boxes of precious rations when we arrived. They were very reluctant to heed our threats, and it took a bit of effort to chase them off their booty. Then we surveyed the damage and found to our great relief that it was minimal. The worst damage had been done to one of our thirty-pound boxes of cheese. Several blocks had been eaten and the rest were strewn across the runway. Toothmarks attested that the wolves had sampled nearly every one of them. Nonetheless, they were carefully collected because every ounce of that cheese had a crucial role in our rations schedule. But as we picked them up, we remembered having been told that the wolves might be rabid. Hmmm, we thought, another interesting dilemma. But the plane was being loaded nearby, the pilots were beckoning us to hurry, and quick decisions had to be made.

Brent suddenly had a brainstorm. "I recently had my rabies shots," he said. "I'll set aside these blocks and make sure I'm the only one to eat them." It sounded plausible to us. We nodded in agreement and headed toward the plane.

THE LAUNCHING PAD

"I FELT LIKE WE WERE LANDING ON THE MOON."

DREP CAMP, NORTH COAST, ELLESMERE ISLAND, NORTH-WEST TERRITORIES—By 10:00 A.M. we were on our way north. Suspense ran high, for Bob, Brent, Paul, and I knew we would be the first of our crew to survey the pack ice that would mark the beginning of our route. The vistas that unfolded below us as the plane flew northward in the the dawn light of the Arctic spring were overpowering. The glistening white mountains and the translucent blue glaciers that laced through the valleys were lightly tinted with oranges and pinks from the faint hint of sun along the southeastern horizon. Looking around at my companions, who were all gazing pensively out frosted windows, I felt a very tight kinship with these close friends.

Mantell and I were sharing thoughts of the first time we had embarked on a major expedition together. He had been my traveling partner during most of an eighteen-month, 7,000-mile journey in 1982 and 1983. The first leg took us by dogsled some 2,000 miles from Baker Lake, near Hudson Bay in the central Arctic, to northern Ellesmere, with a visit to Eureka. After a summer of hiking and dogpacking across the island with another friend, I flew to Yellowknife, Northwest Territories, and sledded to the mouth of the Mackenzie River on the Beaufort Sea. There Mantell joined me again. We sledded along Alaska's north slope, dogpacked over the Brooks Range, and then finished by floating down the Yukon River.

When Paul and I began working full-time on the expedition two years later, Mantell was our first choice as we considered candidates for the team. He was a proven trail companion and a highly skilled handyman. Born in Chicago, he was exposed to the north woods through a scouting program, and had moved to Ely when he was nineteen. He became a carpenter, mechanic, and skilled woodsman. After our Yukon raft trip, he had stayed on in Alaska, where he helped train sled dogs for the famous 1,000-mile Iditarod Sled Dog Race and developed his own dog team. Quiet, thoughtful, methodical, he gains the instant admiration and respect of everyone he meets. Slight and wiry, he shares my physique and my wanderlust. He viewed the North Pole expedition as a proving ground for the variety of skills he had accrued.

It was on my eighteen-month trek with Mantell that the North Pole journey was conceived. He and I were waiting out a blizzard in the center of the Canadian Barrens, the windswept tundra northwest of Hudson Bay. These rolling, treeless plains have the coldest windchills in the northern hemisphere. And on this day they were the coldest I had ever seen—my hand flash-froze when I reached out our tent door for only a second to grab another fuel bottle. To pass the time, we schemed and dreamed about future expeditions. Talk turned to the North Pole. For years it had loomed in my mind as an intriguing challenge, the true test of a dog musher's mettle. But the accepted practice for reaching it, the technique used by the handful of polar expeditions in recent decades, involved heavy reliance on air support. Conventional wisdom held that to do it without resupply was impossible.

As I pondered those thoughts, eighty-mile-per-hour gusts of wind set our tent guy lines vibrating with a high-pitched hum. If we can persevere in these conditions, I thought, we can reach the Pole without resupply. The vision was planted. Its power would carry me all the way to the top. I saw my destiny at the Pole, my niche in history. All my life seemed to have pointed in this direction—my childhood adventures, my wilderness home, the winter trips business, and my fascination with the north and dogsledding. I saw an opportunity to apply everything I had learned to a project whose magnitude would require me to reach my full potential.

Now, as we flew northward over Ellesmere, that opportunity was drawing near. Two hours into the flight, the mountain walls dropped sharply. The plane descended. Stretched before us was the badly broken and heavy frozen surface of the Arctic Ocean. It reminded me of pictures the Apollo astronauts had brought back from their journeys to the moon. Our overheated capsule, filled with the smell of dogs, was in sharp contrast to the lifeless, inhumanly cold scene that stretched below us. From our perspective, hundreds of feet above, it was impossible to judge the height of the rubble. We could only hope it was passable. But what did arouse our optimism was that as far as we could see, perhaps ten miles out, there was no sign of open water. Furthermore, huge gaps of seemingly smooth ice seemed to be sprinkled generously among the ridges and rubble fields. Our pilot, Karl Zberg, a veteran who had flown the Arctic for some twenty years, concurred. It looked as though the Arctic Ocean might deal kindly with its visitors this year. We smiled joyously at each other as the plane coasted to a stop on the smooth shelf ice at the foot of the mountains.

Nearby was our base, "Drep Camp," a twelve-by-twenty-foot hut built in recent years by the Canadian military's Defense Research Establishment Pacific (DREP) for studies on the development and movement of pack ice. The bright orange flat-topped hut was situated on smooth glacial shelf ice, about three miles out from the base of the mountains that define Canada's north coast. The moving pack ice of the Arctic Ocean begins abruptly about a mile north of the hut. Its serrated edge rose before us like the Great Wall of China along the northern horizon. The hut was nearly buried in drifted snow. After an hour or so we had its door, window, and fuel tank shoveled free, and began setting up inside.

Half of the hut is an unheated storage space, which we called the "porch with the ocean view." A low door separates the porch from the ten-by-twelve-foot living area. Packed in it we found two bunk beds, a table, a dry sink and cupboards, and a kerosene heater. Paul stretched out a radio antenna while the rest of us set up stakeout lines for the dogs and organized the gear. Then, as Paul noted in his journal, "Like kids let loose in the park, we all ran off toward the pack ice to explore our new stomping grounds." Our first impressions were of its awesome beauty. The sunlight absorbed by the massive ice blocks piled chaotically was reflected in varying wavelengths, creating emerald greens, baby blues, and indigos that dazzled our eyes. The mammoth proportions of these color-clad ramparts left us feeling like ants negotiating a boulder field.

We'd been similarly humbled the first time we had entered big pack ice as a team. That had been the previous May, when five of us rehearsed among the behemoth blocks of the Chukchi Sea near Barrow, Alaska, the northernmost village of the United States. Barrow was the endpoint for a 5,000-mile training journey that began in Duluth, Minnesota, and crossed Canada to Alaska's north coast during the previous five months. Along the way, I field-tested various generations of clothing and equipment that Paul and Susan shuttled up from our base in Ely. More important, the marathon trek gave me a chance to put thousands of training miles on dogs that were candidates for the polar journey. Paul, McKerrow, Richard, and Mantell rendezvoused with me when I reached the Arctic coast at Inuvik for a month-long "dress rehearsal" across the Beaufort Sea. The ice we'd seen on that journey paled in comparison with the expanse that stretched before us now.

Meanwhile, back at Eureka, the rest of our crew was in a frenzy. Another expedition team had arrived, and now two planes were suddenly freed up to bring more shuttles to Drep Camp. Within a moment's notice, Richard, Geoff, and our media crew, along with Mantell's and Paul's teams and the other tent unit, were on their way north. Only McKerrow and Ann were left behind to look after our remaining three shuttles.

Hearing the planes arrive, Paul and I retreated from the pack ice where we were searching for our "gateway," an opening in the Great Wall that would get us on our way. We were pleased with what we had found—the pack ice seemed passable—but Paul was somewhat shaken by a lapse in caution. As he wrote in his journal that evening, "About an hour into my adventure, I realized how stupid it was for Will and me to be scrambling about separately in dangerous unknown territory with only scattered footprints to mark my whereabouts. I resolved to work in groups until we came to know the 'enemy' a little better." The temperature plummeted into the −60's that evening, but the hut glowed warm and bright as ten of us partied inside, feasting on caribou steaks and sharing a nip or two from the bottles of spirits the reporters had brought with them. The only radio station we could pick up, a Siberian one, was blaring Russian dance music out of our receiver. Several people squeezed onto the top bunk.

Down near the floor it was very cold. Any spilled water froze instantly.

The next morning in Eureka, McKerrow and Ann visited with a French adventurer who had just arrived, Jean-Louis Etienne. He was about to make his second attempt at completing the first solo ski trek to the North Pole. They were very impressed with him, finding him to be a very likable, determined fellow, but persuaded him to make a minor change in his scheme. He planned to ski about ten miles a day, towing a Kevlar toboggan with up to 100 pounds of supplies, and to be resupplied by aircraft every twelve days. His itinerary called for launching his journey a few dozen miles from shore, out beyond the worst of the pack ice. As McKerrow pointed out to him, many expeditions in recent years have used this "head start" technique. It saves them some work but costs them some credibility in the long run. Jean-Louis agreed and decided to embark instead from Ward Hunt, a tiny coastal island seventeen miles east of Drep Camp, where Ran Fiennes's group was now setting up shop.

While Eureka was basking in clear, calm weather, a stiff wind was blowing at Drep Camp. Temperature had moderated a bit— it hovered around −50—so it was another good day for a photogenic Arctic media event. The film crew that had arrived the day before was anxious to see us in action. We harnessed up a couple of dog teams, loaded cameras on the sleds, and took them to the edge of the pack ice, where they could get shots of us hacking a route and driving our sleds over pressure ridges. The wind added drama to their shots, but the chill quickly penetrated their clothing. Staging various dramatic settings, we worked fast to oblige their need for action stories. The scene became increasingly ridiculous, but Jason Davis, the television reporter, saved the best "stunt" request for last. He had us do a series of "stand-up" shots that would be used to promote the news updates on our progress during the coming weeks. One by one, we stood in front of the camera, inserting our names in the brief script and rattling off, "Hi! I'm —————— ——————, on my way to the North Pole. We'll be bringing you a special report tonight at ten." Jason was delighted, but his cameraman, Don, noting our annoyance at Jason's request, mumbled apologies as they loaded their equipment onto Brent's sled for the ride back to camp.

Jason had been covering the expedition ever since our training journey departed Duluth in early December 1984. The on-site reports had often been gathered in odd circumstances. In late April of that year, he flew to Inuvik to capture on film the rendezvous that would mark the beginning of our first journey as a team. Deep snow along the Mackenzie River had delayed my arrival. I was still 100 miles out when he and Don, growing impatient for a news story, chartered a ski plane and dropped in on me as my dogs and I plodded along through waist-deep snow on the frozen river. As they came scurrying toward me with camera and microphone in hand, I knew they were set for a stand-up. Jason, who has a witty knack for television reportage, had a sly smile on his face. I wondered what his opening line would be. "Will Steger, I presume?" he boomed as he drew near.

During our months of training, Jason visited with us many times. His stand-ups on the sea ice near Drep Camp that afternoon were to be his last on-site coverage until our first dog-pickup flight. Paul and I stayed out in the pack ice until dusk, marking a route. In late afternoon a plane arrived in camp. We hoped it was our fourth shuttle, but it was Karl, stopping by after bringing in a load to the group at Ward Hunt. He offered to take the film crew back to Eureka. After a miserably cold day on the sea, they were more than happy to bail out early. Thus the hut was quiet that night as the six of us shared a meal of Arctic char and rice and wondered how much longer our shuttles might be delayed.

By the next morning, March 7, the temperature had plummeted into the minus-sixties again. Those who had slept on the floor had fought a chill most of the night. Wondering whether our half-inch foam ground pads would be adequate for the journey, some team members began eyeing the caribou hides stored in the porch. Paul called the Bradley Air base on the radio to check on the shuttle flights and found that we had another financial crisis on our hands. The flight controller, Rudy, said the Visa card office in New York was refusing to accept any more bills on our account. He intimated, politely but firmly, that without some fast cash there would be no more shuttles. Paul and I were baffled. The cost overrun we had encountered in shipping our supplies to Eureka had cut deeply into the funds we had set aside for flights to the Pole at the end of the journey, but, by our accounting, we still should have had ample funds in our Visa account to cover the shuttles, which were priced at $4,000 apiece. All we could do was have him get in touch with Paul's wife, Susan, now back home in Minnesota, so she could sort out the problem with our Visa agent. Rudy took our word that the money was there—somewhere—and said he'd arrange for our remaining shuttles to come in that day.

I stayed behind for the day to sort and pack gear while the rest of the crew headed out into the pack ice to continue chopping a trail. Our final shuttle flight—carrying Ann and McKerrow, another team of dogs, our folding boat, and the canoe, as well as Jim Brandenburg, the *National Geographic* photographer who wanted to take a few pictures of our base camp—arrived at 4:00 P.M., just as darkness was settling in. Karl and Jim visited with us for a few minutes, wished us well and headed south. Our team of eight was now alone together for the first time.

Over dinner we reveled in the chopping crew's optimistic reports about the sea ice. Though it was badly buckled, they said, no open water had been seen. That meant the pack was relatively stable. A trail had now been marked and chopped about five miles northward. The size of the pans, the rubble-free sections, seemed to increase as they got farther out. The last one they found, the "pie in the sky" pan, as they called it, was nearly a half-mile across. It was bordered by a forty-foot ridge, but they reported that the ice they saw from the top of that looked as if it might be passable without extensive chopping. Our cheery conversation that evening was sprinkled with boastful comments about how we were going to ace it. It's possible, we thought, that we might even knock off some ten-mile days in the first week of the trip. Only Brent, who had seen more pack ice in his lifetime than the rest of us, remained quiet and somewhat skeptical of our mirth. Regardless of what lay ahead, our spirits were high. We were ready for whatever the polar sea could throw against us. The night before beginning our journey, an overwhelming sense of optimism filled the air in our tiny hut.

I captured the moment in my journal: "Here we sit, eight people in a ten-by-ten space, and all of us are happy. In our little shack, well lit and heated, we sit on chairs and bunks, surrounded by all we can eat and all we can drink. Whiskey, sweets of all sorts, meat, both fresh and cured, and cheese. We sit satisfied and ready. What will tomorrow bring?"

WE
MEET
THE
ADVERSARY

DAY 1

"I SAW MY DREAM COMING TRUE IN THE MIST THAT
ROSE FROM THE DOGS' BODIES. WE ARE GOING TO
THE POLE."

On March 8, in the gray dawn light, we lashed our loads with
fingers stinging in the −70-degree temperatures. Like bath water
of liquid nitrogen, super-chilled air was spilling off the mountains and glaciers of Ellesmere and washing over us as it worked
its way out to sea. For the first time, the three tons of equipment
and supplies we had spent three years putting together were
being distributed on our sixteen-foot sleds. The size of the loads
taking shape before us was shocking. When each sled had been
loaded, we estimated the average payload at around 1,350
pounds, one-third again as much as we had planned for. The
weight of each load seemed unwieldy and the volume awkward.
As we surveyed the monstrous loads, we wondered whether the
dogs would be able to pull them. Yet, given the unexpectedly
cold temperatures, we knew it would be foolhardy to jettison any
food or fuel.

I was concerned, but not anxious. I had seen dogs move such
loads before. The sled that Mantell and I crossed the Canadian
Barrens with in 1982 had a 1,700-pound payload on departure
from Baker Lake. The dogs somehow moved it, although they
struggled desperately for the first two weeks until the payload
diminished to manageable size. Experience had taught me to
start out a little heavy—with ample reserves—when venturing
out into the unknown. It usually takes a week in harsh conditions
to get travel and camping systems running smoothly. The extra
fuel and food would buy us some extra time while we got orga-

37

nized. We could always dump weight along the way as necessity dictated.

Earlier that morning, Richard had set out on a three-mile ski to reach the base of the mountains that bordered the shoreline. His assignment was to reach the exposed rocks at the base of the mountains and bring back a small stone for each of us. These "moon rocks," as we called them, served as mementos of our departure. In addition, they served as indisputable proof that we had started from land and would thus dispel any potential rumors suggesting that our expedition, like others, had embarked from a point beyond the chaotic shoreline pack ice, rather than from the beach. The gesture may seem a bit paranoiac, but, knowing that the gossip mill in expedition circles is well greased, Paul and I wanted to preempt any possible efforts by others to discredit us.

Richard returned at noon. Tired and soaked with sweat, he now had second thoughts, he said, about the value of undertaking that exhausting mission just to prevent "some fat hemorrhoidic armchair explorer" from raising doubts about whether we had fudged our departure point. He straddled the kerosene heater to try to dry off a bit. Both he and Brent had awakened that morning with a bit of a chest cold. But, as he noted in his journal, reflecting the stoicism toward health problems that was to become a hallmark of our team, "it's not something anyone would admit to very freely." At noon, Paul ceremoniously turned off the heater in the hut. The umbilical cord to the comforts of civilization was severed.

"This is it," I yelled. "Let's harness the dogs and head north."

The dogs broke the frigid silence with howls of excitement. As the first dogs were harnessed, a wave of nervous energy swept through the teams. As I harnessed my lead dog, Chester, he rolled and squirmed in delight, whining and crying with impatience to begin the epic. His antics sparked the rest of the dogs into wild enthusiasm, and a cacophony of barking filled the air. Team members had to shout over the ruckus to communicate. Thrills of anticipation and chills of apprehension swept over us in waves.

At 2:00 P.M. on March 8, the moment upon which we had focused three years of planning and preparation had arrived. Paul launched his team first. He levered his sled forward with his peavey, a steel-spiked wooden pole, while three other team members pushed along the sides. With a grating squeak, the sled broke loose. His ten Eskimo dogs, a well-behaved team we had received from Igloolik five months before, were throwing themselves against their traces with maniacal frenzy to inch the sled along. Every dozen yards or so, when the dogs ran low on steam, Paul pulled the peavey out to give the sled another thrust. These pry bars, equipment Brent had suggested we carry, immediately proved their value. In fact, they became some of our most important tools. Peaveys are designed for log-rolling, but we had found during our training that with its cant hook cut off, a peavey served admirably as an ice chisel and pry bar. The upstanders on each sled had been outfitted with a short section of plastic pipe in which the five-foot bars could be safely holstered.

With Paul well under way toward the pack ice, my sled was launched next. Richard and Geoff helped with the peavey. My team's frenzied barking stopped suddenly as the sled lurched forward, and they focused every ounce of energy on pulling. Only the enthusiasm of fresh dogs could have moved these sleds. I looked back. Brent and McKerrow—prying, pushing, cursing—could not budge their sled. Brent's team of Eskimo dogs were wildly lunging at their traces. Ann dropped back to help. Another volley of curses followed the eerie squeaking of pry bars being levered against the wind-packed snow. Finally the sled inched forward. Next came Mantell with his nine-dog team, his tenth dog, Jean, having been left behind in Frobisher with an injured foot. But only eight of his dogs were pulling as his sled crept along. The one timid dog on his team, Bandit, had broken loose that morning and was now running alongside the team without a harness, refusing to be caught. Geoff's sled brought up the rear, moving along with slightly less difficulty than the others. His payload weight was somewhat less since his sled was burdened with our boats, a very awkward load. To help protect his delicate cargo, he had fashioned a wooden roll bar over the front of the sled.

The frigid air grew quiet once again as the dogs concentrated on pulling and the team members on pushing. Between us and the wall of pack ice—the mound of rubble that marked the edge of the ocean's active zone—was a mile of snow-covered, landlocked shelf ice that sloped gently down toward the sea. A cloud of vapor enveloped the panting dogs and lingered on, glowing pale orange in the muted light from the sun, which peeked above the mountaintops to the south for a mere twenty minutes that day. Each of the five dog teams billowed steam like locomotives. Exhaled moisture formed a vapor trail that marked the route each sled had taken, and obscured our vision; each team could be heard but not seen. "I saw my dream coming true in the mist that rose from my dogs' bodies," I noted in my journal that night. "We are going to the Pole."

Our elation didn't last long. The real challenge, the pack ice, was still well ahead when our sleds started to bog down in deep snow. The dogs were operating beyond capacity and fizzling out quickly. We teamed up on the sleds—two, three, four, and then five of us on one sled to keep it moving, barely able to inch along, even though this was smooth terrain with a downhill slope. Just a mile ahead loomed the ominous wall of pack ice that rose abruptly and stretched endlessly along the shore. An hour later we reached it. The Great Wall, as we called it, was our induction to the rigors of the polar sea. The combined power of seven team members and ten dogs was needed to inch the first sled through the "gateway," a narrow pass we had chopped as our entry point into the pack ice. Compared to the massive blocks of blue ice aligned in mute defiance across our route north, the five bulging sled loads suddenly looked minuscule.

The moment we stopped heaving against the backs of our sleds, the −70-degree chill would penetrate our clothing. Our cheeks would quickly harden with frostbite. Yet I was confident we would make it. Many times I had been in tight binds like this, but had always come through.

Echoes of history played on our minds as we ventured out on that lonely ice the way many had done before us. Often our thoughts turned to Admiral Robert Peary, who with his black assistant Matthew Henson and four Eskimo companions claimed to have reached the Pole on April 6, 1909, just over seventy-five years ago. Like us, he had relied on sled dogs and received no additional supplies while en route. Unlike us, he had no radio with which to call for help, nor access to airlifts to carry him home. His was a round-trip, while ours was to be one-way. Under Peary's ingenious strategy, all of his team's supplies were relayed out onto the ice by 26 men and 133 dogs grouped in five units. The first four units would blaze a trail and establish a supply line to within striking distance of the goal. As they exhausted their dogs and supplies, one by one these units would turn back, thereby reducing the demands on the rations that had been brought forward. Peary's unit, which had remained somewhat rested and fresh by hanging in the rear, would then launch a dash for the Pole. The key to his strategy was to employ large numbers of people and dogs to spread out the workload. Our crew, including people and dogs, was roughly a third as large as his, whereas our initial sled payloads were nearly three times the 500-odd pounds he loaded onto each of his nineteen sleds.

During our three days at Drep Camp, we had thoroughly scouted, marked, and chopped our first five miles of trail northward. For the first mile or so we found successive ten-to-forty-foot walls of ice separated by snow-filled troughs that ran like moats between them. To establish a level track, we'd chop down the walls and use the rubble to fill in the moats. Our trail took on the appearance of a Roman road heading to the Pole. "Trail" is a misnomer, really, because it was a veritable obstacle course of loose, slippery rubble and deep, soft snow.

After we passed through the gateway onto the ocean, each sled had to be muscled along one at a time. Seven of us would push while the eighth team member "baby-sat" the other four dog teams to keep fights from breaking out. Being stuck with a fairly passive job, the dog-sitter inevitably suffered more from the cold than did the sled crew. A heavy workload was a blessing, since it kept the pushers comfortably warm. To stand around meant to freeze. Within minutes the warm blood would recede into one's torso; fingers and toes would turn numb, and only vigorous activity would send warm blood to the freezing extremities. During the first few weeks of the journey, Richard or Ann often got stuck with the dog-sitting chore. Many times each day we'd look back with pity to see them pounding their feet on the ice and swinging their arms in wide circles to throw precious warm blood to fingers and toes. How lucky the rest of were to be working hard!

Our induction into the polar sea had put a damper on the optimism with which we had started the day. The sleds ground to a halt on every incline. Even the tiniest mound of drifted snow stopped their progress. Often, three people wielding peaveys with four others pushing were needed to get them going. In the frigid air, the surface was as coarse and abrasive as sandpaper. Our state-of-the-art, silicon-imbedded plastic runners offered almost no glide. Moving sleds over the polar snow was like dragging stone boats over boulder fields. And sledding over pressure ridges was proving to be dangerous. Our mukluks offered little traction on the ice blocks. A momentary lapse of attention could result in a paralyzing accident. With sleds careening off blocks and crashing down the back sides of ridges, we had to be very nimble. But sledding up and down sheer ridges proved to be a lesser hell than maneuvering through the sheltered valleys between them, where deep drifts of soft snow had collected. Our sled runners would burrow down in these traps and have to be shoveled free. On that first day we had learned that to get sleds to the Pole would require a rare combination of brute strength and extreme finesse. And if we carried on with these payload weights, we would soon drive ourselves and our dogs into the ground.

Our efforts for Day 1 of the journey had taken us one and a half miles north of Drep Camp. The first pan was a half-mile beyond the gateway. It took us three hours to bring all five sleds up to that point. By the time we had done so, the twilight was all but gone. The temperature had dropped steadily all afternoon, from a high of −58 to −70 degrees. Our body heat drained away as soon as we stopped pushing the sleds. The blessing of the deep freeze is that it's rarely accompanied by any wind. Below about −60 degrees, even the air, like the sea ice, seems to be held in frigid suspension. But as we pitched our camp, a breeze came flowing off the Ellesmere ice shelf, dropping the windchill to something in excess of −100. I had never experienced cold this brutal. Reaching up with a hand to thaw my face, I found that my cheeks were entirely frozen. They felt like cardboard. Brent and Geoff, who'd struggled with tangled dog lines all day, had severely frozen fingers.

While the drivers unreeled stakeouts, the cables and clips to which we secured dogs for the night, Ann, Richard, and McKerrow wrestled with our two dome tents, trying to stretch nylon, stiffened and shrunken in the cold, over the aluminum wands. This was the worst of the camp-setting chores. The cold nylon rendered their fingers functionless. They would persevere for a few minutes, then in rotation each would run in tight circles around the project to generate a bit of warmth.

As I unharnessed my dogs and clipped them in place for the night along the stakeout line, I warmed up a bit and was able to look at the scene more objectively. I remember thinking, "As desperate as this scene appears, we are all going to survive this." The rewards of our intense training were evident. The process was slow and painful, but it was organized. No movements were wasted. Paul set the pace, orchestrating several projects at once. I marveled at his energy. Never have I seen anyone work as hard as he did. Everyone was attending to assigned chores with clockwork efficiency, though at these temperatures each chore took twice as long as it had during training. It was like setting up camp on the dark side of the moon.

After I fed my dogs, they immediately curled up in tight balls, noses buried in their tails to conserve body heat. I scanned the panorama for one last moment, checking for loose ends. Hope surged in me as my attention caught the little sliver of orange afterglow from the sun. It would be rising steadily higher and staying longer each day of our journey.

That brief moment of reverie broke when I crawled into my tent to find a scene of utter chaos. Try as he might, Richard had not been able to get the stoves to ignite and was frantically swapping parts between stoves to track down the fault before his fingers froze. Cookpots, food bags, foam pads, thermoses, and sleeping bags were heaped in piles around him in the tight, seven-foot-diameter space. Soon Mantell entered, and our quarters became even tighter. Our well-being depended entirely on coaxing the stoves into action. Hands and feet were growing numb, moisture from our breath was collecting as frost on the tent walls. Mantell tried his luck with one stove and finally managed to get it to light, though it sputtered reluctantly, with yellow flames. The super-chilled white gas was refusing to vaporize properly. Fumes from incomplete combustion soon left us all coughing. Then Geoff entered. Surrounded by mounds of clothing and sleeping bags as stiff as boards from the cold, we had no room to maneuver.

On any journey, the first night on the trail is always somewhat chaotic. To keep thoughts of misery at bay, I started to work on the second stove. The long dusk had nearly ended. We worked by the light of headlamps that could barely cut through the thick fog from our breath. My stove ignited, sputtering with a yellow, sooty flame. For a moment we allowed it to cast a bit of warmth into the air, but then placed over it a large pot filled with snow that was to be our evening tea. The pot absorbed all heat from the stove. Richard lit two plumber's candles for light to cook by. We quickly yanked off our mukluks and massaged warmth back into frozen toes. Then we sat in the −60-degree silence, waiting for tea and pemmican, a mixture of ground dried meat and fat. Breath billowed out of my nostrils in two steady columns of fog as I wrote in my journal by the light of a headlamp. Pencil lead left only a faint impression on the paper, so I tried a ballpoint pen. It froze up within a minute, so I dug out a few more pens and tucked them in my polar suit to use in rotation. My left palm became numb as it moved across the frigid paper. I wrote about leaving Ellesmere Island, leaving our loved ones, heading north with our backs to civilization, and about the joys and demands of finally getting this expedition under way. What got us through the day, I noted, were spirit and guts.

The fumes from the sputtering stoves burned the inside of my nose and made my eyes water. Richard soon had a rasping cough. But nothing was said. We just waited patiently for the pot of snow to become warm tea. I silently pondered the fact that the hunger and exhaustion we were feeling now were nothing to what we would experience farther down the trail. More than anything, I wished simply that the stoves would burn cleanly, so that they would cast enough heat to warm the tent. I felt the cold subtlely working on my attitude. Two long hours passed before supper was ready. Most of us had a hard time eating much; the fumes, we surmised, were affecting our appetites.

Another hour was spent arranging our tent for the night. During training we had found that sleeping four people with huge bags in these tents was unsatisfactory; someone always ended up crammed against the wall. Fortunately, Paul's and Mantell's sleds, the ones that carried camping gear and daily food bags, were fitted with full-length Cordura covers. Paul had designed these three-foot-high sled bags to double as emergency tents. If someone went through the ice, the load could be jettisoned quickly from one of those sleds to make space in the bag as a shelter. To eliminate the crowding problem in the tents, Paul and Mantell opted to sleep in their sled bags on a regular basis. It meant they had to deal with an extra dose of cold each night— when they left the tents after dinner to make a nest in their sled bags—but they appreciated having the private space and the extra room to stretch out. In our tent, Richard and I slept against the wall, with our heads toward the door. Geoff slept in the middle, facing the other direction. All cooking gear was placed in the tent's entryway, a narrow tunnel, for the night.

Crawling into our frigid sleeping bags was a shock, even though we were fully clothed in parkas, hats, and mitts. Hours of shivering and shuffling about passed before enough heat moved from our bodies to the bags to bring them up to a temperature comfortable enough for sleep. These bags are quite possibly the largest sleeping bags ever made. Produced according to our specifications by Sierra Designs, the bags had twelve pounds of Quallofil insulation and, when fluffed out, were fourteen inches thick. Their modified mummy design was roomy enough to accommodate us with our parkas on. A unique feature was the breathing chamber, an extension of stiff material added to the hood tunnel. With Velcro closures and a drawstring, this formed an open cone about six inches high over our faces—a "preheating chamber" for the air we would breathe as we slept.

The most challenging design consideration in a cold-weather sleeping system, as with cold-weather clothing, is not warmth but moisture transfer. Even while sleeping, our bodies perspire nearly a pint of moisture in an eight-hour period. At room temperature, this dissipates as water vapor into the surrounding air. In cold weather, it condenses as frost inside insulation layers. Thus, winter sleeping bags become heavier and icier day by day unless periodically dried. One system used to circumvent this problem is a vapor barrier, a waterproof bag liner that keeps the moisture against you and your clothing, rather than allowing it to enter your bag. Another is the double-bag system, designed so that most of the moisture is driven by body heat into the outer inner bag while the inner remains relatively dry. These systems are effective, but the overriding design consideration for our system was simplicity—one bag, one zipper.

Our lives depended on this simplicity. On the restless polar sea, we always faced the risk that the ice might shatter beneath the tents while we slept. Therefore, we had to sleep fully clothed, ready to exit the tent and move camp on a moment's notice. Peary's crew had been rudely awakened by such an incident during his 1906 attempt at the Pole. The ice suddenly shifted one night, and before anyone had time to act, part of his crew was cast adrift on a moving ice floe. Fortunately, the gap narrowed and the crew was able to rendezvous in a short time, but that near miss underscored for us the importance of sleeping fully dressed in a simple bag system. A vapor-barrier system would have left our clothing damp, and a double bag, with its additional zippers, drawstrings, and closures, would have hindered fast exits. Our solution to the moisture problem was insulation "overkill"—to design a bag with so much fill that it could take on a substantial amount of moisture, yet still provide warmth. This journey would be its first real test.

DAY 2

"RELAYS. WE'VE DREADED THEM. JOKED ABOUT
THEM. CRITICIZED THEM. . . . NOW HERE WE ARE,
DOING THEM."

That first night I slept fitfully, plagued with feet numbed by the
cold. As I lay awake, pondering plans to begin relaying our
loads, I heard one of our dogs whimper outside and realized that
we weren't suffering alone this night. The stark reality of what
we had undertaken hit me hard. But I was not discouraged. I felt
I could make it, but I wondered about the others. How were they
going to hold up? Thank God for Paul, I thought. Without him
to share the leadership responsibilities, I could not do this.

When morning came, it seemed as if I had never slept. The
night had passed like an endless cold purgatory. Finally, Geoff
stirred as his alarm clock, tucked deep inside his bag, went off
to herald the beginning of Day 2. The other group had had an
equally rough night. "A night I would prefer to forget," McKerrow wrote in his journal. "With four of us squashed into that
tent, Ann and I were pressed tightly against the walls all night.
Very claustrophobic. Had an awful nightmare. The air was so
rarefied I found myself fighting for breath a few times." They
agreed, he noted, that only three people should sleep in the tent.
Paul offered to move into his sled bag the next night. Ann had
additional difficulties. Slipping out the door in her socks to uri-
nate during the night, she had returned to bed thoroughly
chilled. From now on, she would be sharing the pee can in the
tent with the boys.

In the morning we repeated the cold, slow process of getting
the stoves going and melting water. Mantell, who had spent the

46

night burrowed in his sled bag, crawled into our tent and reported that the liquid in the thermometer hanging on his sled was completely congealed in the bulb. It was calibrated to −70 degrees, but the temperature had dropped right off its scale. We sat coughing in the cloud of stove fumes, waiting for a miserable yellow flame to turn −70-degree snow into boiling water for oatmeal. An hour later, steam finally came billowing out of the snow pot. Four pairs of hands crowded over the warm pot lid, soaking up surplus heat. I warmed the pages of my journal against the pot to dry the ink from that morning's entry so that it would not smear when I wrote in it again. My head was pounding from a stove-fume hangover. My mind moved slowly; journal entries that morning were terse: "Fumes in tent. Bad. Slept cold last night. Minus 60 in the tent. Wished the stoves worked."

With warm meals in our bellies, we discussed our "housekeeping" routine. Geoff agreed to be first up each morning and to start the stove's snow pots. Mantell would then look after making tea and oatmeal. Richard and I would take turns making supper. Efficiency was paramount. The more time it took for tent duties, the less time we would have on the trail. Every extra moment on the trail increased our odds of reaching the Pole before spring breakup. It would, I knew, be several days before we had a smooth tent rhythm. Our training rehearsals had never subjected us to these conditions. My goal for the next week was to shave the amount of time we spent in camp. It was equally important to minimize discomforts, lest morale begin to slide. Thus I resolved that until the temperatures moderated a bit, we would keep three stoves burning in our tent, two under the cookpots and one alongside as a space heater.

Breakfast that morning took well over three hours. As soon as Mantell, Geoff, and I had finished our bowls, we bailed out into the cold to begin harnessing up our teams. Richard's morning chore was to pack up the tent gear. The temperature still wasn't registering on our thermometer, but I judged it to be about −75 degrees. Right now, this might well be the coldest place on earth, I thought. In calm air, with proper clothing, that temperature might be tolerable. But this air was sweeping down off the 7,000-foot ice fields of northern Ellesmere, flowing past us in a breeze that dropped the chill factor well below −100 degrees. Our slow progress, we figured, would keep us in the super-chilled wind shadow of Ellesmere's mountains for a week or more. I hoped that once we got away from its influence, the temperature would moderate to the minus fifties, and the constant air flow would cease.

Exiting the tent that morning was a bittersweet experience, as it would be on each day of the trip. Stretching out and bringing circulation to cramped legs was a great relief, but in seconds the cold penetrated clothing that was dampened by the moisture in the tent. Harnessing dogs and loading sleds generated some warmth, but then came the dreaded task of lashing the sled loads in place. To maneuver the lines and tie knots, we had to strip away our warm beaver mitts and work with thin five-finger gloves. In the time it took to tie one knot, fingers would freeze up stiff. Every action was thought out in advance. The price for hesitation was a deep chill, which required a quick jog and frantic gyrations to rekindle warmth.

Both tent groups exited on cue at a predetermined time. This timing was essential, for if one tent was late, the other tent group ended up waiting. And to have one tent standing in the cold waiting is the surest means of building tension among the team members.

That first morning on the trail, it took an hour and a half to break camp, harness dogs, and pack sleds. We all knew that was far too long, but we reassured ourselves that it could only get better. The sun showed momentarily through a mountain valley as we began moving the sleds forward. These were the first rays to reach out across the polar sea in five and a half months. They shed no heat, but they kindled hope in each of us.

After four hours of tugging, yanking, heaving, prying, pulling, and cursing the sleds with their monstrous loads, we stopped for a break, limp with exhaustion. We had gained a half-mile in a herculean effort that McKerrow described as a "nightmare." The −70-degree cold was insidious. Face masks were thick with ice from our exhausted panting. We and the dogs had rarely been able to move the sleds more than a few yards at a time before grinding to a halt, wedged between blocks of ice or mired in deep snowdrifts. Without question, we knew we must move our loads forward a portion at a time. I laid out the plan for relays that I had pondered last night: jettison 250 pounds from each sled and push on for a couple of days. Then send two sleds back to retrieve this cache while the others blazed a trail and set up a forward depot. The team unanimously agreed to this, though there was some concern about the possibility of polar bears pilfering the supplies we had left behind. All of us knew we had no choice. The only way to make steady progress and avoid burning out the dogs was to drop weight.

As the day wore on, the tiny reduction we'd made in our loads proved to make even a smaller dent in our work. True, when we embarked from the drop-off point, it had taken only three rather than the usual five people to break the sleds loose from a standing stop. But within a few hours our exhaustion slowed us right back down to the dismal progress we had made that morning. With each snowdrift and ice ridge we encountered, it still required up to seven of us to push each sled through. We resigned ourselves to another day of dismal mileage and simply did the best we could.

We were all amazed at how much frost collected on our garments from our breath. By day's end, McKerrow's beard had over a pound of ice on it. Our neoprene face masks were sheathed in ice inside and out. Many times that day I found my cheeks cold, white, and hard, stiffened like ice cubes by frostbite. A thick coating of hoarfrost hung from the fur ruffs on our hoods. The vapor from our breath collected on our eyelashes as balls of ice, and frequently froze the lids shut. This was perhaps the most serious frost problem, because it seriously hampered visibility and thus safety.

Careening off steeply sloping slabs of ice, our sleds, with their top-heavy loads, rolled over time and again. After one such incident, Paul smelled gas around his sled. "Help!" he shouted. "Our fuel is leaking!" We all ran over and worked frantically to right his sled and pull out the five-gallon polyethylene fuel jugs that were stowed in the back of the sled, well protected between the sled bag and the upstanders. Relief swept over us when we found they hadn't cracked. The problem, we learned, was that the rubber diaphragms in the pressure-release valves, stiffened by the cold, were allowing fuel to trickle out whenever the jugs were tipped. With no means of replacing or sealing up those valves, we would simply have to avoid allowing the sleds to tip over at all costs. In addition to a small quantity of fuel, the price paid for this incident was Richard's parka. It had been stowed above the fuel jugs, and was now drenched with white gas. He stormed about, frustrated and angry. Yesterday, after his exhausting jaunt for the "moon rocks," he had found that his wind jacket had been thoroughly sprayed by one of the dogs and was caked with yellow ice. Fortunately, we carried one spare parka.

Eight hours of grunt work over tortured pack ice and buckled blocks with deep cracks carried us one solitary mile. During a beautifully calm, clear, deeply cold evening, we set up camp on a large, flat pan bordered by twenty-foot hedgerows of ice. With slightly improved efficiency, we had the dogs staked and fed and tents up and organized in under an hour. Before crawling into my tent I gazed at the domes glowing yellow and billowing steam through the top vents from the stoves and lanterns inside, and felt very, very thankful for this precious shelter.

Tent selection had proven to be one of the most hotly debated issues during our years of preparation. What size was the best? How many should we house in each tent? Which style would best withstand the wind? Which would be easiest to set up?

The first thing Paul and I considered was the number of people to house in each tent. When the expedition was first conceived, my plans called for a four-person team—two tents with two persons each. But as we began to comprehend the extent of the work that faced us, the numbers increased. We would have to enlarge the team to eight to ensure that we would have enough muscle power to reach the Pole. Two four-person tents seemed to be a very workable package. To maximize communication between the tent groups, Paul and I would be housed separately, representing expedition leadership in each group. To have only one leader in a group of this size with two tents would have been very difficult, if not impossible.

For our team, the tent style that offered the best utilization of space and durability in high winds was the dome. Our choice was a customized eight-foot-diameter North Star model by The North Face. The only disadvantage, one inherent in the dome design, was the excruciatingly long process required to set up the tents in the cold. The sections of the six sixteen-foot poles are held together with elastic cords, which, we found, lose all elasticity in extreme cold.

Once pieced together, the poles must be threaded through a maze of sleeves on the tent roof, which is then pulled taut over the poles to form the dome. In the cold, this process can take well over half an hour. Add a stiff breeze and it becomes nearly impossible. Paul came up with the brilliant solution of glueing the pole sections together, threading them through their sleeves, and then permanently affixing one end of each pole to the grommets around the tent base. The resulting system was a tent that could be popped up or dismantled quickly in almost any weather conditions and easily stowed on the sleds.

As good as these tents were, if their thin nylon membranes did not survive the rigors of the polar sea, our lives would be in jeopardy. On the third day of my dogsled journey with Mantell across the Canadian Barrens, a blizzard nearly destroyed our two-man tunnel tent. Winds gusting to eighty miles per hour packed snow as hard as concrete between our tent fly and inner wall. Then one of the back seams popped and a zipper broke open from the pressure. Mantell grabbed the seam to secure it while I bailed snow out. For three days the blizzard howled, while we kept a constant vigil with sewing awl in hand to secure every rip that occurred. When the winds abated we retreated to Baker Lake, the village from which we had embarked, for more substantial repairs.

When I entered my tent that second night of our polar journey, Paul was the only one still outside, finishing some chores. With plans to make a radio check the following morning from inside his sleeping bag on the sled, he had stretched the thirty-foot copper antenna wire between pinnacles of ice nearby, then climbed down into a sheltered crack for his evening constitutional. Taking a dump on the polar sea was not quite as awful as might be imagined, because our clothing system incorporated a couple of special design features. The Quallofil parkas were cut wide and long so that when you squatted, they formed a tentlike shelter around you. From within, you undid a waist belt and pulled down the "trap door" on the back of the one-piece inner suit, tucking it up safely out of range between your knees. Despite these provisions, it was still a cold, miserable job and was always completed in record time. But Paul, mesmerized by the stark beauty around him and the tangerine afterglow of the sunset, dawdled a bit too long that second evening on the polar sea and found himself in a dilemma. Too cold to move and too far from the tents to call for help, he felt a flash of panic cross his mind. What a way to go, he thought. With a burst of adrenaline he somehow pulled himself together and raced back to the comfort of his tent.

As we prepared our dinner, we wrestled again with fumes from sputtering flames on our stoves. The hacking cough returned, but it was a small price to pay for the touch of warmth the stoves brought to our frigid tents. These stoves, Mountain Safety Research's XGK and WhisperLite models, had proven foolproof on earlier treks. I knew there had to be a simple solution to the current problem. The stoves consist of a small plastic air pump that screws tightly into a one-liter aluminum fuel bottle. From this a ten-inch steel tube feeds pressurized fuel to a tiny jet housed in a burner the size of a coffee cup. When operating properly, this frail-looking apparatus puts out a jet of blue flame like a blowtorch. The fuel tube glows red hot where it loops through the flame to ensure that the fuel is completely vaporized before ignition. Thus, to start the stove you prime the burner area with a squirt of raw gas.

Could it be, I wondered, that at these temperatures the fuel feeding the jets was so cold that it never had a chance to vaporize? After all, we had to probe the priming fuel with a lit match to get it to ignite, and often the priming fuel simply doused the flame. Prewarming the fuel bottles might be a solution, I surmised. We allowed them to soak in a potful of "snow water" for a few minutes. When we lit the jet, it sputtered for a few moments and then popped into a clean blue flame. Ah, the joy of victory! The stove roared to life with a sound that made conversation difficult but brought a sense of warmth and security to our tent. Coincidentally, the other tent group hit upon a similar solution that same evening. Rather than soak the bottles in warm water, they tucked them inside warm parkas or sleeping bags for a while.

Our stove problems were not yet over, though. Later, when I pumped the plunger to repressurize the fuel bottle, fuel suddenly began spraying out around the seal. In a flash the escaping fuel ignited and a wave of blue flames swept across the stove box and flooded out across the tent floor. We sprang into action, smothering the flames with our fire blanket. The neoprene O-rings that sealed the fuel bottles, we found, were prone to cracking in the cold. Fortunately we had several spares.

None of us panicked during the fire. We had anticipated a tent fire or two. Nearly every major polar expedition has had one. Mantell and I had a similar incident on our Barrens trek, and Paul's tent group had a serious fire during one of our training journeys near Frobisher. Disaster was averted in the nick of time when Paul dove out the tent door and pulled the flaming stove box out behind him. With those drills under our belt, we responded to this fire reflexively. With split-second timing I slid the stove box out the door while Richard smothered the flames spreading across the floor with our fire blanket, a three-foot-square piece of ceramic cloth called Z-Tex.

The one-gallon tin that served as our potty was a lowly piece of equipment, but invaluable. The humble "piss can" served multiple purposes. Before dinner we would, from now on, be using it as a bucket for warming fuel bottles. After dinner we disposed of washwater, food scraps, and tea bags in it. And then, of course, it would be topped off each night with our final pee before bed. To crawl outside to take a leak was out of the question. Opening the door would release all the heat in the tent. Furthermore, any movement or shuffling about tended to knock down the frost that collected on the ceiling.

In my tent I was the assigned "keeper of the can," and kept it under my watchful eye at the head of my bed when it was not in use. My last chore each evening was to ensure that the can was dumped just outside the door and then returned to its "standby" position. Generally, Mantell would empty it as he exited for his nightly berth in the sled bag. If that crucial task was overlooked—and it was on a couple of regrettable occasions—the can would have to be thawed over the stove in the morning so that its frozen contents could be removed.

DAY 3

"BAD NEWS . . . THE PAD OF ZAP'S FRONT PAW IS BADLY SPLIT."

The goal we set for ourselves during the first week of the trip was just to get through the days and have a few miles of progress to show for it. As long as we didn't take too much of a beating early on, we would make it to the fifteenth round and then, maybe, the North Pole. Our bodies were steadily growing acclimated to the conditions and our minds were slowly beginning to accept the fact that, hostile as this place might seem, it would be "home" for a couple of months.

After being immersed in the cold night and day, we found that even extremes of temperature became relative. For example, consider this exchange of words. Upon waking that morning, I peeked out the tent door to check our thermometer. "Hey, Bob," I shouted cheerfully to Mantell, who was shuffling toward the tent from his sled, "it's only minus sixty today!"

"Yeah," he responded glibly, "I thought it felt warmer out."

Meanwhile, Paul, tucked in his sled bag with the radio that he had warmed during the night, was having a less cheerful conversation with Jim Gasperini, our support staff member who was managing our radio base in Resolute. This was to be the first of our twice-weekly radio checks in which Paul would report our progress, our health, and newsworthy incidents. Jim would pass this on to key sponsors and media groups who held the rights to news coverage of the expedition. A steady tug-of-war ensued throughout the journey between the parties involved concerning these rights. Thus a large portion of many radio checks was consumed by details of the latest gambit. The issue that morning concerned the tape-recorded diary entries Ann and Geoff had agreed to make for the *Minneapolis Star and Tribune,* which would publish portions of the transcripts in its news stories. The KSTP-TV reporter, Jason Davis, was now contending that recordings of any kind were the property of his station. Paul suggested some solutions, nodding in frustration as he realized that the desolate polar sea would offer him no escape from the business side of the expedition.

Contracts and sponsorships had been a constant preoccupation for Paul and me for nearly three years. Fund-raising for the expedition had begun the day I returned home in September 1983 from my eighteen-month trek across the Arctic. By surveying magazine ads, I had learned that the divisions of the Du Pont company that produced fabrics and fibers for the camping industry utilized expedition endorsements in their marketing strategy. All of their ads featured mountaineering expeditions. Perhaps they'd like something fresh and different, like a dogsled trip to the Pole, I thought as I called their Wilmington, Delaware, headquarters on a WATS line. My inquiry was brushed off with a polite but firm "No, thanks." Undaunted, I continued to pursue them with phone calls and letters for months. I traveled to England the following spring to research the route and the Cook-Peary controversy at the Scott Polar Research Institute in Cambridge. I also toured the East Coast, meeting with publishers, marketing representatives, and Arctic researchers. My first big break came when *National Geographic* agreed to buy the magazine rights to the story. Now potential sponsors were more apt to lend me their ears.

By August, my perseverance with Du Pont had paid off. I had my first check in hand. Paul joined on and, with equipment loaned to us by our local power company, we set up an office complete with word processor in the front room of his tiny house. Then we launched our shotgun approach to fund-raising, blasting out hundreds of letters and phone calls to companies all over the country. We lived hand to mouth, often having to do some fast talking to keep the creditors at bay. Twice our phone was cut off as the monthly bills, which often neared $2,000, far exceeded our resources. As our debts started to mount, Paul and I would always remind each other of the maxim, "There's nothing like a good debt to increase your sales power."

When we returned home in early summer 1985 after the training journey to Point Barrow, the expedition was $20,000 in debt—not a very good base from which to start raising the sum of well over $100,000 needed to meet the costs of the charter flights and other expenses on the Pole journey. Since six-figure budgets are difficult to raise in the quiet woods around Ely, Minnesota, Paul and I packed our bags for a series of East Coast crusades. We became experts at budget travel and could pull off a one-week business trip—flight included—for $300 each.

Generally, our first stop was Washington, D.C., home of the *National Geographic*. Since I was under contract to them for magazine coverage of the story, they paid for my flight and lodging. Paul would book a Sunday-night economy flight months in advance and sleep on my hotel room floor. We'd spend the next day paying courtesy calls or meeting with *Geographic* staff, Arctic research firms, Senate staff, or personnel at various embassies, updating them about our plans and seeking information or support.

When we'd completed our rounds, we'd take Amtrak to Wilmington, Delaware, headquarters of Du Pont, whose Fiberfil division was the chief contributor to the expedition. There we would deluge marketing managers with the reasons why this expedition would boost sales of their clothing and camping equipment fibers and negotiate sponsorship arrangements. We scheduled our arrival for noon so that our first meeting could be over lunch, with Du Pont footing the bill. We would eat like wolves, hoping the meal would tide us over until our next business luncheon. On our first trip to Wilmington after the training journey, we had a difficult task. We had already spent $20,000 of Du Pont's money, reaping them relatively little publicity, and were now about to ask for $40,000 more. Before Paul could launch his carefully crafted pitch, they read us the riot act, asking us to account for our use of their funds. Paul and I unabashedly assured them that the payoff was coming—if only they'd give us just one more substantial check. The Du Pont reps gawked at us in disbelief as we rambled on, outlining various publicity schemes in hopes of piquing their curiosity. "Wait a minute!" the leader of the meeting shouted suddenly as he leaned back in his chair, "a lightbulb just went off in my head." He outlined a brilliant series of marketing ideas that would tie the expedition in with their sales strategies. Paul and I glanced at each other and smiled, knowing the deal was cinched.

By late afternoon on the days of our Wilmington visits, we were on the train for New York, where we set up shop in a friend's apartment. Our days there would be spent shaking the money tree and seeking publicity, meeting with potential sponsors and various journalists. Most often we'd travel about the city on foot, shuffling along at a fast clip to make appointments, but pacing ourselves so we wouldn't arrive sweaty and ruffled. During breaks, we would retreat to the midtown offices of one of our sponsors, Borg Textile, which generously granted us the use of a telephone, a typewriter, and a photocopy machine. Paul worked best under pressure, and if we needed a well-crafted sponsorship proposal for a meeting an hour later, he'd have one out in twenty minutes or less. Meanwhile, I'd be on the phone courting interest among journalists or going green-eyed over the copy machine, cranking out expedition press releases and other promotional materials.

By midsummer we felt we had thoroughly covered our bases on the East Coast but we still had more than $50,000 to raise. We decided to try working the Twin Cities some more. Knowing that local media interest would be the strongest, we offered exclusive television and newspaper rights to KSTP Television and the *Minneapolis Star and Tribune* respectively. They emphasized in their negotiations with us that they weren't buying news but were rather seeking priority over competitors in gaining access to it. The catch was to coordinate television and newspaper coverage with *Geographic*'s interest, since their story on the expedition wouldn't come out until months afterward. The pivotal moment came when *Geographic* sent out the head of their news service, Paul Sampson, to meet with KSTP and the *Tribune* and discuss the issues involved. His presence in the Twin Cities lent us some credibility and some bargaining clout. As a conversation piece for the meetings, we brought my sled dog Zap along. For three days we chauffeured Sampson and Zap around in my 1970 Cadillac, which was missing its muffler and, worse yet, had a leaky gas tank. To keep the tank from draining during our meetings, I had to angle the car by parking on a hill or, when one couldn't be found, with the rear tire perched on the curb. Very politely, Sampson never commented on my unusual parking habits, and shortly after his visit, we had the last of our media contracts signed.

A groundswell of support began to build throughout Minnesota. Our souvenir T-shirts and posters sold briskly as word trickled to virtually every household in the state about our plans. To enhance our visibility, we put casters on one of the dogsleds and entered a few parades. These were always a calculated risk, since you never knew how the dogs might respond in a crowd. One such event was set up as a celebrity race between two of my dog teams in downtown St. Paul, with our state's lieutenant governor driving one of the sleds. Rounding a corner, one of the teams took a shortcut over the sidewalk, smashing the sled into the curb and sending its passengers flying Fortunately no one was injured and the event reaped good press coverage.

To help fill the coffers on the home front, we launched our Minnesota Support Campaign and printed T-shirts and posters to sell as souvenirs. That eased our cash-flow problem. Our U.S. senator, Dave Durenberger, took a personal interest in the project and helped arrange for sponsorships from many local companies. We put our sled dogs and equipment on tour at fairs and shopping malls, and soon our plans were known in every corner of the state. Hundreds of people sent contributions and dozens of volunteers arranged fund-raising events of various kinds. All told, these grass-roots efforts accounted for nearly a fourth of our budget. The remainder of our needs for cash, equipment, and services were met by some sixty companies worldwide that caught the enterprising spirit of our project. But cost overruns would plunge us increasingly into debt as the journey progressed, adding another nagging anxiety to our overload of stress.

Those events seemed a lifetime away as we lashed our sleds on the morning of Day 3. I noticed the damage the cold had already done to us. Brent was wincing in pain when he handled the lines or did intricate jobs like unclipping dogs from the stakeout cable. His fingers had been badly frostbitten. I was particularly struck by what a mess McKerrow's nose was. It had been broken during training when his sled careened down a steep pressure ridge and he was slammed face-first onto the ice. Swollen and crooked, it was covered with a hideous thick mat of dead flesh, blackened with frostbite. Pus oozed out of cracks formed when the swollen, frostbitten skin had thawed and contracted. But what amazed me most was that the damage and suffering that accompanied it had done little to dampen McKerrow's robust spirit. His great heart radiated vitality even when he was in pain. Listening to him rattle off endless quips and cheery comments in his lyrical New Zealand accent as he worked on the sled with me, I suddenly felt warm. I was heartened by the fact that no one was complaining about the cold or discomfort.

The best part of the day was when the sleds were levered free and the dogs moved out. The sense of power and spirit in the dogs would fill us with pride and excite our souls. Toes and fingers were always nearly frozen after the tedious stationary job of lashing sleds, and thus we leaned into the uprights with vigor when it came time to launch. Moving sleds meant work for us, and the blessing of heat that it brought. But the departure of all five sleds had to be coordinated on cue. If some carried on in advance, they would pay for it later with a frigid wait when it came time to rendezvous.

The sleds were proving to be remarkably durable, withstanding the stress of the cold, the monstrous loads, and the pack ice with no sign of weakness. We had borrowed heavily from the traditional Greenland *kamotik* in designing them. Sixteen feet long, they had two eight-inch-high runners spaced thirty-four inches apart, with slats lashed across their tops. For maximum strength and resilience, Mantell and Brent had laminated the runners from twenty-four layers of Sitka spruce, an extremely lightweight and straight-grained wood, bonded together with a special cold-weather epoxy resin. Lateral strength was increased by sheathing the sides of the runners in an extremely light aircraft-grade plywood made in Finland. A three-foot "upstander," or handlebar, was lashed in place on the rear of each sled. No nails, bolts, or screws were employed in the construction, as these would shear off when the sled flexed. One-eighth-inch nylon parachute cord was used throughout to bind the parts together. Well over a thousand dollars' worth of materials had gone into each sled. Among the most expensive components was the special friction-resistant plastic known as silicon-embedded ultra-high molecular weight polypropylene, with which we lined the runners and slats. Despite its impressive name, this material was as humbled by the extreme cold as we were. It held up fine but didn't glide well on the snow in temperatures below −40 degrees. We suspected that nothing could be designed to glide at the temperatures we encountered.

To further lighten our sleds that morning, Day 3, we left behind an additional 100 pounds from each sled at camp that morning, making for an average payload of 1,000 pounds. Our

plan was to push ahead for another full day before sending sleds
back to retrieve the two caches we now had on the ice. But this
had little impact on our progress. Each yard gained was still a
hard-fought battle. Throughout the day, we ran back and forth
from sled to sled, prying and pushing over the pressure ridges
and slogging through deep snow on the flats. We were now in
virgin territory, beyond the trail we had blazed while based at
Drep Camp, meaning that three or more team members had to
be diverted to scout and chop a route, thus reducing our pushing
power.

The workload, the cold, and the relentless stopping and starting thoroughly frustrated the dogs that day. Their irritation
surfaced in growls, scuffles, and some rip-roaring fights. Like
wolves, these dogs have a pack order, with the alpha male or
"boss dog," as the Eskimos call it, at the top. Generally the fights
that erupt in the pack are mere skirmishes, the result of irritations from exhaustion or hunger. But if the fight results from an
underling challenging the boss dog, it can be a life-and-death
matter. A driver who knows his dog well can immediately tell
the cause of the battle. Often a quick voice command will restore
order, but if they are locked in a death struggle, then the driver
has to start swinging, kicking, pounding, and clubbing—anything to pull them apart. This may seem cruel, but it is the only
means of saving the dogs from possible mutilation or even death.

While I was out in front scouting, leaving Ann to handle my
team, Zap picked a fight with his son Chester. The two were
running in lead together. It was just a domestic squabble. Zap
was feeling irritable and decided to vent his frustrations on whatever was nearest. But though Chester was the smallest and mel-
lowest dog on my team, he was no slouch when it came to a
battle. Even the big Eskimo dogs respected him. Hearing the
growls, I ran back to my sled while Ann, who felt such affection
toward my dogs that she hated to be forceful with them, was
vigorously yanking them apart. I was furious, knowing they had
taken advantage of the lapse in discipline to pick a fight. "Bad
news, Will," she said. "The pad of Zap's front paw is badly
split."

As I examined the deep wound, my heart sank. He was one
of my favorite dogs and had been on every dogsled trip I had ever
taken. A friend had given him to me nine years before. I remember well the day I hitchhiked up to Ely with him tucked in a shoe
box. Standing there on a freeway entrance, I looked down at that
little ball of black and white fur with one blue and one black eye.

He was shaking, terrified by the cars roaring past. "Poor thing," I said, sheltering the box under my pack, "you look just like a crazed bolt of lightning. I think I'll name you Zap."

Unfortunately, his puppyhood at my cabin in Ely was not a happy one. He became very attached to a young female dog named Gretchen. One day when Zap was four months old, he and Gretchen took off on a romp. Four days later, a neighbor five miles away found and returned Zap, but no sign ever turned up of Gretchen. Zap seemed deeply affected by this and fell into a melancholy mood that lingered a long time. A year later he suffered an injury that permanently changed the profile of his head. During a snowstorm, a huge branch broke from a tree in the kennel and fell on him, leaving a dent in his skull. To make matters worse, Blacky and Soapy, two brothers who ruled the kennel with an iron paw, had singled out Zap for abuse. During his first winter these gangsters, the toughest, meanest dogs on my team, jumped Zap a number of times. Each would grab one of his ears and shake him in opposite directions. The tip of his left ear was slowly whittled away in the process. All I could do was try to keep those three apart.

With his blue and black eyes and chewed-off ear, he looked like a real street fighter, but he was one of the most sensitive, affectionate dogs I have ever met. He seemed to win the hearts of everyone who met him. And on expeditions he proved to be one of my most valuable dogs. Many times, for example, when I would be crossing thin ice and the team would begin to panic, Zap's loyalty to me would shine through. He would set an example by pulling steadily along while the others were freaking out.

But he did himself in one day in 1985, and became regionally famous as a result. I was sledding across Canada's Great Slave Lake in a howling blizzard. While stopped for a rest, I noticed that Zap was frantically licking his groin. His penis was fully extended, frozen solid. "Oh no, Zap!" I said. "What were you daydreaming about this time?" I nearly panicked, distraught over the pain he must be in and fearing he might die. Fortunately, the weather warmed the next morning and I was able to get him to an Indian village and have him treated. He healed up just fine, but that trail story ended up a week or so later on the front page of the *Minneapolis Star and Tribune*.

Zap was now a household word in Minnesota. Everywhere I went, people asked about him. Thus he became our mascot during preparations for the Pole trip. His face appeared on buttons, T-shirts, and posters. At fund-raisers the crowd would chant, "Zap to the Pole! Zap to the Pole!" when he was brought on stage. Paul and I always found it amazing that despite his banged-up, scarred gangster face, nearly everyone who met him commented on what a beautiful dog he was. Apparently they saw through to his warm heart.

His fame spread to the East Coast. Zap accompanied Paul, Susan, and me when we stopped in New York for a press conference luncheon at the Explorers Club on our way to Frobisher Bay in mid-January. On a shuttle flight, New York Air allowed him to sit on a seat in the passenger section. At La Guardia, a gleaming silver limousine was waiting for us. Zap, proudly sporting a bright red cape that Susan had made for him, emblazoned with a huge gold *Z*, hopped in and settled into the prime spot between the bar and the television set, as if this were his customary means of travel. But his greatest honor was yet to come. At the Penta Hotel, the desk clerk could not find our names among the reservations. Several times he searched. "Ah, might this be it?" he finally asked, holding up a VIP registration card in the name of "Zap the Wonderdog." That evening we walked Zap down to Times Square to oblige press photographers who couldn't resist the opportunity for an ironic setting. The next morning the *Minneapolis Star and Tribune* sported a picture of Paul, Zap, and me posing at the world's most famous intersection with the title "Publicity Hounds Hit Broadway." A few days later they ran another photo from Zap's Broadway debut, a picture of him nose-to-nose with a toy poodle, perched on its tiptoes, whom he had encountered on Fifth Avenue. I had Zap securely tethered in my hands on a heavy steel chain while the delicately manicured poodle, which apparently had no understanding of relative size, was frantically emitting a threatening squeak, restrained by what looked like a gold necklace in the hands of a distinguished though somewhat rattled older woman. With the utmost patience, Zap ignored the challenge and thoroughly sniffed the perfumed creature with a look of complete disbelief.

We all desperately wanted Zap to reach the Pole. But as I looked down at his bloodied paw, I knew that was no longer in the cards. Ann bandaged him up and put him on antibiotics. We could only hope that over the next few weeks until the dog pickup, his injury wouldn't become more severe.

Most of the dogs on Mantell's and my team had much thinner coats than the Eskimo dogs. Our two teams were basically of

Alaskan husky stock, but over the years a variety of breed lines had been mixed into them, including Eskimo dog, Mackenzie River husky, and timber wolf. Mine averaged around seventy pounds, while Mantell's, most of them Iditarod race dogs he had purchased in Alaska, weighed only fifty to sixty pounds. My goal in selecting and breeding dogs over the past dozen years has been to build the high spirit of a racing dog into the frame of a freight dog. And since it's hard to strike the right combination of spirit and power through breeding, I'd help ensure that it was built into my team through the mixing of personalities. On my Pole team, my lead dog Chester and a Mackenzie River husky named Sam were the sparkplugs. Though light and lean, they were always brimming with spirit, barking and dancing, anxious to pull in any conditions. Choochi, Yeager, and Leif were my intermediate dogs; they combined a fair spirit with a good coat and good size, and ran as a group in the back half of the team. They'd been sired by a huge Eskimo dog I'd obtained from Arctic villagers during my eighteen-month journey. These three had pleasant demeanors, something lacking in my other three intermediate dogs, Zap, Tim, and Slidre, who were sometimes moody or irritable. In "wheel," the position nearest the sled, I had two Eskimo dogs, Mongo and Capone, who were huge and powerful but needed the spark of Chester's antics to keep them motivated. Mantell also used two Eskimo dogs in wheel position with his Alaskan dogs.

The Eskimo dogs, ours and the ones that Brent, Paul, and Geoff were handling, were ten to twenty pounds heavier than the Alaskans. Paul's dog Ciarnuk, a handsome, powerfully built dog of 115 pounds with a playful, humble demeanor, was the largest on the expedition. Moving along with slow, steady gaits like little Sherman tanks, the Eskimo dogs provided the bulk of the power for moving our heavy loads over the horrendous pack ice we encountered early in the journey. To compensate for our dogs' thinner coats, Mantell and I brought chunks of sleeping pad foam for them to curl up on. And Zap, our team mascot, wore his red cape every night.

To see how the Eskimo dogs would do with our Alaskans, we had brought the team Paul was now using down from Igloolik to Ely in September by plane, train, and truck. Their first encounter with a woodland environment was a memorable one. The smell that arose from the mossy forest floor baffled their noses. Having never seen trees before, they looked as disoriented as if they were on another planet. One of them, Mongo, staged a standoff with a young birch. Growling and pawing the ground, he threatened it until he felt it had shown proper submission, and then, responding to an instinct he didn't know he had, he thoroughly hosed it down. In the dogyard, many of them set to work chewing up fallen branches, apparently thinking they were bones.

In the early afternoon of that day, March 10, I turned back from scouting trail to check in with the team and, topping a head ridge, was captivated by the sight of our five teams steaming northward across a large pan. What a fantastic sight it was! Dogs, sleds, and drivers enveloped in fog, with vapor trails stretching out behind each team. They looked like a wagon train inching across a dusty prairie. The drivers were issuing a steady stream of commands and words of encouragement to their dogs. "Hup! Hup! G'dogs! Let's go! Straight on, now! Hubba Hup! Out front!" I was struck by what a huge operation this expedition was. Perhaps, I thought, this is the last time in history a dogsled expedition of this size will travel the polar sea.

Represented among the dog team was nearly the whole range of sled dog types and, among the drivers, a wide range of Arctic experience and travel systems. For example, the five teams employed a variety of hitching techniques. Mantell's Alaskan dogs were hitched in the tandem system, with the dogs clipped two-by-two to short paired tuglines that were spaced at six-foot intervals along a fifty-foot gangline. The beauty of this system is order; it minimizes chances for tangles. The disadvantage is that with the dogs stretched out over a long distance, some power is lost. To minimize that problem, I employed a modified tandem hitch. My dogs were still linked by tuglines to a central gangline, but the rear dogs were grouped in threes or even fours. Thus, though I ran a somewhat greater risk of tangles, my gangline was only about thirty-five feet long. Paul also used a modified tandem hitch with his team of Eskimo dogs.

The most compact system, the one Geoff and Brent employed with their Eskimo dogs, is the traditional Eskimo fan hitch, in which the dogs run as a pack. Separate traces of staggered lengths, the longest being around twenty-five feet, link each dog directly to the sled. The system gives the dogs much freedom for jumping cracks and securing good footing on sections of rough ice. But the same freedom produces tangles, and the traces of a fan hitch inevitably become a knotted mess after a few hours of travel.

The driving techniques for the hitch systems differ as well.

With the fan hitch, voice commands are punctuated by the snap of a whip. The pack is sort of herded along like sheep by snapping the whip to the right or left of them to get them to turn. The whip never touches them. It is merely an extension of the driver's voice, a turn signal of sorts. The traditional Eskimo whips that Brent and Geoff used were twenty-foot-long strips of bearded seal hide cut in a steady taper from the wooden handle base to the tip. The rest of us, with our tandem hitches, used only voice commands, though we had only one dog, Mantell's lead dog Critter, who responded well to "gee" and "haw," the traditional mushing commands for turning right and left respectively. With one team member out front scouting the trail all the time, voice-command lead dogs were not essential on this trip.

Throughout training we debated endlessly the merits of the various systems. In general, it seemed that the fan, with a tighter grouping of dogs, offered the most power in big pack ice, while the tandem offered the steadiest progress on the straightaways, with the dogs pulling like a train. The determining factor, though, was the driver's preference and the type of system each team of dogs had been accustomed to. For Mantell, Brent, and me, who had dogs we had trained ourselves, our teams were truly extensions of our own personalities, and so they ran best in the system in which we had conditioned them.

Brent was by far the most daring sled driver in our crew. Steering generally from the front of his sled, he would jump deftly from side to side, pushing its bow to maneuver it around blocks of ice. Tall and lanky, he always seemed only inches away from getting his legs trapped and crushed. On smooth sections of ice, he would amble along with a sauntering gait, with the carefree look of someone pushing a shopping cart. He seemed perfectly at home in the Arctic and had great rapport with his team of Eskimo dogs, herding them about with simple commands and a snap of his whip. Most of them he'd raised himself.

Born and raised in Edmonton, Alberta, he was attracted to Canada's north and had moved to Baffin Island nine years before. There he married an Inuit woman, Nala, had a son, Nigel, now seven, and started Nun-Kuuk Outfitters, a dogsled and kayak trip business. Four months before the expedition, he and Nala had their second child, Crystal. Brent had been recommended to us as a team member candidate by Ken MacRury, a government administrator on Baffin whom Paul and I had contacted a year before while looking for a site for our final training base. We paid a visit to Frobisher to meet Brent and consider it as a training base. We were pleased with what we found. Brent agreed to join the team, and Ken, who was very receptive to our plans, generously offered to provide housing and coordinate a two-month stay during our final training. Brent, in turn, agreed to include his team on the expedition and helped us arrange to get additional Eskimo dogs through Ultima Thule Expeditions, an outfitting business in Igloolik.

Although Brent may have been our most intrepid sled handler, Geoff, who was in charge of the renegade team we had added a week before departure, had by far the greatest challenge as a dog driver. As he noted in his journal that night, "They are like a pack of juvenile delinquents, completely unsocialized and very difficult to handle. They exist only as a pack, getting along well among themselves but viewing the rest of the world as the enemy. They don't give a shit about me and hate to be touched. I can punish them by petting them."

One serious handicap Geoff faced was that he simply didn't know their language. In the rush of airlifting these dogs from a remote Arctic village to our training base, we had received no information about the commands they were accustomed to, nor had we been told their names. Geoff set about rechristening each of them, and experimented with several intonations, hoping to hit upon ones they might respond to. He finally settled upon the words "Ite! Ite!" and, using this in combination with the snap of the whip, he was able to herd them along. However, they had a terrible habit of milling about uncontrollably whenever the sleds stopped, knotting the lines up in a horrible mess. These knots could only be undone with bare fingers, a very painful and dangerous job. Several of Geoff's fingertips were blackened with frostbite during the first few days of the journey. Geoff has the patience of a saint, but their antics left him infuriated. "The only solution," he noted, "is to make them lie down whenever the sled stops." And so he would corral them into a bunch and make them lie low by snapping the whip in a circle around them. "But when I discipline them," he continued, "they challenge me with growls and I'm sure there's not too much of a separation between their growls and an attack. Pretty exciting stuff! What could be more interesting than driving a team of wild dogs to the Pole!"

Geoff's dogs were a real slice of history. At the turn of the century, most Eskimo and Indian sled dogs were as wild as these dogs. They were never treated as pets, but rather played a strictly utilitarian role in the harsh boom-and-bust life cycle of the Arctic. In times of plenty, the dogs feasted. In times of hardship, they were fed to each other or eaten by the villagers. When they were ravenous, they were dangerous. During my visits to Arctic villages over the years, I had often heard stories about instances of a person who slipped and fell in front of a hungry team of wild dogs and was killed and eaten. Thus, though they are an essential part of the development of northern cultures, many natives have a natural fear of them. Indeed, most of us were nervous around Geoff's dogs from time to time. They simply had no respect for us. Once when I was running along in front of them, I turned around and saw them eyeing me like a pork chop. It took a very rare person to handle these dogs, and we all felt very lucky to have Geoff on board.

We had met Geoff, an Arctic wildlife biologist, at the end of our expedition training journey in Barrow, Alaska, where he had seasonal employment with Alaska's North Slope Borough. His job was an intriguing though somewhat tedious one: counting whales that pass by the coast during their spring migration from the Pacific Ocean to calving grounds in the Beaufort Sea. We found him spending his days in a lawn chair on top of a pressure ridge ten miles out to sea, counting the flukes and blowholes of whales that surfaced in the lead in front of him. The information was used to monitor the stability of bowhead whale populations, and for determining the annual hunting quota for North Slope Eskimos. We knew we needed more team members—our exercises in the sea ice had persuaded us to go with eight rather than six—and the census bureau staff highly recommended Geoff.

Born and raised in Wyoming, this big, strapping, soft-spoken man had two young daughters, a pleasant Western drawl, a ready wit, and a thorough knowledge of sea ice. He had one other impressive credential—a week before I met him, he had deftly thwarted an attack by a polar bear. That night, while he and his colleagues were asleep at the survey site, a young bear ambled into camp and nosed his way into a tent where Geoff's colleagues were sleeping. Abruptly awakened and caught without a rifle, they grabbed a steaming teapot off their stove and hurled it at the bear. Bristling with anger, he reeled back out of the tent. Hearing the commotion, Geoff stepped out from a nearby tent with his rifle. The bear charged directly for him. Shouldering his rifle and preparing to fire, Geoff found the safety jammed. Running full tilt, the bear was within an arm's reach of him when Geoff swung the butt of the rifle around with all his might like a baseball bat, smashing the bear over the nose and sending it rolling backwards. Before it could regain its footing, his colleagues grabbed another rifle and shot it. Considering the responsiveness Geoff displayed in that episode, we knew he would be a good candidate for our team.

Late in our third day on the sea ice, a haze blanketed the sky, the temperature warmed slightly, to −55, but soon a stiff crosswind developed. These conditions were the most torturous I had ever experienced. We were driven faster and faster to generate sufficient warmth. Parka drawstrings were pulled taut; any exposed flesh would flash-freeze. Survival alone seemed to require all of our energy.

In six hours we covered two miles. We all had hacking coughs, and many of us were spitting up thick green phlegm. Stress had given Paul, Brent, and McKerrow flu-like symptoms—nausea, stomach pains, and, the worst of all curses in the cold, diarrhea. Believe me, there's no greater drag in life than having the runs at −70 degrees. And my tentmates and I were battling headaches and sore throats. I suspected these resulted more from fumes of faulty stoves than from exhaustion. In the tent that night, I surveyed our frostbite injuries. Geoff was fighting intense pain from four blackened fingers. I cringed when I looked at them. His unruly bunch of dogs had created such knots in his lines that day that he had repeatedly had to stop and, stripping down to his light gloves, undo the macrame of tangles. Mantell had several frozen toes, the victims of an unforeseen equipment disaster. The snow and ice were as sharp and coarse as heavy sandpaper. The grit was cutting through the moosehide soles on our mukluks. Mantell's had already worn through, so he had switched to his sealskin boots, intended only for warmer conditions, when sea water seeps up on the surface. While he waited, time and again throughout the day, for the sleds ahead of his to inch forward, the cold had numbed his toes and heels like novocaine and frozen them.

The frost had dealt its severest blow to me on my face. Flesh to nearly a quarter-inch deep had been frozen on my cheeks, nose, chin, and forehead. But I was thankful that my damage was limited to cosmetic features rather than functional parts like fingers and toes. I wondered how Mantell would fare. The slow but sure demise of our mukluks was a very serious matter. We could repair them, but that required long hours of stitching each night, costing us precious sleep as well as gas to warm the tents as we worked. Geoff's mukluks were deteriorating as quickly as

Mantell's. The damage to Mantell's feet had put us all on notice that footwear systems could not be compromised. As a result, long, cold hours of sewing became a standard ritual for many team members every evening.

That night I counted my blessings. Chief among them was the fact that my mukluks had not worn out, and so I could go to bed right after supper and get seven hours of sleep. Several times during the early hours of the night I awoke to hear the sound of roaring stoves as the other team members labored on for hours stitching damaged mukluks.

None of us questioned the value of the mukluk for this journey. It combines light weight, comfort, and warmth in a way that no modern winter footwear has matched. Made from various types of hides, the mukluk is basically a roomy bedroom slipper in which you wear numerous layers of thick, knee-high Eskimo socks known as duffels. The soft, flexible bottoms don't conduct heat away from your foot as hard-soled winter boots do. And the hide breathes well, minimizing perspiration buildup in your socks. We each carried three types: sheepskin, moosehide, and sealskin, this last type being called *kamiks*. The moosehide mukluks were our basic walking boot. The sheepskin mukluks were worn as over-booties during the coldest days of the trip, while the sealskin kamiks, which were waterproof though not terribly warm, would be used later in the trip, when temperatures would moderate a bit and we would hit wet conditions.

It came as no surprise to us that the sheepskin booties were wearing through. On the trail they lasted only a few weeks—about as long, we hoped, as the severely cold weather. As added insurance I carried extra pairs of them as part of my clothing allotment. The damage being done to the moosehide boots, the mainstay of our footwear, was the chief source of our anxiety. They were produced for us by a crafts co-op in the western Arctic. Because of various delays in production and shipping, we hadn't received them until the last few weeks of our training in Frobisher. They had been well crafted from good-quality, smoke-tanned hides, but the soles had looked suspiciously thin. However, at that point it was too late to make changes; we could only hope for the best. And now, unfortunately, the surface of the sea ice was proving to be much more abrasive than we had anticipated, grating away at our mukluk soles.

I'd been introduced to mukluks six years before, when my mushing partner Dave Olesen and I had sledded 700 miles along the coast of Hudson Bay. Two hundred miles north of our start-

ing point, we sledded into our first native village, Eskimo Point.
The locals were impressed to have white men, or *kabloonas,* as
they called us, arrive by dogsled, but they were amused by our
clothing system, which featured army-surplus wool jackets and
white felt "bunny boots." This system was adequate for Minnesota winters, but we found it barely marginal for the subarctic
conditions we then faced. The old men of the village provided
us with hide mukluks and skin clothing, showed us how to
construct and lash komatik sleds, and introduced us to eating
meat raw, rather than cooking it, for added nutrient value. We
left the settlement a few days later far more comfortable and with
a stronger appreciation for that vast land and the people who call
it home.

DAY 4

"NOODLES, CHEESE, PEMMICAN, AND OATS IN
REHEATED DILUTED TEA WATER. YUM, YUM."

Over breakfast the next morning, I consulted with Mantell and
Geoff about some ideas I had tossed around in my head the
evening before. To avoid burning out the dogs, we needed to
relay even more weight. I suggested we move our sleds forward
with half-loads and then, every few days, send empty sleds back
to retrieve the caches. In essence, we would make two trips. With
the empty backhaul, this plan would triple our mileage, but at
least we would be able, with light loads, to keep the sleds moving
at a pace that would keep the dogs' spirits up. At our current
pace I estimated that our dogs would give up within the week.
And our own morale might bottom out as well.

Despite the extra mileage, relays offer certain advantages. By
reducing payload weights, we would increase the safety margin
substantially. The heavy sleds were not only unwieldy uphill but
were also uncontrollably dangerous on the downgrades. And
lighter sleds could be handled by fewer people. Furthermore, the
monster payloads might overstress our laminated Sitka spruce
runners and cause them to crack or split. The size of our expedition, forty-nine dogs and eight people, lent itself well to relays.
It allowed for various combinations of units.

With the stoves functioning well, our breakfast routine proceeded much more quickly and smoothly. There was one little hitch. Our tent group decided to have dinner leftovers for breakfast. As we reheated the frozen lumps, the largest one turned out to be oatmeal. "Noodles, cheese, pemmican, and oatmeal reheated in diluted tea water. Yum, yum!" Richard quipped in his journal. We ate very little. Our appetites were marginal, but I knew that within a week or so we would be ravenous. A breakfast like this would be wolfed down and the bowls licked clean. On Arctic expeditions it always takes a week or so for the cold and the workload to take their effect on one's body. As body reserves are burned up, exhaustion sets in along with a keen appetite.

To ensure adequate body warmth on journeys such as this, a diet high in animal fats is essential. In fact, I have found that as the weather gets colder my body increasingly craves fats. Many times on the trail, I have found myself munching sticks of butter as if they were candy bars. Gram for gram, they pack in three times as many calories as carbohydrates. And, like huge chunks of cordwood in a furnace, they release energy slowly and steadily during their long digestion process. Since weight was such a crucial consideration on this journey, we selected food items that would pack the greatest number of calories in the smallest weight and volume. Our staple was pemmican, which, though largely unheard of nowadays, was a staple in the diet of the American plains Indians, who made it from buffalo meat. The early explorers recognized its virtues and adapted it for expeditions. Because the meat is raw, pemmican provides the full complement of nutrients and amino acids. You can sustain yourself indefinitely on a well-made mix. And because it is dried, it keeps a long time.

McKerrow had arranged for our supply to be made by Dawn Meats, a packing house in Hastings, New Zealand, that used a recipe provided by Sir Edmund Hillary, the New Zealand explorer who was a member of the first group to climb Mount Everest and who was one of the leaders of the first motorized surface traverse of Antarctica. Ours was 60 percent finely ground beef and 40 percent rendered fat with small amounts of wheat germ, molasses, and rose hips mixed in for added nutrients. It was fairly tasteless and had the color and texture of liver sausage. We would thaw blocks of it every evening and mix in cheese, butter, and noodles to form a pasty stew.

We had set our rations for the trip at two pounds, four ounces per day per person. Nearly a pound and a half of that was animal fat in various forms. Breakfast consisted of cooked rolled oats with four ounces of butter and three ounces of peanut butter. Lunch was a six-ounce lunch bar that we had made from dairy butter, dry milk, and various nut butters. Supper consisted of a half-pound of pemmican with two ounces of butter, four ounces of white cheese, and a cup or so of cooked ribbon egg noodles. The beverage was herbal tea made with melted snow. For added nutrition, most of us took Shaklee Vita-Lea supplements. No sugar or caffeine was included in our standard rations. These stimulants throw your body's metabolism on a roller-coaster ride of booms and crashes, which in the long run can have very detrimental effects.

For treats, we allowed each team member to bring six pounds—about two ounces a day—of personal rations. The selections were varied and interesting. I brought ten ounces of brown sugar, forty ounces of lemon squeezings—pulp and juice—for my tea, thirty-four ounces of raw dried seal meat, and sixteen ounces of Jack Daniel's. Paul brought raw dried caribou meat, popcorn, and raisins. Mantell brought a hardtack bread known as "pilot biscuits," and brown sugar. The others brought various sweets: candy, cocoa, mints, chocolate, and Shaklee energy bars. A few team members scrupulously metered out their treats day by day. Others gulped them down in large quantities, quickly diminishing their supply. That would lead to some interesting negotiations later on.

Unfortunately, most of us, being very lean, started this trip with minimal reserves. Having been thoroughly stressed by expedition preparations, I weighed in at only 135, ten pounds under my normal weight. This left me somewhat concerned because on previous expeditions I had always tried to maintain at least seven pounds of extra muscle weight that my body could burn up in the event of a food shortage. While traveling alone on a dogsled in the western Arctic in 1985, I ran out of food on Great Bear Lake. There was no sign of any game. And though the nearest village was only fifteen miles north of the lake in a valley, deep snowdrifts made the trail there impassable. My only option was to retreat 150 miles over well-established trails to Fort Franklin. Fortunately, I was in great shape and carrying my normal weight, so the three-day journey proceeded without incident. Being underweight on this polar journey, though, left me feeling very vulnerable.

Each of our bodies responded differently to the cold, depending on our metabolisms. Lean and wiry, weighing only 135 pounds, and having less than 10 percent body fat, I was on the "cold" end of the scale. Whenever I stopped working, my body had little resistance to the cold. I always slept with my insulated parka on—something the other team members almost never did—and I was still cold. I shivered for many long, miserable hours and shifted about to generate enough warmth to heat my sleeping bag. On the plus side, my low metabolism meant I rarely overheated. During the day I seldom had to unzip my wind parka to cool down as the others did. This may seem contradictory, but even at −50, while wrestling heavy sleds over pressure ridges, we often roasted in our polar suits. Mantell and Brent, with builds very similar to mine (though Brent was much taller), also had very low metabolisms and managed to stay relatively dry. Mantell's sleeping bag showed the least moisture gain. He credited this in part to sleeping outside, away from the damp air in our tents.

Geoff and McKerrow, with large frames and high metabolisms, were on the other end of the comfort scale. Though they suffered from cold fingers and toes as severely as any of us, they had little difficulty keeping their trunks warm. In fact, their major problem was overheating, a serious matter since it caused heavy perspiration, which dampened clothing systems. To keep from sweating, Geoff always shed his wind parka on calm days, regardless of the temperature. Nonetheless, at the end of each day his clothing was thickly coated with frost from condensed perspiration. He brushed it off as best he could, but when he entered the tent at night he looked like a snowman. McKerrow had a similar moisture problem. Both of them found their sleeping bags heavily caked with ice and frost early in the trip.

In between were Richard, Paul, and Ann. With his lean athletic build, Richard tended to generate little heat—at times he sweated at night—but he monitored it well and scrupulously avoided letting any frost collect on his clothing. Paul, who was tall, with a medium build, had a very high metabolism and was often scantily dressed in a makeshift system of vests, hats, hoods, and mitts that he would adjust to avoid perspiration. Nonetheless, as he scampered about, attending to a dozen projects at once, he was generally enveloped in a cloud of frost and steam, which prompted Ann to christen him "Pigpen" after the dust-clad character in the "Peanuts" comic strip.

Among the eight of us, Ann had the best body type for cold weather: short, medium-framed, with a low metabolism and—thanks to female physiology—an extra layer of body fat. Having the right amount of body insulation and a low metabolism struck a good balance between the opposing dangers of being over-chilled and overheated. This is not to say she didn't suffer from the cold, but I sensed that she had greater resistance to it than did those of us with leaner bodies. She also managed to maintain one of the driest clothing and sleeping systems in the group.

Our metabolisms were reflected in our appetites. Geoff and Paul ate the largest portions at each meal, ingesting between 6,000 and 8,000 calories apiece each day to fuel their demanding furnaces. Ann needed the least food, perhaps averaging 4,500 calories a day. I, too, ate small portions, mostly as a result of digestion problems with the high-fat diet that later would nearly debilitate me with diarrhea. Thus, while we had rationed out equal amounts for each team member, meals were informally reapportioned according to need on a daily basis.

On the morning of Day 4, we shaved twenty minutes off our tent time and, best of all, exited into the frigid air without the stove-fume hangover we had suffered with the first two days. Outside, it was again a −60-degree day, but somehow it didn't seem as brutal as the day before. Our bodies and minds were slowly adjusting to the conditions. With adaptation came more time and energy. Little time was wasted as we attended to one pack-up chore after another. We were no longer preoccupied with survival; rather, as I looked around I realized we were beginning to click as a team. The well-oiled machine we had sought to become during training was starting to take shape on the polar sea. Each of us tailored systems for increasing our comfort and warmth. Face masks were donned instantly, since we had found that would conserve body heat and keep fingers warm longer. We'd alternate stationary chores, such as taking down tents or lashing sleds, with active ones like hooking up dogs and shifting heavy loads among sleds to balance payload weights. If departure was delayed, those waiting would quickly grab a pickax and begin grooming the trail to maintain warmth.

The dogs, too, were now growing trail-wise. They became accustomed to the long workday and were slowly learning to pace themselves for it. But they could do nothing to minimize the frequent stops and long waits as sleds would bottleneck in rough sections. Unlike us, they were helpless to continue work-ing and generating heat when the sleds stopped. At best, they could slowly mill about in their traces, causing horrendous tan-gles that would just lengthen the delay as drivers had to sort through the web of lines.

That morning, Paul and I established a procedure for a team

huddle that we followed throughout the trip. When the sleds were ready to go, we would gather around the middle sled for a quick meeting. This gave us a good vantage point from which to monitor all five teams for fights and tangles as we talked. A meeting at −60 degrees running in place and talking fast and to the point.

My routine each morning was to mull over a plan for the day with my tent group and present it to everyone at the meeting. We'd assign certain sleds to relays and backhauls, others to pushing forward, and set a tentative quitting time based on the weather and the group's well-being. Despite our eagerness to hit the trail and generate warmth, each day's plan was often debated or discussed if team members had misgivings or other options. Our strength lay in our combined vast Arctic expedition experience.

At this morning's meeting, I described the plan to go ahead with half-loads. I also suggested that we should send one sled all the way back to Drep Camp to get some of the additional fuel we had left there. Because of the cold, we were burning more than we had planned to. Geoff and Richard agreed to take two teams back to retrieve the 1,600 pounds of supplies we had dropped along the trail the last few days. Mantell and Ann would go all the way back to Drep Camp. Our tents would be left in place while the rest of us took light loads ahead to establish a forward depot.

With work assignments agreed upon, the next agenda item— as it was most every morning—was establishing dog-food rations. We fed the teams varying amounts of Science Diet Maximum Stress dry food and pemmican each night, based on the temperature and workload, and we would decide on the amounts each morning to avoid confusion at quitting time. Paul and I also tried to weave into these meetings some overview of the general scheme for the next several days, as we saw it: the rotation of work assignments among sleds, the length of the working day, and the number of miles to shoot for. He and I would make a point of traveling together the first hour of the day to discuss strategy and assess group morale. Dogs were also a key issue at these meetings. Each driver would briefly summarize the state of his or her team, noting dogs that were showing signs of injury or burnout and would thus require special attention or extra rations.

Discussing these issues was very important, but the greatest value of these cold, hurried meetings was that they provided a forum for team members to vent frustrations and anxiety, a stopgap to prevent conflicts down the trail. Debate was encouraged if disagreements erupted. But Paul and I found that most of our teammates were so quiet and soft-spoken that we had to pry concerns out of them—all of this while we stomped our feet, jumped up and down, and whirled our arms to keep our limbs from freezing.

We adjourned that morning with plans to meet back at the same campsite around midnight, thus saving the time and energy of packing up tents and sleeping bags. With that, our crew split, half heading north and half south. I marveled at the sight of Geoff's wild dogs rocketing out of the camp with Geoff and the empty sled bumping along behind. With a lightened load, my dogs, too, pulled with new vigor. They radiated excitement with a lengthened stride, and their tails and ears perked up straight. "At last," I said to myself, "we are cooking."

Soon we hit a mile-wide stretch of rubble ice through which we chopped our way for three hours. Hell's Gate, we called it. Working together, Paul and I wrestled with doubts. As he noted in his journal that night, "Had a real lesson in life out there today: fighting doubt consumes more energy than blazing trail through rough sea ice. . . . But, thank God, hope springs eternal!"

The rubble ended in our first big break of the journey. A large pan opened up to the north, stretching as far as we could see. I thought about the massive disappointments Paul and I had plodded through in organizing this expedition. We had learned to charge headlong into insurmountable odds with perseverance and faith in ourselves. It's not the goal that counts, it's the process, I thought as I looked out across the smooth ice. The pan was, of course, just a temporary reprieve. More struggles awaited us over the horizon. But this oasis recharged my faith, bolstering it for the next challenge.

Our advance group blazed seven miles of trail that day, dropping 1,400 pounds at the depot. On the return trip, a biting wind came up, dampening our exuberance. We hit our first thin ice that day. Brent nearly went through while crossing a narrow gap covered in ice only about an inch thick. Though we'd regularly heard muted grumblings from beneath the ice, we hadn't yet felt any movement. Nonetheless, the precariously angled slabs of ice hinted at the ocean's tremendous power, which might be unleashed at any time.

"I think the ominous thing about the ice," Brent noted in his journal, "is that it's always letting you know that it's alive. When

[you] travel on refrozen leads and see the recently formed pressure ridges, you realize the power. The huge thick ice, piled twenty to thirty feet high, must have cracked with the sound of thunder. The bits of open water let you know that as stable as everything appears there are a million trapdoors out there, some of them disguised ingeniously, like the one I stepped into, broken ice covered with two inches of soft snow, but underneath, water."

We arrived in camp at midnight, the backhaul teams staggering in about an hour later. Richard arrived last, having driven Paul's team with a heavily laden sled alone. I felt very proud of him. Our training in Ely was his first exposure to dogsledding. But he approached that skill, like every other, with methodical determination. That same relentless self-discipline had won for him several national medals as a cross-country skier for the Canadian national team. He had sacrificed a shot at competing in the Olympics to push this sled to the Pole. But his connection to our team owed more to his father, Hans Weber, than to his skiing. Hans is a geophysicist with the Canadian government who has conducted research throughout the Arctic and at the Pole. A colleague of his in Minnesota, Robert Lillestrand, had been advising us on ice conditions and navigation on the Arctic Ocean during our first year of preparation. At the time, Paul and I felt we should have Canadian representation on the team. Lillestrand recommended one of Hans's sons.

We called Hans. He concurred, and told us that Richard was finishing an undergraduate degree in engineering at the University of Vermont. Then we called Richard, invited him to be a candidate, and told him that the prerequisite was to join us on a six-week training journey that spring across the Beaufort Sea. Sorry, he said, senior exams were coming up, and to miss those would cost him his degree. We hung up, wondering what other avenue we might try to find the right Canadian candidate. Five minutes later, Richard called back. "I will be there," he simply said, having arranged to take all his exams within a few days before leaving. Our Canadian connection was made.

That night the tent scene had a little cheer. Though we were camped only five miles out to sea, we had a depot twelve miles out, and the ice we had seen beyond that looked encouraging. Outside, the temperature had warmed to −45 degrees, and now that the stoves worked, we enjoyed a bit more warmth inside as well. When the cookpots were on, absorbing all the heat, the temperature still hovered well below zero, but as we ate our supper we pulled the pots off for a few minutes so that the open flames could briefly warm the tents. Our eyes no longer stung from fumes, but we were still coughing up phlegm, which we assumed was a lingering effect of the stove problem.

That evening I reflected on how we were steadily adjusting to some of the severest temperatures and surface conditions on earth. The resilience of the human body and mind always amazes me. After the initial physical shock of immersion into the polar winter, we had rebounded. The first adaptations were psychological; not only would we survive, but we would steadily push forward with the heavy sleds. Momentary reflections on the seeming futility of the effort did creep in, especially as we lay limp with exhaustion in our icy bags before sleep recharged us each night. But none of us fell prey to doubts very long. The goal remained unquestioned.

I was also pleased as I thought of how our campsite and travel efficiency had steadily improved. As we tuned our travel system, the long stretches of waiting were gradually diminishing. We focused on saving time—time that we desperately needed to edge forward and reach the Pole before the advancing spring set the ice in motion. On Day 2, I recalled, we had mistakenly positioned a sled carrying one of the tents at the back of the caravan. Thus, at the end of that workday, that tent group had stood waiting miserably in the cold for their shelter to arrive from the rear of the pack. With that lesson etched in our minds, we positioned the two sleds carrying camp equipment in the second and third slot from then on. And we streamlined our "road construction" system by allocating tools and choppers among the sleds according to conditions. Each day we had shaved a few more minutes off the time needed to make and break camp.

Tent discussions each evening centered on economizing time and energy. In the interest of efficiency, we rarely varied camp assignments. Drivers looked after their dogs while Richard and McKerrow looked after the two tent units. Ann was our "floater," assisting where needed. Repetition minimized the need for communication—no reason to shout instructions over the wind or through a face mask encrusted with ice. Furthermore, exchanging chores would also have opened more grounds for conflict and disagreements over whose system was best for organizing the tent, or whose turn it was to cut snow blocks. When coupled with high stress, such minor annoyances can magnify into mutiny.

While I jotted these thoughts down in my journal that evening, Geoff tended to mukluk problems once again. He had securely patched the holes the night before with *ujuck,* the thick, tough hide from a bearded seal, a patch of which Brent had brought along for personal repairs but had generously offered to Geoff and Richard, since their boots were showing the most damage. Unfortunately, that day Geoff had found the ujuck soles to be very slippery and possibly dangerous. He was now scuffing up the soles with his knife in hopes that that might gain him some traction. He got only four hours of sleep that night.

DAY 5

"DON'T WORRY. IF MY SNORING DISTURBS YOU, THROW A SHOE AT ME."

The next morning found Paul's group in a dour mood. Brent had tried a stint in the sled bag that night and had gotten almost no sleep. Ann, fighting a cold, had got her period, though she didn't let on to the rest of the crew the cause of her deeply melancholy state of mind. And Paul and McKerrow had locked horns over how to organize the cooking gear inside the tent. But amends had been made and, to bring spirits up, Paul introduced his group to "The Doggy Song," a tune that had become a favorite among participants on his camping trips. Sung in three verses to the tune of "The Church's One Foundation," it goes:

> The dogs they had a party, they came from near and
> far.
> Some dogs came by taxi and some dogs came by car.
> Each dog signed his name upon a special book,
> And each dog hung his asshole upon a special hook.
>
> One dog was not invited and this aroused his ire.
> He stormed into the party and loudly shouted "Fire!"
> The dogs got so excited they all forgot to look,
> But grabbed the nearest asshole from off the nearest
> hook.

This is a sad, sad story, for it is very sore
To wear another's asshole you've never worn before.
And that is why when dogs roam o'er land or sea or
    foam,
They sniff each other's assholes in hopes they'll find
    their own.

From our tent we couldn't hear the song, but we could hear the burst of laughter afterwards. My crew was a fairly quiet bunch. Often I was the only one who did much talking, strategizing out loud about various means of moving our loads ahead. Tent 2 proved to be very gregarious. McKerrow's endless supply of stories, poetry, and jokes helped ensure a steady banter among them morning and evening.

Our connection with McKerrow was a result of pure chance, or fate. Paul had met him in New Zealand in 1983 when he and his wife, Susan, were bicycling across the country. They'd been asked to speak at an outdoor leadership conference at the New Zealand Outward Bound School where McKerrow was about to assume duties as the director. After spending some time with him at the school, Paul was very impressed, and when he and Susan returned home that winter, he suggested to me that McKerrow would be an excellent candidate for the team. His credentials looked good—he had completed numerous expeditions all over the world and had wintered in Antarctica as part of a research team. Paul fired off a letter offering him a chance to join the training journey we were planning. McKerrow replied immediately that he would make arrangements with his family and his new employer to take an extended leave.

As it happened, McKerrow was touring Outward Bound schools in England the following spring when I was in Cambridge, collecting information from the Scott Polar Research Institute. We visited together for two days and, over beers in an English pub, he regaled me with stories from his wealth of experiences. For years he and his wife, Joan, had traveled the world as relief workers for the International Red Cross. In fact, each of their five young daughters had been born in a different Third World country. We got along famously, and I found that he had only one serious flaw—he snored. A very sensitive sleeper, I am disturbed by the slightest sounds during the night. This could bode ill for the expedition, I thought. Furthermore, McKerrow was no average snorer. His nose, broken numerous times in rugby battles, was severely constricted. At night he breathed with tremors and snorts in a roar that would resonate off the ceiling of the dorm we were staying in near Cambridge.

"Don't worry," he quipped with his elfin grin as we went to bed the first night. "If my snoring disturbs you, just throw a shoe at me."

I dutifully lined up three pairs of shoes next to my bed and slipped into pleasant dreams. Soon these were transformed into scenes of earthquakes and destruction. I awoke and found the source of my nightmares was McKerrow's nightly roar. A well-aimed tennis shoe silenced him. I drifted off, but was abruptly awakened again. I launched a second shoe and stuffed tissue into my ears. But it was to no avail. Within three hours I had exhausted my supply of shoes, and I moved outside to sleep in the car. I informed McKerrow that he was welcome to join us on our training journey, but, I added, he and I could not be tent partners. The next year, during our month traveling together across the Beaufort Sea, he proved to be a cheerful and competent member of our team. Short, stocky, square-jawed, and swarthy, with a bristly beard, he looked more like a pirate rogue than a polar explorer, but with his pleasant demeanor and entertaining stories he ingratiated himself with all of us.

The strategy for our fifth day was to strike camp and carry everything forward to our depot seven miles ahead. It was a tall order, but we now had a good trail broken through Hell's Gate, and beyond that lay the Great Plains, with hard-packed snow and fast travel. Ann and I took a light sled forward so we would have time after reaching the depot to scout a trail through some massive pressure ridges I had seen in the distance. Meanwhile, the rest of the group would, by carrying fairly heavy loads, try to bring forward our camp and the rest of our supplies and meet us that evening.

It proved to be an overly ambitious plan, and this was by far our toughest day. It took the main crew nearly all day to get to the edge of the Great Plains. Ann and I, having finished our scouting, waited at the depot with darkness settling in upon us. A faint sliver of moon appeared overhead. We were desperately anxious to hear the sound of dogs pulling the sleds that contained our tents, fuel, and sleeping bags. Leaving my team at the depot, we walked back down the trail at midnight to offer help. Three miles later we found them staggering along, thoroughly tired. They could go no farther and began to set camp while Paul accompanied me back to the depot to retrieve my team. We were finally in our tents at 2:00 A.M., after fourteen hours on the trail. Though the temperatures had only been in the minus forties that day, a steady southwest breeze had taken an exacting toll on fingers and faces. All of us had severe frostbite damage.

That evening, as we did each evening on the trail, we chose as our campsite a stretch of multi-year ice whose surface had been smoothed out by being repeatedly melted and refrozen over several seasons. Gray in color, it contrasted sharply with the blue-green angular plates of young ice. It was also much more stable and consequently offered less risk of breaking under us while we slept. In addition, old ice offered one other substantial advantage. Because sea salt leaches out as the ice ages, this ice offered a source of fresh water that melted faster than snow.

One of the first things we did each evening was to stock blocks of this ice near our tent site. As we set camp, we would feed them into our snow melter, set up just outside the tent door. A device we affectionately called the "Weber Cooker," since Richard had fabricated it, the melter consisted of a two-gallon aluminum pot set on our stoves and sheathed in a tall sheet-metal flange that prevented any heat from escaping. Fumes vented out through a small hole in the wooden disk that covered the heat shield. When it came time to enter the tent, we would dismantle the flange and bring in just the stove and the water pot.

Our dogs would be put to bed by being clipped into position along a stakeout line kept on each sled. These were fifty-foot lengths of three-sixteenths-inch aircraft cable with short lengths of chain on swivels attached at four-foot intervals. We used mountain climber's carabiners—large, spring-loaded clips that can be maneuvered with gloves on—to attach each dog's collar ring to a chain. Harnesses were removed from dogs that chewed—there were a few chewers on each team—and rival dogs were well separated along the line to prevent disturbances at night. The important thing was to ensure that each end of the cable was securely anchored. If one end came loose during the night, the dogs would begin milling about and end up in a seething ball of cable, chain, and fur. So we would generally attach one end to our sleds, which we staked in place for the night with peaveys or steel spikes driven into the ice, and the other end to a "deadhead," a block of wood buried deeply in the snow or jammed in a crack in the ice.

Then came feeding time. Full rations were two pounds per dog per day, though these would be tapered down on a sliding scale as the journey progressed. Generally the Eskimo dogs, which were accustomed to an exclusively meat diet, received more pemmican, while my team and Mantell's, which had been raised on dry feed, received a larger proportion of Science Diet. Feeding time was always a cause of unbridled excitement among the teams. As soon as they would hear the clink of the feeding cans being pulled off the sleds, they would break into fits of howling and crying and jerk wildly on the stakeout line. It was a tense time for the drivers, because if the line broke, the dogs would swarm and fight viciously. Grabbing gunnysacks from the sleds, we would quickly meter out the rations. The dogs tugging the hardest were fed first to relieve the tension on the line. Like vacuum cleaners, the dogs would literally inhale the food, growling and snapping at their neighbors between gulps. Even the most mild-mannered dogs turned into scowling, ravenous brutes during feeding time. But once fed they instantly settled into sleep, the silhouettes of their curled bodies along the line looking like beads on a rosary.

DAY 6

"THE GLOW OF THE WOODSTOVES AND THE SMELL OF EMBERS MAGICALLY CHANGED THE ATMOSPHERE OF THE TENT TO A WARM, COZY HOVEL."

The bitter southwest wind prevailed again the next morning. We left our tents in place and sent Ann and Richard back with my team to pick up supplies dropped along the Great Plains during the forced march last night. Zap was left in camp. With his injured foot festering badly, it was now apparent that he would go out with the first dog pickup flight. The rest of us loaded our four sleds with half of the remaining supplies, about 1,800 pounds, and spent the day pushing forward some seven miles to set up a new depot.

These relays posed a calculated risk. Supplies spread out across miles of ice could easily be buried in a storm, ravaged by polar bears, or scattered randomly if the plates of sea ice began to shift. Fortunately, polar bears are rarely found along the northern shore of Ellesmere, because the coastal ice is generally packed tight, with few gaps where the bear's favorite prey, seals, might surface. As we got farther out to sea, where there were more cracks in the surface, our chances of encountering bears would increase. However, there have been exceptions. The Japanese polar explorer Naomi Uemera had the most frightening experience of his life just off Ellesmere's shore during his 1978 solo dogsled trek to the Pole. A bear came into camp looking for food while he was tucked into his sleeping bag. Ignoring the dogs, which were barking and howling in alarm, it went right for the tent. Hearing the bear scratching the walls, Naomi grabbed his rifle, but found that it was jammed by the cold. All he could do was burrow down in his bag and pray while the bear pawed through gear stored just inside the tent. Miraculously, it soon lost interest in him and wandered off into the pack ice. Each of us harbored fears of a similar encounter. We carried two Remington .300 Magnum rifles on our sleds for protection.

The deep cold served as our ally during the relays. It held the ice in frigid suspension, preventing it from breaking up and moving the supplies left on the ice. However, with team members spread out for miles, a sudden blinding blizzard or whiteout could still obliterate the trail, separating us from each other and our precious supplies of food and shelter. To minimize the chances of losing our trail in storms or shifting ice, we marked it with ski poles flagged with gunnysacks from our pemmican boxes. Extra tools, such as ski poles, pickaxes, and pry bars, also made good markers. But since these were in limited supply, they were only used as long-range markers, propped up on pinnacles of ice or hummocks of snow every quarter-mile or so. Stretches in between were marked with trail flags, short wire wands with patches of brightly colored material tied onto their ends.

When we returned to camp that evening, March 13, we congratulated ourselves on making Arctic history in an odd sort of way. With plans to burn packing materials and wood jettisoned from our sleds as we shortened them with a wood saw along the way, we had brought along tiny sheet-metal woodstoves. We stoked these for the first time that night, undoubtedly establishing the northernmost wood fires ever.

The notion of carrying tiny woodstoves had occurred to me years before while traveling through the forests of the western Arctic. I was surprised by how little wood was needed to heat my large trapper's tent, even on −50-degree nights. Just a few handfuls of splinters, I surmised, might warm the interior of a compact dome tent. And the wood jettisoned from our sleds as the payload decreased would provide ample fuel. Stoves would give us an option for driving frost from clothing and sleeping bags, and offer a means of sustaining warmth in the tents for long periods. This represented a tremendous safety margin, a means of treating someone who had succumbed to hypothermia or of drying a set of clothes if someone fell through the ice.

The breadbox-sized stoves, made for us by our hometown high school shop class, were fitted with three-inch pipes that vented through a circular ceramic cloth patch that we stitched across the back doorway of our tents. Geoff referred to these stoves as our "secret weapons," noting in his journal that between packing material and sled wood, we were hauling around 1,300 pounds of fuel for them. Later in the trip we would begin shortening our sled runners, which we could use for fuel, but on this night, Geoff and I donated our sled boxes for the fire. These thirty-pound boxes provided a safe place to stash fragile equipment such as cameras and fuel bottles, as well as a spot to stow parkas, thermoses, and other gear needed through the day. But we had found we could do without them, and within minutes our two boxes lay in a pile of splinters alongside each tent.

Also in the pile were sticks of mahogany. These came from the gunwales of our canoe, which, the day before, had become a victim of the extreme cold and a sledding accident in Hell's Gate. Geoff had carefully designed a set of roll bars to protect the canoe, which rode like a cover over his load. But despite his utmost precautions, the sled rolled and the canoe was impaled on a shard of ice. The gaping wound in our gleaming red boat was beyond repair. So we salvaged the wood trim and set the Kevlar shell ablaze on the ice.

The canoe, specially designed for us by the Wenonah Canoe Company, was outfitted with sled runners on the bottom. Serving as an "insurance policy," this fifty-pound sled/boat was intended for use in a last-ditch effort. If we ran out of sea ice, most of the crew would turn back while two would paddle the canoe through gaps and pull it over ice cakes to attempt to reach the Pole. But this small-capacity craft would be of little use in shuttling the entire expedition across the wide-open cracks or leads, as they're known, that we expected to encounter during the first weeks of the journey. It was too light and unstable. For that purpose, Geoff carried a second craft on his sled, a plastic folding boat. Though it weighed about 100 pounds, it fit neatly on the bottom of the sled, adding only a little bulk to Geoff's load. The decision to carry these boats was very controversial during training. Most team members fully accepted the need for the folding boat. Without it, the expedition might come to an end even a few miles out to sea if we hit open water. But many were disgruntled about having a canoe, fragile and bulky, on board. As Geoff noted in his journal, "Bringing this will go down as one of the dumbest mistakes this expedition made." In addition to making for an awkward sled load, the canoe had also become a source of underlying tension because if it had to be used, most of the team members would have to turn back. Having it along represented a threat to their shot at the Pole. I think a bit of relief was felt in camp that evening as the canoe was dismantled.

Frost accumulation in our clothing was taking a heavy toll on our warmth, so Day 6 became our first "party night." We were in the mood for it, having pushed ahead seven miles mostly over young ice with little snow cover, and returned to camp in only seven hours. McKerrow, the team poet, noted in his journal, "What beauty we saw today in such a God-forsaken place. Crystals play in the light, shimmering with white shades of the sinister."

The prospects for an evening reprieve from the threatening cold filled our camp with cheer, and the lighting of the stoves was attended with much fanfare. We each carefully placed ourselves among personal piles of frost-encrusted clothing and waited and watched as the stove came alive and glowed red through its thin sheet-metal walls. Our spirits soared as the tent warmed, clothing began to drip, and a festive evening got under way. Various team members shared special treats from their personal rations. Soon our tin snow-melters were resonating with the sound of corn popping. The smiles on faces and the pleasant aroma of woodsmoke lifted the tensions that had knotted up our bodies and minds. The smell of burning pine conjured up memories of campfires and my cabin stove in Minnesota. Outside, the steady whine of the polar wind was broken by loud bursts of laughter from our tents.

After three hours, with our wood supply nearly gone and eyelids drooping, we let the stoves slowly burn down. When the last embers went out, the stoves were tossed out through the tent doors and we dove into our sleeping bags before the cold sapped the warmth that lingered. Our tents, which minutes before had been cozy little hovels glowing with warmth and cheer, instantly became deep freezes shrouded in the windswept blackness of the polar night.

I thought of the previous parties we had shared as a team. The first was a Halloween party in Ely at the beginning of our training. Relations were a little stiff and formal just after the team and staff had assembled for training. To loosen things up, Paul and I took advantage of a friend's party invitation and made attendance mandatory for our crew. They pieced together costumes from dog-food bags, stakeout chains, harnesses, and prototype expedition clothing and face masks, then, taking the party by storm, danced on through the night. The ice was broken. By mid-December we were due for another break in our intense training schedule, and held a Mexican party night to brighten up the winter darkness. We brought in a bluegrass band, the Vermillion Varmints, hung piñatas from the workshop ceiling, and served up gallons of tequila fruit punch from plastic garbage cans. The band quit at two in the morning, but the team danced on to tunes from a tape deck until they dropped in their tracks and were snoring on the floor.

DAY 7

"WHEN THE GOING GETS ROUGH, LIKE WHEN IT TAKES ONE AND A HALF HOURS TO GO 100 YARDS, I START TO QUESTION THE SANITY OF DOING THIS."

The wind was gusting stronger yet when we awoke on Day 7. But the moderate temperatures continued—it remained around −40 that day—so we decided it was time to trim our fuel consumption by running two stoves rather than three in each of our tents during mealtimes. While we broke camp, the last remnants of the canoe and the sled boxes were set ablaze. Heaped on the pyre was every ounce of equipment that had proven to be unessential: tent pegs, spare ropes, pulleys, spare parts for the sleds, anchors, packing boxes, and tarps. Some 200 pounds of gear were burned or jettisoned. Team members scurried back and forth between their sleds and the inferno, offering up additional garbage and unnecessary gear and pausing to warm fingers and toes. As I finished lashing my sled, I looked back and saw Geoff squatting in the snow on the far side of the fire, framed by leaping flames. He was taking advantage of our incinerator for a warm morning potty break.

Something about the orange flames and billowing black smoke, standing out sharply against the flat light of an overcast sky, excited me. A quote by the Norwegian polar explorer Fridtjof Nansen came to mind. The secret of his success, he said, was to "demolish my bridges behind me. Then one loses no time in looking behind, when one should have quite enough to do looking ahead. Then there is no choice for you or your men but forward."

It proved to be a reflective day for the team members. Several found themselves amazed at the wide range of emotion they experienced as they trudged along, pushing their sleds. As Brent noted in his journal, "It's amazing how much my mood swings on this trip. When the going gets rough, like when it takes one and a half hours to go 100 yards, I start to question the sanity of doing this. But then when the ice is less difficult and we start moving efficiently, there is nothing but optimism and a strong drive to go north. Though I've answered the question 'Why do you want to go the Pole?' a hundred different ways, to be honest I don't know why. But it sure is one helluva way to have an adventure." Ann found herself thinking about Christa McAuliffe, the schoolteacher-turned-astronaut who was killed in the space shuttle disaster while we were training in Frobisher, sensing that she was experiencing the same kaleidoscope of emotions that Christa must have felt about the adventure she was to have undertaken.

Ann had a lot in common with Christa—she was also a schoolteacher, and was attempting a monumental achievement no woman had yet accomplished. I knew Ann through her father, Dick, whom I'd met in 1970 on a winter camping trip at the Minnesota Outward Bound School, where he was serving as a trustee. We struck up a close friendship, and the following summer I visited with him and his family at their home near St. Paul. Ann was only fourteen, a shy tomboy who was developing a knack for tackling big adventures. Throughout the following years, I frequently heard Ann's name mentioned among mountain-climbing friends. She was known for her competence in various outdoor pursuits, and had proven herself in a harrowing incident while climbing Mount McKinley in 1983. On the summit, her partner became severely hypothermic. Delirious and babbling incoherently, he could easily have died in the extreme cold and windchill. Ann took control, warmed him with some soup, and guided him down to a camp several thousand feet below, where he recuperated, thus saving his life.

I didn't really get to know Ann until the summer of 1985. In

June, as I was flying into Minneapolis following our polar training journey to Point Barrow, I looked down from the aircraft as
we flew over the suburbs and spotted the Bancrofts' wooded
homesite. I hadn't heard from Dick in more than five years, and
decided to give him a call from the airport. He listened with keen
interest as I filled him in about our plans for the North Pole
expedition and our eight team members, which at that point
included Jorg Mattner, a Dutch geologist I had met in the
Yukon, who was very skilled in dogsledding and Arctic travel.
The next day Paul and I learned that Jorg had to withdraw from
the team because of a knee disorder that required immediate
surgery. We were saddened to lose him, but by this time word
of our plans had traveled among adventurers worldwide, and we
had numerous highly qualified alternate candidates. Over the
next month, Paul and I pondered our many choices. Then one
night in early July, I dreamed that we had selected Ann Bancroft
as our eighth team member. It seemed an omen, and the next day
I discussed with Paul the possibility of having a woman on the
team. It was a big risk; with seven men on board, she would
definitely be the odd one out. But we felt that female representation would lead to a stronger sense of "family" among the group
and add to the significance of the project. It would also, we felt,
widen our circle of support, which, considering our shortage of
funds, was an important consideration.

Paul and I established as an additional criterion for Jorg's
replacement that that person should be locally based. We desperately needed someone nearby who could assist with the fund-
raising burden. To have someone in Minneapolis and St. Paul,
the hotbed of our support, would be ideal. We were delighted to
have an international team, but the problem was that the other
members could offer very little practical assistance to the project's organization from their distant homes. Paul and I were
saddled with the entire organizational responsibility. Ann fit the
bill. She had no Arctic experience and had never worked with
a dog team. But those skills were well represented among the
other team members.

Paul and I knew we were about to make one of the biggest
decisions of the expedition. Our concern centered on protecting
our credibility. To add a woman would magnify press coverage
of the project, but would leave us vulnerable to accusations of
tokenism. We knew there would be no tokens on the sea ice once
we hit our first day of intensely cold weather and rugged pack
ice, but, I wondered, would the press understand that? Very few

women are represented in the history of Arctic expeditions. Thus the woman selected for our team would be in the vanguard, helping to break stereotypes about women's abilities to handle cold weather and extreme conditions. I knew Ann to be a warm, stable person, and envisioned the positive impact that she, as a role model, would have on men and women worldwide if she reached the Pole. But what if she couldn't adjust to being with seven men, or couldn't handle the physical demands of the polar sea? If she had to be flown out, it might only serve to perpetuate a negative stereotype. Before approaching her, I sought advice from several of her acquaintances. They all assured me she would do fine. She was a team player, they said, and had the mental fortitude for this journey.

Finally, in late August, we invited her up to our base in Ely and dropped the invitation on her. "Count me in!" she responded without hesitation. After returning home, she set to work on our fund-raising campaign and then joined us in October for the training. With her ready smile and quick wit, she soon became a friend of all of the team and support staff and diligently applied herself to every project assigned to her. With no Arctic skills, she had an immense amount to learn before departing with us for the polar sea, but as we learned later, Ann was accustomed to overcoming barriers. Plagued by learning difficulties in grade school, she had been diagnosed as dyslexic. Growing to resent classroom learning, she turned to sports and the outdoors as her medium for building self-image. The confidence she gained from her proficiency in basketball and tennis as well as mountain climbing gave her the boost she needed to pursue college studies. She obtained a teaching certificate, and a few months before we began considering her as a candidate, she completed her third year as an elementary physical education teacher at a public school in Minneapolis with programs for disadvantaged students. She helped show them the route to self-confidence through sports and recreation.

During our training in Ely, Ann impressed us all with her persistence. She mastered the art of dogsledding in just a few weeks. I felt fortunate that Ann was to be my sledding partner on the trip, because she showed much affection and compassion for the dogs. This would help counter the heavy demands I often placed on them. Initially my team ignored her commands, but through firm determination she gained their respect and thereby crossed the paramount hurdle in mastering a dog team.

* * *

Now, on Day 7, Ann was handling my team like a pro while I pushed ahead, scouting a trail, deep in thought. The expedition was becoming a way of life for me. Thoughts linking me with the outside world had been steadily severed. With Paul in charge of the radio, I no longer had a direct connection with the press or the lingering business complexities of this project. Shedding that stress left me feeling like I was on vacation. Despite the size of our group, I began to think of the expedition as a single unit of life alone in the universe. Except for occasional thoughts about loved ones back home, the outside world no longer existed for me. My world now was the polar sea.

Concentrating on route-finding, I soon found myself well ahead of the rest of the crew. Turning back, I saw Paul hurrying toward me, looked a bit miffed. "Do you think it's fair," he asked as he approached, "for you to be walking ahead out of sight so much of the time while the rest of us are pushing our asses off behind those sleds?" Yes, I agreed, group morale would be better served if I was back with the crew. Trail conditions were such through this stretch of ice that little scouting was needed. We called it a "pick as you go" area.

Generally, it was imperative that I be out front. Often the group had a hard time understanding and accepting that. Geoff and I had much pack-ice experience and were therefore better qualified than the others to serve as trail scouts while we learned the essentials of the polar sea during the first few weeks of the trek. But Geoff had his hands full cajoling his wild herd of Eskimo dogs into pulling a sled awkwardly laden with our two boats and hundreds of pounds of supplies. Thus the trail-scouting job fell to me, and I took it very seriously.

Thorough trail scouting was the best investment of time and energy we could make to minimize our workload. The onerous necessity of scouting was accentuated by our need to relay the loads in two units. Forward with half a load, backhaul empty, forward again with the rest. Every step of the trail was now being trekked three times. Every obstacle the scout and choppers could not circumvent would agonize the team three times over.

Climbing the nearest pinnacle, I would search for a gap in the ridge just ahead, mentally map out passages that looked promising, then run ahead to assess the amount of chopping each would require before it could be negotiated by the sleds. The process usually required scampering across the spine of a heaved-up formation of ice, from one high point to another, trying to connect possible routes. While climbing these lookouts, I had to check my exuberance constantly and remind myself to focus full attention on my feet. A sudden slip could mean a broken leg, and, separated as I was by miles from the rest of the group, that could be fatal. Climbing over and around these slippery car-sized blocks with numb hands and feet, visibility severely limited by hood and face mask, required the concentration of a trapeze artist. The deep fissures between the blocks, often hidden by drifted snow, were traps that could snap the legs of the unwary.

Once I decided upon a general course through the ridges, I would tumble over ice blocks, marking the possible trail to the end of the next pan with flags. In doing this, I became thoroughly familiar with the lay of the ice over the last quarter-mile or so, and would double back, fine-tuning the trail around drifts and blocks. Then I'd shoot ahead to work over the next section.

On the sections of smooth older ice, covered with undulating, wind-packed snowdrifts, I would meticulously navigate a gently curving trail that avoided crossing as many drifts as possible. These seemingly benign mounds of snow were as exhausting an obstacle to forward sled progress as were the ridges of ice. As our sled runners cut into the ridge, the coarse snow would grab the sides of the runners as surely as a parking brake. To free the sled required concerted pushing, prying, and cursing. But among trail obstacles, sharp turns were dreaded as passionately as drifts and ridges. The dogs' traces ranged in length up to fifty feet, so, through curving sections of trail, much of the power of the front dogs was lost as the lines caught on ice blocks. On sharp turns, all forward power was lost and each sled would have to be manhandled around the bend. A winding course was arduous work. The straighter the course, the less energy would be expended and the greater would be our chances of reaching the Pole.

Many evenings I would mark about three miles of trail beyond the point where camp was to be set. That way, if the morning brought poor visibility, we'd have an established trail to follow for much of the day, and we'd eliminate the chance of having the sleds bottleneck while drivers waited for a route to be selected. By that hour we were growing limp with exhaustion. Like a mouse in a maze I would scamper along, slowing to a walk on occasion to catch my breath. As the nightly hours of scouting wore on, a point would come when exhaustion manifested itself in a persistent chill that no amount of running would shake. This was the body's final warning that it was time to return to camp.

Backtracking had its own dangers. Visibility would often be

washed out by the dimming daylight and drifting snow. All sense of perspective was lost, and visibility was often restricted to less than eight feet. The only way back was to follow my blurred footprints, playing a life-and-death "connect the dots" game as I pieced together the long series of flags I had set. They were often a hundred or more feet apart. As drifting snow blotted out my footprints, the flags represented my only link to warmth, food, and survival. The painstaking process of retracing my path required total concentration. Countless times I lost the trail. Then, keeping panic at bay, I would slowly retreat, footstep by footstep, until I found the last life-giving flag. After breathing a sigh of relief I would try to connect it with the next one, driven on toward the warmth of our tents. Whiteouts, periods of drifting snow and haze that minimized visibility, would obscure my sense of time, so that the camp often seemed to appear as if out of a dream. What a glorious sight it was! Like returning to the spaceship after venturing onto the moon. Home again to a camp buzzing with evening chores and tents emitting the muffled roar of gas stoves thawing snow for an evening pot of tea. Another day on the polar sea, another few miles gained in our pursuit of the Pole.

Scouting was a far colder job than driving a sled. Much of the time was spent standing still, surveying the terrain and mulling over route options, in temperatures as low as −60 degrees, with windchills often exceeding twice that figure. I was tightly encased in my wind jacket and my insulating parka with both hoods drawn securely around my head, caribou mitts and beaver overmitts and moosehide mukluks sheathed with sheepskin overboots. It was a cumbersome ensemble that required a delicate balance of activity to avoid overheating and sweating, the scourge of winter travel. If clothing systems become dampened by perspiration, they lose their insulation value. I kept my body temperature at an equilibrium by trotting along at a jogging pace whenever possible. When I was tired and slowed to a walk, the cold would cut through my clothing in minutes. Carrying additional clothes in a backpack for moments of scanning and deliberation was out of the question because a pack would restrict movement and, worse yet, would cause my back to sweat.

The effect of the cold would begin with my extremities. Grasping the cold bundle of steel flag wands grew unbearable. The heat from my hand would melt snow caught between my glove and the wands. Soggy mitts conducted the cold directly into my hands. We considered fashioning some sort of a quiver for the

flags, but holding them proved to be the only efficient means of
having them readily available. Scanning the terrain from pinnacles often meant facing into the wind. Any exposed patch of flesh
would be flash-frozen in seconds and would require thawing
against a bared palm.

Adding to the physical misery of scouting was that it often
proved to be a thankless job. Team members who were thoroughly exasperated with the horrendous workload of chopping
ice and prying, pushing, and pulling the thousand-pound sled
loads inch by inch for endless hours each day, often thought the
scout had the easier job. Minor grumbling erupted from time to
time when day after day I was often out of sight of our caravan.
Some felt I was copping out of the brunt of the work.

Granted, the stress I endured during our final months of
preparation had taken a heavy toll of my health and strength. In
this state I felt I was not as effective as many of the others in
maneuvering the sleds. More important, I felt that scouting,
especially in the frequent whiteouts, was a very specialized job
for which I was the best qualified. Until all of us had spent ample
time on the sea ice, I didn't want to jeopardize someone else's
life by sending him or her out front. Spending a day or two
behind the sleds to assuage bad feelings seemed like a token
move, and I wasn't willing to do that, given the dangers that
scouting involved.

Our chopping system, like our scouting one, settled into a
routine during our first week. Each day after breakfast, two
choppers went out ahead on the trail I had flagged the night
before to smash a trail through the ridges. When the sleds caught
up, other team members would grab tools and join in with road
construction. Chopping was a specialized and dangerous job.
During our months of training in the pack ice, we had experimented with chopping tools of various shapes and sizes and
found that the most effective tool for shattering blocks of sea ice
was a standard double-pointed pick of the kind used for digging
ditches in hard-packed ground. We cut off the end of one point
of the pick to reduce weight as well as danger from errant blows,
and sharpened the other end to a pinpoint wedge.

Essential as they were, these five-pound picks represented the
single greatest safety hazard of the expedition. A glancing blow
could instantly turn them into lethal weapons. Time and again
during training we drilled ourselves on safety procedures for
storing, carrying, and swinging the picks. The ways in which
they could cause damage were considerable. A pick improperly

secured on the sleds might puncture a fuel canister, leaving us several gallons short of a crucial commodity. We arranged to store them between two sheets of plywood lashed to the uprights on the back of a sled. The only safe way to carry them was to let them hang from one arm, with the head toward the ground and the tip pointing back. If slung over one shoulder, a pick might easily embed itself in your back if you slipped on the ice. While using them, we insisted that choppers be at least ten feet apart. We practiced this configuration during training until team members instinctively spread out when chopping was under way.

Like every other aspect of our lives, the dangers were exacerbated by the work conditions. Fumbling for footing on sharply angled, slippery ice, with hoods drawn tightly around one's face, eyelashes frosted over or frozen together, and ax handles and mitts glazed with ice, multiplied the dangers of chopping. However, our extensive training paid off: the chopping proved to be one task, probably the only one, that we performed more efficiently than we had anticipated. We could enter some impossible-looking ridge system with a crew of two to six people and, in a very short time, pulverize a towering ridge or hundreds of yards of rubble into a passable trail.

The steady road construction progress didn't alleviate the annoying discomforts brought on by hours of chopping at extreme temperatures. Cold was conducted from the pick handle to the palm of the hand, while the rest of the body overheated from the exertion. While arms and shoulders ached with exhaustion, our bodies were invigorated with long, hard breaths of cold polar air. These had to be taken in—somewhat painfully—through the nose, because if one's mouth was open, a flying piece of ice could knock out a tooth. Care was taken also to avoid splinters of ice hitting the eyes. Goggles and sunglasses that frosted up and slipped out of place from the constant swinging motion of chopping proved counterproductive to safety, so these could not be worn.

The sleds would creep forward as the choppers progressed. Driving a 1,000-pound sled through pack ice was by far the most difficult work any of us had ever done. Again, total concentration and confidence were required. During a momentary slip of the driver's attention, a sled might roll over into a ravine, requiring long delays and extreme effort to right the load and carry on. Or it could mean a paralyzing accident. One of my greatest safety fears was that team members might get crushed by sleds rolling off huge blocks of ice. Like the chopping system, techniques for safely maneuvering the heavy sleds through pressure ridges were practiced extensively in Frobisher. In difficult stretches, it required perfect rapport between the driver and the dogs. They must give you full power while threading through the ridges, with the bow of the sled glancing off one ice block after another. If the lines went slack at a critical time, the sled might lose momentum and slip sideways over a precipice.

The key to success and safety in trekking to the Pole, we were finding, was total awareness and concentration on the task at hand. Any small mistake could spell defeat: an overlooked leak in a fuel-bottle seal could result in a disastrous tent fire; a misplaced swing of an ax might puncture a foot; a bit of frostbite left unattended could develop into serious tissue damage, requiring evacuation; a momentary lapse of attention while driving a sled could result in an arm or a leg being caught under the runners and crushed.

These thoughts rolled through my mind as we pushed on. Our plan for Day 7 was to haul everything seven miles forward to One Ton Depot, the cache we had set up the day before. We reached the depot in six hours. While the others set up camp, Paul and I attempted to push on with a couple of small loads. Throughout the day the haze had become increasingly thick. Between the flat light and the drifting snow, discerning a passable route through the rubble was now all but impossible. A quarter-mile from camp we saw, looming across our route in the distance, a huge wall of ice perhaps forty feet high. "We better wait till morning and hope for better light conditions before trying to negotiate that monster," I said to Paul. He shook his head with disappointment as we turned our sleds around.

The day was not without its rewards. Mantell's dog Bandit was finally back in harness, pulling enthusiastically with his teammates. The only Alaskan dog in the group that was afraid of people, he had been running loose since Drep Camp, evading every effort to capture him. But Richard, spotting him playfully sparring with some of Mantell's other dogs as they were pulling along, moved stealthily up alongside. Taking a headlong plunge, he landed squarely on top of Bandit, locking his arms around him in a bear hug. Bandit turned and snapped at Richard's head, but fortunately got only a mouthful of his thick beaver hat. Then he acquiesced and offered no resistance as Mantell slipped him into harness and clipped him in position on the gangline. Mantell was delighted and, in a rare display of emotion, playfully took a similar plunge at Richard, tackling him in the snow.

We were all grateful and relieved. Loose dogs are a serious nuisance on the trail. During the day they distract and often pester the working dogs, and at night, roaming free around the campsite, they cause a lot of barking, disrupting sleep. Worse yet, they may jeopardize the journey by pilfering supplies from sleds at night. If that begins to happen, the only option may be to shoot them.

The day of his capture, Bandit was living on borrowed time. Just before he was caught, some team members had suggested we dispose of him. He had been living up to his name, digging in one of the sled bags. We were torn over the decision. For one, Mantell needed him. Without Bandit, his team was seriously underpowered. For another, something about his wild spirit was very appealing. Many of us had grown fond of him during training. A big, strong, handsome dog with a thick, tawny coat, he was one of the most determined pullers on Mantell's team and would lean into the harness with such passion it often looked as though he was about to fall over forward.

Bandit was born at my kennel in the spring of 1985, while I was on our five-month training journey. When I returned home in June, I anxiously ran down to the dogyard to check out the new puppies that streamed out of their boxes to scamper about my feet. I noticed one hiding at the edge of the woods. My efforts to entice him over to me were to no avail. Throughout the summer, he developed into the tallest and huskiest dog of the litter, but eluded our attempts to capture him with various snares and nets. When the team members arrived that fall for training, Mantell caught site of him and, impressed with his size and spirit, was determined to subdue him and add him to his team. But even baiting him with heavy doses of tranquilizers failed to blunt his wariness. In early November, Mantell finally outsmarted him. He hid a small foothold trap in the doorway of a storage shed and tied a female dog in heat just inside. An explosion of howls and whines late that night signaled that Bandit was about to join Mantell's team.

His skittishness was a product of his puppyhood. Dogs that aren't well socialized as puppies carry their intense fear of humans throughout their lives. My best dogs are the ones that had children to play with during the first months of their lives. Giving sled dogs ample attention and affection as puppies pays big dividends later in their responsiveness to people. The bond with people must be formed early, because it is nearly impossible to tame them as adults. Mantell, applying his boundless patience, befriended Bandit as much as he could during our final months of training, but made little progress in gaining his trust.

CROSSING THE SHEAR ZONE

DAY 8

"WHEN I CLIMBED ONTO A PILE OF RUBBLE ICE, I
COULD SEE LARGE BLOCKS MOVING. YEP, IT WAS
HAPPENING."

The first morning of our second week on the trail opened with
a minor snafu. For the third time in eight days we'd had a
screw-up with our alarm clock; my tent crew awoke late, throwing off the day's schedule. The other tent crew was a bit irritated.
The first such incident had been excusable. Geoff had worn the
tiny electric clock in his hat while he slept, so that he would hear
the alarm, but it had tumbled out during the night, frozen up,
and quit running. On the second occasion it was set wrong, and
today we simply hadn't heard it.

While we hurried to catch up on our morning chores, Paul and
Brent took two light loads forward to scout and chop a trail
through the wall of ice we had seen the night before. Fortunately,
the weather had cleared and we broke camp in calm air, with the
temperature still hovering around −40. Leaving only 1,200
pounds behind, we loaded up our sleds fairly heavily and hurried
along to catch up with the scouts. We found to our delight that
Paul and Brent had been able to do an end run around the wall
by veering about a mile to the west. When we caught up with
them, they were hacking a trail through rubble that was apparently the result of very recent pressure beneath the ice, since it
had only a light covering of new snow.

For six hours and seven miles, we struggled with the sleds over
this field of shimmering, baby blue ice blocks. In midafternoon,
after crossing a ridge system onto the first old pan we had
encountered all day, we stopped to take a break and wait for Ann

101

and Geoff to come up from behind. Little did we know we were about to witness an awesome display of the power of the polar sea. This was the day we first experienced the shifting of the ice. As we stood sipping tea, huddled together for warmth, the ice began to creak and groan. Then it began to pulsate, emitting a steady drumming rhythm with the frequency slowly increasing. Our attention was riveted to the vibrations beneath us. The dogs, curled in the snow, perked up their heads in alarm. Soon a forceful noise, like that of a rushing wind, came from a nearby ridge of ice. As the pressure increased, the ice beneath our feet began to heave and shift. Scampering to the top of a nearby pinnacle, we watched as the ice gave birth to a forty-foot ridge just to the east of us. Huge plates of translucent blue ice were slowly thrust skyward, as blocks of rubble spilled off the top and rumbled down along the plate walls.

Ann and Geoff were bringing the last sled across a ridge onto the pan on which we had parked as the movement began. They felt the plates of ice shift underneath them. Charged with adrenaline, they rammed their sled across the ridge and scrambled to safety on the pan. Then, awestruck by this spectacle of power, they watched as their sled tracks on the far side of the ridge were shifted thirty feet to the east.

"We must be entering the shear zone," murmured Brent in alarm, sending a wave of nervous tension through the group. Throughout our training we had anxiously pondered how the fates would deal with us through this part of the polar sea, where slowly drifting ice plates of the outer ocean meet plates held fast against the shore and above the calmer waters of the continental shelf. The shear zone churns up a band of ice many miles wide paralleling the shore some ten to fifty miles out, depending on the year. Some years it exists as a belt of open water up to a mile or more in width. Such a formidable barrier stopped Peary on his 1906 attempt at the Pole. He waited for five days along a mile-wide gap before it closed shut and he could carry on, only to be turned back a few days later by a raging blizzard. On his return journey the shear zone again wreaked havoc on plans; he and his men were swept eastward and nearly drowned before they stumbled onto the north coast of Greenland.

When Ann and Geoff arrived, we called a quick meeting. Humbled by what we had experienced, and fearing the loss of the 1,200 pounds we had left behind, we opted to make camp where we were and send the sleds back to retrieve the gear before our trail shifted any further. Five people and three sleds embarked on the backhaul while Richard and McKerrow began setting camp. I pushed ahead alone on foot for a few miles to find out what surprises this area might hold for us tomorrow. I found that the shear zone was dealing more kindly with us than it had with Peary. I spotted no sign of leads, no telltale ribbons of mist rising above the ice to the north. It appeared that the devastating cold that had sapped our strength and health was now proving to be our ally. The firm grip it held on the ice was minimizing its movement. Thank God for the bitter cold, I thought as I stopped to thaw a frostbitten fingertip.

The weather slowly closed in as I scouted a trail northward. Soon I found myself caught in the worst whiteout I had ever experienced. The blowing snow and flat light of a heavily overcast sky had obliterated all surface features and shadows. Immersed in a skim-milk haze, I groped along, half running, half crawling, retracing my footprints, frantic to reach camp before it was covered in drifts. An eternity seemed to pass before I reached camp and, exhausted and frozen, tumbled into my tent.

Inside, Richard and McKerrow were tending pots of hot water, waiting for the crew to return from the backhaul before making dinner. They offered me a cup of soup made from a nutritive mix that the Shaklee Corporation had provided. I was amazed at how fast it revived my limp body. In my half-frozen delirium, that cup of soup seemed like the greatest luxury I had ever had in my life. In my journal that evening I wrote, "The only reality that exists is the present moment, one of hardships and struggle, one of lengthening days and the promise that the goal can be reached. I thought about this when returning in the whiteout. My life depended on every single step I took. Each step held promise of a warm tent and laughing teammates, each step contained the future."

Later that evening, after the other sleds had returned, I thought again about how good that soup tasted. Paul's tent crew had brought a supply of it, but because I have never cared for "health foods," I had rejected including any in my crew's rations. In fact, my resistance to using nutritional supplements had become a standing joke with the team. However, I now saw how valuable our packets of Shaklee's Slim Plan soup were for quickly regenerating us after the long, cold days on the trail. My tent crew, as well, were keen on having a supply. Fortunately, on their return trip to Drep Camp for extra fuel a few days before, Mantell and Ann had grabbed an extra case of it. Discarding the case to reduce bulk, Paul had dispersed the packets among various bulk food bags. I asked Richard, who kept track of our tent group's provisions, to check how many packets had ended up in our group's provisions. Sifting through the food bags, he produced nine packs, far short of half a case. We looked up at each other and, sitting there tired, cold, and hungry, exchanged suspicious glances. The stage was set for the team conflicts we were to experience in the days to come.

That evening I lay in my bag listening to the titanic forces of ice smashing and grinding nearby. The tremors rumbling beneath us felt like locomotives charging across our pan. My ears were attuned for any sound of wind, which would hint of changing weather and swiftly shifting ice, but to our relief it remained calm. Though the shear zone was rumbling, it didn't appear to be breaking up.

DAY 9

"NORMALLY, −35 WOULD BE A MISERABLY COLD DAY, BUT THIS FELT LIKE SPRINGTIME."

In our tent, it was Geoff's duty to rise first each morning, light the stoves, and prepare tea water. It was a miserable chore but, true to his nature, he never complained. He slept in the middle of our tent, feet toward the door, with Richard and me on either side. Upon rising, he would fold his bag and pad in half, forming a couch and clearing a cook space near the entry way. In this space he placed the stove box and cookpots, which were stowed in the entry tunnel each night.

He reached through the tunnel and grabbed blocks of crusted snow and ice that had been stashed just outside. After filling the water pot with ice, Geoff would pour water from the thermos that had been prepared the night before. This would speed the melting process and prevent the fire from scorching the pot. The roar of the stoves was my cue to get up. In forty-five minutes, Geoff would have our first round of tea prepared. After making a seat from my sleeping bag and extra clothing, I'd begin my one-hour morning writing session. As heat from the stoves caused the frost that lined the ceiling to rain down on us, I always felt as if I were writing in a cellar. During this morning "meltdown," I would crouch over my journal to keep the drops from falling on the pages. My left palm would begin to freeze as it moved across the frozen pages. I'd use two pens in rotation, warming one in my crotch. And unless I warmed the finished pages on the stove to dry the ink, they would smear. By the time tea was ready, the meltdown was over, the tent somewhat warmed, and I could continue writing in relative comfort. I seldom gave any thought to the unusual circumstances the cold imposed on routine activities. They seemed almost like reflex responses; it was just what had to be done to get along in this environment.

Personal hygiene, washing and shaving, also required some adaptation. Since fresh water was a precious commodity, requiring much fuel to produce it, we used it very sparingly. I learned to give myself a quick sponge bath with just four ounces of water. The trick was to wash with a tiny, threadbare patch of cloth, one that could absorb only an ounce or less or water. My five-inch square swath was so worn you could see through it. I would bathe every other day, usually in the morning.

My evening hygiene chore involved cleaning my contact lenses. After scrubbing my hands with an alcohol swab, I rinsed the lenses off, secured them in a tiny case, and then tucked the case and bottle of lens solution into my polar suit to keep it from freezing. The process took time, but I'm convinced that the unobstructed vision that contacts offer make them far superior to glasses for use on the trail. Glasses fog, restricting vision to the point of danger, and the frames conduct the cold to the face and make the cheeks highly susceptible to frostbite. Extended-wear contacts that require little maintenance are the best option. Geoff and Brent used these on the trail with much success. Unfortunately, I had found before the trip that my eyes were only comfortable with conventional hard contacts.

Once a week I took a little extra time to shave. Using my teacup as a washbasin, I'd lather up my face and hack away at the stubble while looking into the mirror on my compass. The sensation of a clean face was luxurious, an adequate substitute on the trail for the pleasures of a shower. In the cold, beards prove to be a mixed blessing. They offer some insulation, serving as a filter to break the intensity of the wind against exposed cheeks, but they collect a lot of frost from one's breath. More than a pound of it can collect on a cold day, which, when one enters the tent at night, has to be picked or melted off. When a face mask needs to be worn over a beard, the problem is exacerbated, because moisture is held tight between the flesh and the mask.

Paul opted to keep his beard, but paid dearly for it because the mask constantly froze to his chin, which became severely frost-bitten as a result. A tuft of whiskers would come with his mask when he pulled it off each evening. That irritation, coupled with frostbite, left a gaping wound on his chin after a few weeks on the trail. It took weeks for it to heal after the journey, and left a quarter-sized scar on the tip of his chin. McKerrow and Geoff, who also kept their beards, partially overcame the frostbite prob-lem by shaving around the cheeks and mouths in the style of Amish farmers.

For dental care, we allotted ourselves three ounces each of toothpaste for the trail, and squeezed all but that amount from our tubes before leaving Ellesmere. My brand was Colgate. It may or may not be a great cavity fighter, but I selected it because on earlier expeditions I had found that, unlike other brands, Colgate did not freeze. Needless to say, that makes it a real winner on the trail. Some team members had brands that didn't offer that advantage. Ann ended up melting her toothbrush by holding it near the stove's flame to thaw a lump of frozen paste.

Most of us would get up when the stoves were first lit, to allow time for personal chores. But Richard, the one true athlete on our team, was always concerned about getting enough sleep. He would sleep until the first round of tea was being served, or if the day before had been exceptionally hard, he'd wait till the second round. Mantell, who found sleeping four in the tent to be misera-bly crowded, slept outside in his sled bag. When the tea water neared boiling, Geoff would bellow out, "Robert, water is on!" Five minutes later, Mantell would crawl in through the side tunnel, bringing in the first fresh air of the morning. I'd immedi-ately query him about the wind and the visibility. From his report we'd each draw a mental picture of the day ahead. The words "calm and clear" were the ones we longed to hear. The temperature was of secondary concern. If he reported poor visi-bility, we knew our scouting challenges would be compounded. A whiteout meant no travel at all. A wind meant that our faces would be tortured all day and we'd have to contend with the annoyance of face masks.

I drank a quart of water each morning, one pint of tea and one pint of a lemon drink. It was essential that we drink ample fluids. Breathing heavily all day in the extremely cold, dry air drained much moisture from our bodies. Dehydration would bring weakness and could lead to hypothermia. The trail habit I've developed over the years is to drink like a camel in the morning and then sparingly for the rest of the day. I've found that my body runs most efficiently that way. I scrupulously monitor my workload to avoid perspiring, so a quart of water often lasts me through the workday. My lean body offered no resistance to the cold, but the lack of fat did offer one advantage in that I rarely overheated. And a sweat was a more serious matter than a chill. We had no easy means of drying saturated clothing, but we could always work a little harder to ward off the cold.

On the morning of Day 9, as we gulped down our bowls of oatmeal, I could hear Paul outside rummaging through sleds and shifting our five-gallon plastic jugs of white gas. I wondered what was up. An hour later we assembled for our group meeting, braced against a nasty wind. Group 2 had stern faces. Paul announced that his inventory indicated we only had thirty-two gallons of fuel left. This was several gallons short of our projected needs. Before he finished, Brent interjected, "This is a serious shortage!" Ann, scowling in agreement, said it was Group 1's fault and accused us of burning too much fuel. My mind flashed to the missing packs of soup mix, but I decided it wasn't time to bring that issue up.

I reminded them that throughout our training I had encouraged both tent groups to be liberal with rations during the first ten days on the trail. Consuming a little extra food and fuel would help keep morale up during this initiation period. Furthermore, I pointed out, Mantell and Ann had retrieved an additional seven gallons of fuel from Drep Camp. We had more than we had rationed for. Unfortunately, during those first two weeks, our tent groups had taken opposite approaches to supplies. While we were splurging to cut weight and increase morale, they were conserving to stretch our supplies. The issue had now come to a head. My tent crew had, admittedly, been a little liberal in the use of gas. But that was due in part to mukluk problems. Geoff, the heaviest member of our team, had worn through his mukluk soles early on. Richard's, too, were wearing out quickly, so they both sat up an extra two or three hours every night sewing with a stove going to keep their fingers from stiffening up.

Paul laid out his concerns about our use of fuel objectively. Brent was almost in a panic. Ann, with her angry accusation, surprised all of us. She pointed a finger at me as the one responsible. I tried to reassure them that we had ample supplies. As the one in charge of fuel rations, I knew how much we had left. All of our stove bottles—some two dozen one-liter tins—had been filled the night before. Thus we had several gallons in reserve, in addition to the amount Paul tallied in the jerry jugs.

Nonetheless, the debate—conserve or splurge—raged on. The argument pitted one tent against the other, leader against leader. Perhaps, I commented, if Group 2 hadn't scrimped on their gas, they would be in a better mood. That comment didn't sit well with them at all. I was confident that our fuel supplies were adequate. On three other expeditions I had traveled through the winter and into spring. The advancing season would drastically reduce our fuel needs. With air temperatures now as low as −70 degrees, we had to heat our ice and snow blocks nearly 100 degrees before they would begin melting. As the weather warmed, less fuel would be needed for preparing water. Furthermore, the sun, which inched higher each day, would help heat the tents. I predicted that in the second half of the trip our fuel needs would be cut in half. And, if we had to, we could stretch meager fuel supplies a long way. Once, on a mountain-climbing trip in South America, three climbing partners and I stretched a quart of fuel over three days. So I didn't see a pending fuel shortage as a cause for panic.

I respected their concerns, however. It was a sign that we had a healthy system of checks and balances. But the intensity of Brent's and Ann's anger concerned me. I knew where Brent was coming from. Brent's camping practices had been gleaned from the Inuit of the eastern Arctic, who depend on abundant fuel supplies. They routinely dry all of their clothing by stoves in their tents every night. On their short hunting forays, they can afford to carry large quantities of fuel. Brent's experience hadn't taught him how to factor rations over a trip as long as this one. I pointed out that our woodstoves and ample supplies of sled wood offered another option for heat. My group conceded, though, that it was now time to cut back. We agreed to limit our use to three and a half bottles a day. But that still left Group 2 feeling shortchanged.

The cold drove us back to work. We broke camp under a perfect, clear, calm, polar day. The ice movement had subsided and we were in great spirits, delighted that this year the shear zone, so far, was proving passable. I noted in my journal that I now felt we were going to make it. Richard noted in his that the night had been our first without any darkness; twilight had lingered until the sun rose again this morning. We pushed forward four miles through more fresh rubble with "thousands of blocks strewn across the surface like dice tossed from the hand of an angry giant," noted McKerrow.

Ann took my sled while I worked with Paul so that he and I could review our situation. We agreed that it was time to start bracing the troops for disappointments that we felt lay just ahead. Paul and I knew we were not going to get the break in conditions that some had expected when we crossed the big lead. In fact, the terrain we were now traveling on was the worst we had seen. It was highly fractured with crevasses and enormous pressure ridges. Paul and I also felt we needed to cut back on tent time. Camp efficiency had to be improved. Every moment counted if we were to reach the Pole before the ice gave. Some team members didn't seem to share our passion for saving time. Paul and I knew we had to speed up their morning routines, but it was a delicate issue. To slice more minutes off tent time or add time to the travel day might raise tensions. Of course, the determining factor was the well-being of the dogs; we could only squeeze as many work hours into the day as their energy would allow. Talking with Paul this morning helped clear some of the tensions between us over the fuel. As always, the problem stemmed from lack of communication. The two groups had different perspectives on use of rations, but the brutal conditions of the polar sea had allowed little time and opportunity for discussing those differences.

That day we crossed numerous small crevasses that varied in width from a few inches to ten feet and dropped down ten feet or more in the big rubble ice. Chester, my lead dog, panicked when he saw these fissures across his course. He would lunge back into the other dogs and, knowing this angered me, would duck and dive among the dogs to avoid my wrath, upsetting them and tangling their lines. These were awful, exasperating moments. I worked feverishly to restore order to the team and to untangle lines and harnesses.

I dreaded these crevasses with a passion. After straightening the lines, I would tug Chester across the void. Then the others would sense Chester's alarm, and panic would again sweep through the ranks. Yeager was as bad as Chester in his paranoia about crevasses. After a while he shied from crossing even the tiniest cracks.

Straddling a crack, my dogs and I would engage in a tug-of-war. I would pull and curse with all my might while they would firmly plant their feet, with their necks stretched by the taut lines. Tim was the one dog who was willing to jump, but his reluctant teammates would hold back. His lead would be cut short and he'd end up dangling headfirst in the crack. This would only intensify the fear and resistance of the others. Once I managed to drag the first four dogs over, I had the upper hand. The momentum was now on my side of the crevasse and the rest had to come, like it or not. Yeager would be gripped by panic right up to the brink, and then, like a coiled spring, he would explode into the air, desperately flailing his legs as he reached the other side.

Late that afternoon, after dropping our loads at a prospective campsite, Geoff, Mantell, and I returned with our sleds for the backhaul while the others continued northward. We returned from the shuttle earlier than planned, so while Geoff set camp, Mantell and I continued forward with our loads on the trail that the advance group had broken. Soon we met them, returning with empty sleds and smiling faces. "Great news!" Brent shouted. "Easy miles over smooth ice lie just ahead." A huge gap that had opened in the shear zone weeks before had since re-frozen as smooth as a skating rink in the frigid temperatures. What had obviously been a lane of water many miles wide—the Big Lead—was bridged by ice nearly a foot thick.

We all stopped for a quick tea break to rejoice at this respite from the endless task of road construction. Few expeditions had ever gotten even this far onto the polar sea. Those that had were often severely hampered by the leads. But we had been blessed with the right weather. "Are you game for a little late travel this evening?" I asked Mantell. "Yep," he said with his usual economy, and we prepared to continue forward with our two loads out onto the new ice. Richard said he would have supper ready when we returned. We secured our face masks and waved good-bye to the group returning to camp.

The new ice was indeed like a highway. Excited by the vista of open space, the dogs sprinted with their 800-pound loads. The red sun rolled below the horizon, promising to return earlier the next morning and set later the next day. A half moon, sharply defined in the blue polar sky, hinted of the coming spring. The sleds rumbled northward with little resistance.

Many miles clicked by before Mantell and I reached the depot where the others had dumped their loads. On the return trip, a south wind penetrated our clothing and froze our faces. Our bodies, drained by the long day, had no reserves to ward off the chill. My fingers became so stiff I couldn't remove my gloves to thaw my face. At best, I could turn away from the wind from time to time to limit the damage.

I ran alongside my sled to generate warmth. The cold exhausted me more than the running. We were moving at a brisk pace, but time passed slowly as I fought the pain. My thoughts retreated home and fixed on the image of eating a meal in a warm room. I wiggled my fingers to keep them from locking up and freezing stiff. Finally the dogs, sensing that camp lay just ahead, picked up their pace, and I hopped into the sled to gain shelter from the wind. We heard howls and barks as we topped a ridge and spotted our tents glowing yellow. My temper was short as I scrambled to bed down my dogs, but when I peered into the tent with its stoves roaring and pots steaming, my mind instantly unwound. How pleasant it was to be back home.

Inside, pleasant chatter abounded. "This has been the nicest day," Richard commented. The temperature had edged up to −35, and there had been no wind. "It's funny how relative temperature is," Geoff noted in his diary. "Normally, −35 would be a miserably cold day, but this felt like springtime." The real bonus, he added, was not having to wear our neoprene face masks, which turned into a thick sheath of ice around our faces after a few hours' use. Mantell, reflecting on the "skin-searing cold" a few days earlier, also commented in his journal on how relative cold is. "Occasionally we were blessed with a −50-degree warm spell. It felt warm, too."

Over my years of travel in the Arctic, I have come to categorize relative comfort levels in ten-degree increments. Twenty below and warmer is Hawaii-type weather; when the wind isn't blowing, you can almost carry on in shirtsleeves. Thirty below is perfect for skiing and dogsledding. Working hard in this range, you remain comfortably warm without overheating. Forty below is a good travel zone as long as it's calm. After a heavy dose of extreme cold, −40 degrees can seem almost like spring weather. Fifty below, as well, is tolerable, though the slightest breeze will freeze you up.

It's not until you hit the −60-degree range that the temperature becomes downright hostile. The upper −60s are miserable. But wind is, of course, the most important factor. Windchill, the relation between wind speed and heat loss on the body, is a primary consideration when assessing travel conditions. Fifty below on a clear, calm day is pleasant if you are working hard, such as wrestling heavy sleds over rough pack ice. At that temperature you can easily balance heat loss with preventing perspiration. But add a wind and the day is transformed into a night-mare.

The key to comfortable dress for cold conditions is to maintain a thin, dry insulating layer next to the skin. The enemy is body moisture. Under normal conditions and activities, the body gives off about two pounds of moisture through the skin and lungs in a twenty-four-hour period. The more active a person is, the more moisture is released. In cold conditions, this moisture accumulates in the clothing, reducing insulation value and conducting body heat to the outside. Unless the clothing is dried out day by day, this moisture accumulates as a thick layer of ice.

The traditional Eskimo parka system employs two layers of fur garments, primarily caribou hide. The fur of the inner garment faces the skin as a moisture collector, while the outer shell is reversed. Without question, it is the warmest system of dress for the Arctic, but it requires a tremendous amount of maintenance. In traditional hunting camps, Eskimo women spend much of their time producing, maintaining, and repairing skin clothing. In addition to mending the tears and abrasions to which the soft hides are susceptible, they have to beat or scrape out the frost that accumulates in the fur of the inner garment. If this is not done on a daily basis, the garment's insulation value is soon lost.

For a journey such as ours, in which every minute counted, the maintenance requirements of skin clothing made it unsuitable for general use. Other drawbacks with hides are their weight and bulk, which limit maneuverability. Our activities—pushing, chopping, skiing, and lifting—determined our selection of light, supple clothing that would offer the least resistance to movement. In contrast, Eskimos, on their hunting forays, rarely entered areas of rough pack ice and thus avoided having to chop and push their way through obstacles. Most of the time they rode their sleds until they reached a hunting site, where they would stand for hours waiting for prey.

During my early years of winter travel, I relied upon wool. It is durable and reasonably resistant to accumulating moisture, but not enough so that body heat alone is sufficient to keep it dry day after day. On long trips I found wool clothing to be clammy unless I had access to a woodstove each night. The dampness would leave me feeling chilled whenever I stopped moving.

Searching for a solution to the moisture problems, as well as sponsors for the North Pole journey, I approached Du Pont in June 1985 to ask if we might field-test clothing systems made from their synthetic fibers in return for a small sponsorship. They agreed to help. Their new fibers had undergone lab tests and some highly controlled field tests, but never under conditions of rugged use and extreme weather conditions. One of the first materials we tested was their new underwear fabric called Thermax, which Du Pont claimed was superior to any others on the market for wicking moisture away from the body. After using it extensively on training journeys, we were convinced as well. Light and thin, yet very durable, Thermax continued feeling warm, dry, and as comfortable as flannel after weeks on the trail. A bonus is that the chemical components of its fibers do not react with body sweat and body oils the way wool or most other synthetics do. We found we could wear Thermax garments for weeks on end without getting "ripe."

The next layer we added to our Arctic dress system, and the key piece, was our polar suit. Basically a glorified union suit, this one-piece jumpsuit had a torso-length zipper in front and a "trapdoor" flap in back that was held in place with Velcro closures and a belt. During the five-month training journey, I field-tested numerous versions of this garment, which Susan produced from various combinations of materials. The design we selected for the polar journey, produced for us by Wilderness Experience, incorporated three layers of fabric: two layers of Thermax between which was sandwiched Thermolite and Thermoloft, Du Pont's new thin insulation battings. Like Thermax, these fabrics are superb in their ability to wick perspired moisture away to the outside. The thickest part of the suit, the torso suit, had a little under an inch of loft. These battings were also incorporated in our knee-length duffel socks and our mukluk insoles, a neoprene pad with Thermolite and Cambrelle affixed to it, marketed as the Insolator by the Surefoot Company of Grand Forks, North Dakota.

Our undergarment system, the suits and Thermax longjohns, was designed to maximize moisture transfer and generally worked well. Only on days when we allowed ourselves to overheat badly and perspire heavily did we find that ice collected within the layers of the garment. On most days, body heat would effectively drive perspired moisture to the exterior, where it condensed as a dusting of frost that could easily be brushed off. This was crucial because we had no sure means of drying iced-up clothing. And because of weight considerations, we had only a minimal supply of spare garments. This system was designed to be worn night and day, like fur on an animal. Our fears about the ice breaking beneath us as we slept necessitated this consideration. It would allow us to exit the tents in an instant without scrambling to find clothing. The trade-off, as mentioned earlier, was that at night the garments would transfer perspired moisture to our sleeping bags, which day by day were growing slightly heavier from accumulated frost. So far, this was not proving to be a serious problem. The bags felt a bit clammy, but we were usually able to get adequate rest in them.

In addition to staying relatively dry, our undergarment system also proved to be very warm. On days with no wind, it was often all we had on. When a breeze came up, we'd slip on an extra-large zippered parka that The North Face adapted for us from one of their designs. The shell fabric was Du Pont's Cordura, a tough, abrasion-resistant fabric commonly used in backpacks. The choice of such a durable fabric was based on our need to minimize time needed for repair work. For added windproofing, Gore-Tex laminate was bonded to the shell.

During our field testing, we debated at length the relative virtues of zip-up versus pullover parkas. The pullover certainly offers maximum simplicity, but it allows you only two options for adjusting ventilation and body heat—you put it on or take it off. Parkas with zippered fronts allow you to regulate your comfort level over a wide range. In the cold, though, zippers are very vulnerable to breaking and often become jammed with frost, so we had Velcro closures on our wind shells as a backup. Velcro closures were also used for the pockets, cuffs, and hood. We had so much Velcro that we joked about all eight of us getting stuck together in a ball and having to radio in for a rescue. Wind pants were simply baggy trousers of Cordura and Gore-Tex, with a drawstring waistband. With conventional cold-weather clothing such as snowmobile suits, the outer wind-shell fabric is generally bonded or quilted directly to the insulation layers. Moisture is blocked from reaching the exterior and becomes trapped as frost or ice within the garments. The advantage of our system was that the insulation layers and wind shell were two separate units.

Whenever we stopped working during the day, for breaks or delays, we put on parkas that, like our sleeping bags, were insulated with Quallofil batting nearly three inches thick. A slightly modified version of The North Face's Brooks Range model, these zippered garments extended almost to our knees and had detachable contoured hoods with fur ruffs and a breathable Cordura shell fabric for durability. Pound for pound, Quallofil is nearly as warm and stuffable as down, but it far surpasses down in its handling of perspiration. For a journey such as ours, in which very little fuel could be allocated for drying clothing, this was a primary consideration. These massive garments, which we referred to as our "portable mobile homes," were far too warm to wear while working, but offered instant comfort if we stopped and an important edge of emergency protection if someone was injured. To enhance the photographic documentation of this journey, all of our garments were made of bright red material, which offered a sharp contrast to the stark white Arctic setting.

DAY 10

"AMAZING TO SEE DOGS PULLING 1,000-POUND LOADS UP A 45-DEGREE SLOPE. THE AIR BRISTLES WITH THEIR BARKING AND SNAPPING."

On the morning of March 17, we shot out onto the Big Lead, the freshly frozen skating rink of smooth ice on which we had stashed supplies the night before. What a joy it was to sail across the polar sea, stumbling along, trying to keep up with the excited dogs. What good fortune we had struck! In less than an hour we made the four-mile distance to our cache from the night before. There we loaded everything on the sleds. For the first time since those first desperate hours after leaving Drep Camp, our entire expedition was on a one-way course to the pole. Our spirits soared, and the dogs caught the excitement and pulled ever faster. For once we were enjoying travel on the polar sea.

But the fast track came to an end only one mile ahead. The smooth new ice tapered off into old pans covered with hellish-snowdrifts and interspersed with fresh pressure ridges. I felt it was time to resort again to relays. But, brimming with exuberance from the easy miles, several team members campaigned for carrying on with full loads, grunting it out. A heated discussion ensued. I insisted on lightening the sleds rather than risk burning out the dogs. Brent countered that the Eskimo dogs run better with heavier loads, that they are built for the slow grind. I reminded him that he had never had to sustain a team on meager rations in harsh conditions for two months or more. "As much as we want to avoid relays today," I pointed out, "we have to consider our situation weeks from now, farther down the trail. We've got to meter out our energy and the dogs' energy." The group agreed. We dropped 1,250 pounds and pushed on for three miles over conditions that became steadily worse, with frequent ridges and pockets of deep, soft snow. Teetering along the sharply angled ridges, the sleds often tipped over. McKerrow was caught under one as it rolled, taking a sharp blow to his rib cage. He sensed he had torn some muscle or cartilage, but though the pain was severe, he gave no thought at the time that the injury might later cost him the trip.

By the time we stopped that evening, the joy of the morning's easy travel no longer lingered in our minds. We had crossed the shear zone, and it became painfully obvious that the ice beyond it was the same as the ice we had crossed before, or worse. In fact, that day we encountered the largest pressure ridges we had ever seen. Some towered sixty feet above the pans. Yet, despite their awesome size, some gap could always be found through which we could pass with minimal chopping. Scouting was the key. In a difficult spot, three or four of us would go off in different directions to find the best route. Using hand signals, we would indicate promising passages and then send someone forward for a final check. With a route flagged, we would regroup and then, armed with picks and axes, head out into the pack ice again. As backbreaking as it was to wield those five-pound mauls in the extreme cold, chopping duty was often a welcome break from pushing sleds, as well as a chance to vent frustrations.

Even though we moved everything forward seven miles that day, we were a bit discouraged as we set camp. A wind was coming up and a whiteout was settling in around us. Hopes harbored by some team members that conditions would improve a bit after the shear zone had now been dashed. Our moods sank lower when the scouting crew returned to report that another mile or so of even bigger ice, which Mantell estimated had ridges rising 60 to 100 feet above the surface, lay just ahead.

As I melted snow for hot drinks, Richard dug in our sled bag for some packs of Shaklee soup mix. Only a few were left among our tent group's provisions. As we stared at that meager handful of precious soup packs on the tent floor, the suspicions we had shared a few nights before were aroused once more. Sitting there cold and hungry as the wind snapped the tent walls like a whip, we grumbled among ourselves, certain that the other group was hoarding more than its share of the additional supply we had gotten from Drep Camp. With a storm raging outside, another one was about to erupt inside our tents. As our suspicions evolved into anger, we shouted over to the other tent group, demanding our full share of the soup. They were appalled to be accused of hoarding rations and countered that the only hoarding going on involved the few ounces of dry milk that Mantell had gotten from Drep Camp for my tent crew to use in our tea. "And what about that caribou hide?" Brent shouted, referring to the piece Mantell had grabbed to use as an insulating floor cover in our tent. Tempers flared. Accusations shot back and forth through tent walls over the sound of the wind. The storm precluded a face-to-face confrontation, so the resentments and suspicions festered throughout the night.

DAY 11

"TO UNDERSTAND PATIENCE ONE MUST LASH SLEDS IN THE EXTREME COLD. EVERY MOVE MUST BE CALCULATED."

During the night a polar high pressure system moved in from the top of the world, bringing bitter cold temperatures and even stronger winds. The sky remained clear all night as the gusts shook and rattled our tent while the moon, nearly full, brightly lit its interior. Despite the weather, we were all anxious to exit the tents in the morning and settle the score. When breakfast was finished, both groups tumbled outside on cue and huddled together for the showdown. Anger filled the air, though we all braced ourselves against any open hostilities. We were riding the brink of a serious crisis, one with dimensions well beyond the few ounces of supplies being debated, for we faced a dangerous disruption in group unity. The pitting of one tent group against another might plague us for the rest of the trip. Dissension within the team could block us from reaching our goal more surely than any physical barrier.

Despite the charged emotions, the cold still proved to be the ruling force. We stamped our feet and windmilled our arms as we debated the issue heatedly. As the accusations shot back and forth like darts, it slowly became apparent to all of us that, in our state of perpetual stress, hunger, and exhaustion, it was impossible for us to look at the issue objectively. When the smoke cleared, it proved to be an innocent matter with a simple explanation. On Day 4, when the extra soup was brought in from Drep Camp, our appetites had not been the voracious monsters they were now. No one had given any thought to how Paul dispersed the packets between the two tent groups' food bags. But as the days wore on, that soup, which offered instant warmth and sustenance after a hard day on the trail, had become a precious commodity. Having vented our frustrations, we all groped for words to bring the matter to a quick resolution. Ann and Richard agreed to collect all the soup and come up with some means of distributing it equitably among the team. A tinge of bitterness lingered, but rather than stand there in the brutal wind, we loaded up our sleds and carried on.

On breaking camp that morning, we suffered the coldest wind-chills of the journey. I noted in my journal: "To understand patience one must lash sleds in the extreme cold. Every move must be calculated. The body temperature must be high in order to compensate for the heat loss from the gloved fingers that are only exposed for brief moments. If the body is chilled, the fingers' resistance to the cold will be down, and upon exposing them to tie a quick knot, they will freeze. A frozen finger means excruciating pain for the remainder of the trip, or if they are refrozen it could lead to evacuation. Full concentration is needed when doing a little task like tying a knot. The cold rapidly seeps in, numbing the fingers. If close attention is not paid, that knot will have to be redone. After one such move, the arms are vigorously shaken to get blood to the fingers, and then, quickly, another knot is tied."

To capture the brutal reality of polar travel, I photographed scenes such as this windy morning. The prerequisite for performing such an intricate task is to saturate one's clothing with enough warmth to give the body a slight edge on the encroaching cold. I would run a hundred yards or more with my bulky beaver gloves on to build up heat. As I closed in on my subject, I quickly dropped the mitts in my thin work gloves and clicked off three or four rapid-fire shots with just my thin work gloves. Intricate adjustments would have to be made on the camera body or lens as I wildly shot film. Then I slipped the camera back in my holster belt and sprinted off, cramming my hands in my beaver gloves as I ran. Sometimes I repeated the process three or four times before I felt I had an adequate shot.

This journey was giving me a chance to develop my skill in outdoor photography in a big way. It had been one of my earliest pursuits. When I was eight, I saved three months of allowances to buy my first camera, a Kodak Brownie Deluxe with a flash. I spent most of my Saturdays filming planes landing and departing at the Minneapolis/St. Paul Airport. Soon my interest turned to nature photography. I spent many evenings at a pond near our house, floating on my raft, filming sunsets and reflections on the water. As my savings accumulated I invested in a 35mm camera and various lenses. However, my early expeditions took a heavy toll on my growing collection of camera gear. On one trip I flipped a kayak, dumping my best camera in the drink. On another I took a bad spill on a hiking trail in the mountains and smashed my new telephoto lense. That loss caused me far greater agony than my bruised ribs.

Eventually, cold-weather expedition photography became my forte. I find it very rewarding, but it is a difficult and painful task, and often not a very popular one with other team members. The most trying times on the trail offer the most dramatic photo opportunities. Tensions can easily arise when one person is off shooting photos while the others are struggling and suffering at capacity. We discussed this problem numerous times during our training. On the Pole journey, the team accepted the fact that I would occasionally have to drop back from the action to capture it on film. The person running the movie camera, primarily McKerrow, also had to relinquish his trail duties frequently. The price that thorough documentation of the journey would cost us in manpower was one of the reasons we opted for a large group size. With a team of eight, we could occasionally spare a person or two without seriously breaking our momentum.

During my years of Arctic travel I have field-tested many models of cameras. The Nikon FM2 has proven to be the most dependable and durable. The standard off-the-shelf model functions well in temperatures as cold as −40 degrees. For journeys in colder conditions, *National Geographic*'s photo department winterized my camera bodies, a very expensive procedure in which lubricants are removed from all moving parts. I opted to carry a zoom lens rather than separate 35-, 55-, and 105-millimeter lenses. The *Geographic* initially questioned my decision to use a zoom lens. They felt certain the slide would stiffen in the cold and become impossible to maneuver. I felt that the zoom offered tremendous advantages. It eliminated the weight problem of carrying multiple lenses. And it eliminated the miserable task of having to change lenses frequently in extreme conditions. A zoom offered the best chance of getting the right picture in every setting. On previous treks I had used zoom lenses in temperatures down to −55 degrees without any problems. The experts were still skeptical, so we decided that Ann, as backup photographer, would carry fixed lenses. As it turned out, the zoom worked well even on our coldest day, at −72 degrees. During the course of the expedition and the training runs that preceded it, I took some 3,000 pictures. Kodachrome 64 was used exclusively. Its color renderings were superb and, aside from cracked leads on a couple of rolls, no problems resulted from using it in extremely cold temperatures. Though the equipment worked flawlessly, loading a camera in temperatures below −60 degrees ranks among the worst tasks I have ever had to perform in the Arctic. Meticulous attention and speed is required to get the film wound through the sprockets before one's fingers are frozen.

For our first mile on Day 11 we threaded a circuitous course among ice ramparts that towered dozens of feet above us and then broke out onto undulating pans with occasional short stretches of refrozen lead that allowed for bursts of fast travel. Paul persuaded us to try going with full loads over these windswept plains. Though the surface was smooth, our runners would sink down several inches into the snow. The abrasive, freeze-dried corn snow, with a texture like styrofoam, would grab the sides of our runners like brake shoes. We had to constantly lever the sleds forward with the peaveys to make any progress. After three miles, exasperated by the work, we dropped our tent units and part of our supplies and went about four miles with 500 pounds on each sled to set up a forward depot.

Interspersed throughout this zone of old ice, which stretched on to the horizon like rolling farm fields, were towering pinnacles trapped in the pans when they formed. Gracefully fluted by snowdrifts and polished by the wind, they looked like statuary, an ice sculpture garden, or, as Paul put it, "an iceberg graveyard." The diversity of sea-ice forms and colors was incredible. As Richard noted in his journal that night, "Now I can see why the Eskimos have 200 words for ice. Every day is different out here."

The ice piled and shattered in an endless array of beautiful and ominous shapes. Traveling over the refrozen leads and struggling up the ridges, we gained immense respect for the ocean's power. Passing by forty-foot-high blocks that had been sheared in half, we tried to imagine the thunderous roar that must have erupted when they cracked. As Ann noted in her journal, "As solid as this surface may seem, it is always letting you know that it is alive."

In his journal, Geoff aptly compared the ice profile with mountain ranges. Young ice, like young mountains, is marked by sharp, steep ridges. The older ridges we hit farther north he compared with older mountain ranges that have been worn smooth.

In preparing for this trip, I had dug up all the information I could about the nature of the sea ice north of Ellesmere. The best descriptions from a dogsledder's perspective are to be found in Peary's journals. He vividly describes the herculean challenge of maneuvering sleds over mammoth pack ice that bent and cracked the sturdy oak runners of his kamotik sleds. However, his team's greatest obstacle was a large lane of open water, which he dubbed the Big Lead, found in the shear zone, the transition area between land-fast ice and moving sea ice that we had crossed two days before. He took soundings in the area with a coiled steel wire. Finding that the ocean floor dropped off sharply after the Big Lead, he concluded that this phenomenon was caused by an ocean current that flowed along the deep edge of the continental shelf.

Beyond the shear zone, Peary found the ice to be moving generally eastward, creating the huge open gap along its edge. The Big Lead represented the greatest barrier and variable in his efforts to reach the Pole. It was in constant flux, varying in size year by year and week by week. He had found it to be very wide during his 1906 trip, more than a mile across. His team waited nearly a week for it to narrow and freeze. The delay cost him his shot at the Pole that year, and very nearly cost his life and the lives of his men. With an early spring that year, the ice movement was so rapid that after crossing the lead, the team was almost swept eastward into the Greenland Sea, where there would have been little hope of returning to shore.

Nearly all of the early polar explorers reported encountering open leads in the area around the shear zone. In fact, open water and swiftly moving ice thwarted many of these journeys. To gain a more thorough understanding of what we were up against, I gathered satellite photos of the sea ice from research centers in Cambridge, England, and Washington, D.C. By comparing various photos taken over several weeks and juxtaposing them with weather maps for the same period, I quickly saw what had taken

Peary sixteen years of polar travel to learn. After numerous attempts at the Pole from various points along North America's northern coastline, he had concluded that currents and ice conditions mandated that the only feasible departure point for the Pole was northern Ellesmere. The photos I studied clearly illustrated the pattern of leads and ridges, indicating that the most active ice zones lie east and west of the seventy-fifth meridian. Thus, travel up that line of longitude, which runs through central Ellesmere, would offer the most stable ice. Researchers call it the Convergence Zone, where two huge spiral currents or "gyres" meet. To travel northward on the west side of this zone, you might risk being swept into the Beaufort Sea, north of the Mackenzie Basin. To travel east of this zone, you might—as Peary had found—risk being swept into the dangerous waters of the Greenland Sea.

Ice in the Convergence Zone is buckled in monstrous ridges as it is pressed against the shoreline for the first 100 miles or so. On satellite photos I studied, the shear zone, laced with leads, lay conspicuously some five to fifty miles out to sea, depending on the year and the season. Some years, even during the dead of winter, gigantic lanes of open water were evident. The nature of the ice differed on either side of the zone. To the south it lay in wrinkled heaps above the shallow waters of the continental shelf. To the north the ice sheared off to the east or west. Weather maps confirmed that ice movement north of the shear zone corresponded generally with major weather systems and in particular with the prevailing winds. I pored over the maps, discerning the trends in the ice with hopes that they might be predictable, based on local weather. I followed a large low pressure system in mid-March, the first influx of warm air from the south that particular year, and observed soberly that the advancing south wind opened up large lanes twenty miles wide off the shore of northern Ellesmere. The first influx of spring winds pushed the ice north, shattering it and setting it in rapid motion. Following the path of this anticyclone, I noted that the encroaching cold of a polar high swept down to compress the ice into mammoth ridges off the coast of Ellesmere and seal the leads shut with its −50-degree cold.

The shear zone was definitely not the place to be in such a storm. I concluded that winds from low pressure systems were real cause for concern on a polar journey. South winds scattered the ice and set it adrift, and north winds crushed it together and caused shearing action in the area of the Big Lead. I compared weather maps and satellite photos from other years and observed that on occasion the Big Lead stayed open for a week or more at a time. The odds we were up against left me uneasy. Carrying boats gave us a little edge, but did not guarantee safe crossing of a lead. The ice was in greatest motion, I noted, just after storms, when pressure from the winds slackened and the ice "rebounded." This was true throughout the polar sea. Thus the biggest threat to our journey would be an early spring bringing south winds and open leads as well as warm weather that would prevent the cracks from refreezing.

I understood the mechanics of the ice intellectually, but I knew I wouldn't develop a "sixth sense" about it—as Peary and Henson had—until we traveled on it. The first few weeks of our journey would be our classroom. For the first five days of the trip we had crossed a huge pressure ridge interspersed with old pans. In this zone, stretching a dozen or so miles out to sea, the ice is violently thrown against the continent, lifted and twisted by the global forces of titanic winds and currents. In the shallow shore-line waters, the surface was compacted by pressure welling up from below. On Day 6, Ann and I had scouted a region of intense recent pressure that marked the southern border of the shear zone. The garage-sized blocks of blue ice, covered only in a light dusting of snow, rose fifty feet or more. "I'm glad I wasn't around when these were formed," Ann commented. Our lives seemed microscopic in comparison. That first sight of the power of the shear zone was etched indelibly in our memories. We crossed over the zone during the following three days, experiencing our first moving ice and our first freshly frozen lead many miles wide.

On Day 10, nearing the end of the shear zone, we encountered the highest ridges on the trip, some up to sixty feet. During the previous few days, some thirty miles out, the ridges had tapered down a bit in height. Most of the time we were crossing old, multi-year pans of rolling, snow-drifted ice. We felt certain we were now beyond the continental shelf and above the deep moving waters of the outer ocean. The pattern of pressure ridges was becoming more random. They no longer were aligned in sequence like huge frozen waves. The pans were now heavily drifted with deep, coarse snow that gripped our sled runners and added immensely to our burden. We inched along at a miserably slow pace, pushing constantly. Our largest ice axes, the ten-pound Crusher and Big Mac, were no longer needed, so they were jettisoned to reduce weight.

It was becoming painfully apparent that the entire journey would be a long, hard grind. The end of the shear zone would not diminish our struggles. Relaying was starting to take a toll on morale. The group mood would swing with the weather and ice conditions, but was steadily growing more gloomy from the effects of exhaustion and frostbite.

DAY 12

"IT'S TIME TO FACE THE MUSIC, FOLKS."

After loading sleds in the morning, we held a quick huddle. Paul and I felt that, while the team was putting out 100 percent on the trail, camp chores and mealtimes were still taking too long— up to four hours, morning and evening. "It's time to face the music, folks," Paul told them, stressing the need to economize on time spent doing chores so that more of our day could be spent pushing northward. There had been a lot of chatter among the troops about how the ice would improve once we passed the shear zone. The cold fact was that there was no improvement; ridges were farther apart, but snow depth increased. Paul and I proposed increasing the travel day to eleven hours. The plan was accepted with only a few grumblings. To gain the extra time, we would have to shave an hour off camp chores. If this couldn't be done, we would have to trim our sleep time. The only way we'd make the Pole before the ice gave out in the spring was by putting in longer trail hours. The workday, so far, had averaged around eight hours, though we'd had occasional twelve-hour marathons. With moderating temperatures and ample twilight each morning and evening, it was time to hit a consistent stride. Paul and I feared that if the pace didn't pick up soon, our only alternative for reaching the Pole would be to send some team members back. As he noted in his journal, "Will and I wondered again today if we'd make it as planned. . . . It's apparent that we can make it one way or another. But it might require stretching the rations an extra twenty days by sending most of the team out. That would be a difficult decision, I wonder what sort of mutiny we'd face." Driving the team harder seemed the only means of saving us from having to make that dreaded decision.

As I looked at the faces huddled around me during our meeting, I felt like I was in a scene from a horror movie. Ravaged by frostbite, everyone was getting uglier by the day. Black scraps of dead skin hung from cheeks, noses, and chins. Some had pink blotches where scabs had peeled off, exposing new raw flesh below. Without the scabs to protect it from the lacerating wind-chills, the new flesh would also soon be dead. The freezing of new growth is always more painful than the original frostbite because the healing flesh is much more sensitive.

None of us had been spared. Brent, an Arctic veteran, noted in his journal, "Will and Paul have the worst frostbitten faces that I have ever seen. It makes me feel very fortunate to have just a few scabs on my cheeks and nose." Geoff said I would win the "Most Ugly Face" award if we held a contest. My face, which I had seen for the first time the day before when I shaved, looked as though it was covered by a black mask. McKerrow's nose was painfully swollen and black. Richard, Mantell, and Brent also had black noses and frozen cheeks. Ann, who was very meticulous with her face mask, had suffered the least frostbite. But the damage to our faces was merely cosmetic compared to our frozen toes and fingers. Geoff, Brent, and Mantell had the most serious cases, though everyone had frost-nipped fingers, which, in various states of healing, were now either numb or in excruciating pain.

As we talked, McKerrow, our team cameraman, bobbed in and about our shivering circle, shooting film with our Canon Super 8 battery-powered sound camera. His previous efforts to gather footage had been thoroughly frustrated by the cold. Within seconds after he turned on the camera, the motor stiffened up and ground to a halt. But he had tucked the camera in his sleeping bag the night before, and now, giddy with the joy of success, he was able to shoot several three-minute reels of our morning routine.

The next item on our agenda concerned selecting candidates for our first dog-pickup flight, which was scheduled for April 1, fourteen days away. The dogs had ample body reserves to run for a few weeks on meager provisions. To extend our supplies, the strategy called for diminishing their rations as the journey progressed. We identified the strongest twenty-three dogs and agreed that the other twenty-six, the injured and spent that would be airlifted out, would go on reduced rations that night.

Their standard two-pound daily feed—one pound of dry feed and one-pound of pemmican—would be lopped to a pound and a half. In another week their rations would be cut further, to one pound.

I reported to the team that we had shed 1,700 pounds from our total payload since Drep Camp, and were now set up for lighter relays. We had started with more than 5,000 pounds of food and fuel, our heaviest component—some 3,700 pounds—being dog food. On the face of it, it seems self-defeating; a lot of dogs are needed to pull that much food. But, as Geoff noted in his journal, the logistics of an extended dogsled trek are oddly similar to that of travel by rocket. Most of the payload is engine and fuel that are, respectively, jettisoned and depleted during the course of the journey. Like booster rockets, the dogs that helped propel the expedition through the worst of the sea ice and the brutal weather would be sent back. Only a small "capsule," a few sleds and roughly two dozen dogs, would carry on to the top.

Warm, −30-degree air and an ice fog moved in as we traveled that day, and a whiteout settled upon us. In three hours we reached the depot at the end of the five-mile trail we had marked the evening before. Visibility was now severely diminished. Fortunately the breeze was westerly, making it unlikely that this gloomy weather would bring a storm. But the whiteout was still a troublesome matter. The blowing snow and haze reduced visibility, which hindered navigation and sometimes made it impossible. At this stage of the journey we were totally dependent on the sun for navigation. In some areas of the polar sea, the *sastrugi*—snowdrifts aligned with the prevailing winds—are often useful for navigation. But in this area large hummocks, crusted drifts of snow, and pressure ridges prevented their development.

Though we had been advised that compasses would be of little value on the polar sea, we found that they could be used to determine north as a last resort. The needle was very slow to settle, and declination had to be carefully adjusted. But when the sun was not visible, we found we could rely on the compass to keep us headed generally northward. Using it, though, required time-consuming line-of-sight navigation. We had to align the compass reading repeatedly with some prominent ice formation to the north, which would serve as our target. In heavily ridged areas, a new fix was required every few hundred yards. Thus use of the compass cost a lot of time. We often found that our depth perception was severely diminished in whiteouts. On one occasion I skied right into a wall of ice. Our habit of pushing a trail forward a few miles each evening was insurance against delays that might occur if we awoke to a whiteout the next morning. With a marked trail we could be assured of making at least a few miles on days of bad visibility.

Anxious to make good progress, we carried on blindly through the whiteout, groping our way over and around ridges. Out in front, Paul pressed forward, stumbling over ridges and drifts, trying to thread a trail through the rubble. Having been in white-outs before, I felt his efforts were futile, but I let his boundless momentum keep us inching along. By now his reserves were starting to dwindle. He had literally worked himself into the ground and was becoming sick. Headache, nausea, and stomach rumbles plagued him all day and steadily worsened. My energy was returning, I told him, and I assured him he could now hang back and let me lead the charge for a while. His journal that day reflected his misery: "The slow tedious crawl through the rubble . . . chilled thoroughly most of the time. Generally miserable. Tended cold feet and hands in the tent this evening and cleaned up my trapdoor from an unfortunate accident—had the shits and missed. I almost cried, then Ann came by with some words of comfort. There's nothing worse than having the runs at minus 50. The trail is no place to be sick."

Flu-like symptoms were running through many of the team members. All of us continued to cough up green slime. Brent had a bad case of diarrhea. I pitied him. He was a tough man, but was now put to the test of wrestling with the worst curse on the trail. Some nights, Brent would have to exit the tent quickly, to return minutes later thoroughly chilled and nearly hypothermic. Everyone was suffering, yet they were all hanging in. Tempers were short, but we still worked as a team. Our determination to make the Pole never faltered. Though doubts crept in daily, no one ever really gave up hope.

For five and a half hours we fumbled along through the white-out, gaining only a mile and a half. The only thing that kept us going was that McKerrow's birthday was coming up—he would be thirty-eight on March 21—and we had agreed to take that day off. So we trudged on. Late in the afternoon we came upon a high wall and agreed to stop. McKerrow and Paul, now feeble and nearly delirious from exhaustion and stomach cramps, set camp. While the other team members set out with three sleds on the backhaul, Richard and I pushed on ahead to scout. But we found it nearly impossible to scout a passable route and, fearing that we might lose our way, soon returned to camp. The mood in camp that evening hit bottom. At our "pep rally" that morning we had built up a good head of steam, but were now stopped in our tracks.

Summing up our situation, I noted in my journal that night, "Exhausted again. Today was one of your typical Arctic situations where you think you can't make it another 100 yards, or over the next pressure ridge, but you go on for miles and miles. Struggle and perseverance are the names of this trip. There is nothing real exciting to write about these past twelve days, just a hell of a lot of work for very little mileage. For a pessimist this expedition would be labeled 'impossible.' For an optimist, 'maybe possible.' Mathematics are against us with the slow mileage, averaging five miles per day with hundreds to go."

As part of our efforts to ration gas, we now agreed to pull the stoves out from under the snow-melting pot for only five minutes to blast heat into the tent while we ate our dinner. The rest of the evening the temperature inside the tents hovered at around −40. For someone wrapped in a parka, protected from the wind, this would normally be a tolerable temperature. But our exhausted bodies were now much more susceptible to the cold; −40 felt like the −60 we'd had at the beginning of the trip. Despite the hardships, no one complained. The miseries and hassles were just accepted as part of the daily routine. Perhaps in survival conditions stoicism holds things together better than open sharing of concerns and discomforts. We all seemed to feel compassion for each other, but it was rarely expressed.

McKerrow, sensitive and loquacious as ever, was the one team member who continued to express his daily joys and agonies to anyone who would lend an ear. Sometimes I would draw energy from that; empathizing with him helped relieve my burden. Ann also showed sensitivity in our hardest times. I particularly liked the kindness she showed to my dogs. Generally, though, the bond of brotherhood was not keenly felt among us. Perhaps that was an advantage. If we had grown as close as brothers and sisters, we might have been more inclined to fight like them, as well, during times of great emotional stress. In group survival situations such as this, it's possible that close friendships may be more detrimental than beneficial. Some team members surmised that the less we knew about each other, the less vulnerable we might be to conflicts when under pressure. For my own part, I wished we had been closer.

DAY 13

"THIS IS REALLY LIVING."

We had planned to rest on McKerrow's birthday, March 21, but upon awakening to bad weather the next morning, we declared his birthday to be a day early. This rest day was badly needed. Tempers and tensions were mounting among us and our dogs. Nerves relaxed like released rubber bands when the decision to lay over was made. A festive mood replaced our dour spirits when Group 2 set plans for a party that afternoon.

Through the morning we repaired sleds and clothing and inventoried supplies. There was plenty of work to be done, but at least it didn't include pushing sleds. Most of Group 2 was plagued by diarrhea and nausea and severely weakened. My group was in better shape, though battered by frostbite. Some of us set up the woodstove while others pared wood from the sleds for fuel. Brent removed the rearmost two slats from his sled, Geoff removed his plywood decking, and I removed my sled's uprights and shortened the runners by three feet. That lightened my sled by nearly seventy pounds.

The polar sea witnessed strange sights, sounds, and smells that day. Some 2,000 miles from the nearest tree, the sounds of bow saws cutting wood filled the air. While working on my sled in the stark −50-degree surroundings, I soon heard the warm sputtering and cracking of woodfires through the stovepipes. The smells of burning pine and birch made me nostalgic for my home in Minnesota.

With plans to combine a team meeting—our first major one since Eureka—with McKerrow's birthday party, Paul and I set about inventorying all of the supplies, to give a status report on rations to the team. Using a double-check system, we ran briskly in circles around the sleds to ward off the chill as we counted boxes and burlap sacks of bulk-packed pemmican, dry dog food, butter, cheese, oats, and noodles, as well as gallons of fuel in jerry jugs and stove bottles. Time and again our totals conflicted. On the fourth try, by then thoroughly chilled and exasperated, we found our numbers jibed.

It was time to celebrate. Like an excited kid about to get his first snort of moonshine behind the barn, I grabbed a one-pint plastic jug of Jack Daniel's whiskey—frozen as solid as a rock—from my sled bag and dove into our tent. My plans had been to save it for a celebration of warmer weather, dipping into it the day its contents thawed. But I couldn't wait any longer. As my tentmates gazed on with eager anticipation, I brewed up a strong pot of tea, mixed in the whiskey along with a few ounces of sugar from my personal stash, and served up a round in our tin cups. "This is really living," I mumbled as we sank back in our little nests of sleeping bags and clothing and sipped the steaming amber liquid while the stove glowed red hot. As the liquor relaxed our bodies, we talked and joked, relishing the chance to converse without fighting the roar of the jet stove. The tensions of the past week had built barriers among us, but the collective heart was shining through once more. From Richard's carefree laughter, Geoff's gentle wit, and Mantell's quiet respectfulness, I drew the strength I needed to revive my weary body.

At 3:00 P.M. Paul shouted over that popcorn was on in Tent 2. Bearing the gift of our remaining brew, we headed over for the birthday party. Inside, like a king on a throne, McKerrow sat perched on a stack of folded sleeping bags, generously dispersing the gifts he had received—a bag of licorice allsorts from Brent and a pack of Oh Henry! candy bars from Ann. Paul had contributed the popcorn and was carefully tending McKerrow's sleeping bag as it thawed and dripped, suspended on a latticework of ski poles lashed across the ceiling of the tent. Sitting together shoulder to shoulder on a caribou hide that Brent had spread across the floor, we belted out a crackly, hoarse rendition of "Happy Birthday." Tears rolled down McKerrow's cheeks, his thoughts, I'm sure, fixed on his family back home, who would be celebrating his thirty-eighth birthday without him. The popcorn was delectable. To eat something crisp, dry, and crunchy after meal upon meal of pasty oatmeal and pemmican stew was a rare pleasure. McKerrow entertained us with rugby songs, and as the party wore on, sewing kits came out as team members decided to capitalize on the warm space and time off.

When the treats were finished, we opened the meeting. Paul reported that we had shed nearly 1,600 pounds from the two-and-a-half-ton load with which we had left Drep Camp. Our 3,400-pound payload now comprised 1,980 pounds of dog food, 280 pounds of fuel, and 420 pounds of equipment, as well as 730 pounds of people food, which, at two pounds per person per day, worked out to a forty-five-day supply. The amounts seemed about right, we told the group, as long as we religiously followed our ration schedule. I emphasized that that meant metering out dog food cup by cup each night. If we carelessly dispensed even a few ounces too much each day, we would end up several pounds short in the last week of the journey. That could be the decisive factor in our chances for success.

We might be able to shed a few more pounds, I added, if we each scrutinized our personal gear and jettisoned items that hadn't proved useful or, with warming temperatures, were no longer necessary. McKerrow nodded toward the empty five-gallon dog-food tin Mantell was sitting on and said jokingly, "How about that?" Mantell smiled, and the rest of us laughed. We all knew how important that tin was to him. Mantell thrives on organization, and that container represented his only means of organizing his world on the sea ice. In it he stored all of his clothing and equipment, and since he didn't keep a sleeping bag in the tent, it gave him a spot to perch on during breakfast and dinner.

Next we discussed the dog pickup. It was still slated for the first few days of April, depending upon the weather, but Paul had learned in the radio check the night before that the charter service had decided it would have to make two trips rather than one to airlift all twenty-six dogs that we had earmarked for departure. The extra plane meant our debt load back home would take a jump, but it opened up a new strategy. Our plans had called for dropping to twenty-four dogs and three sleds with initial payloads averaging 650 pounds after the airlift. I pointed out that if we sent the dogs back in two shifts, a week or so apart, we could extend the usefulness of the stronger ones and end up with lighter payloads when the teams were cut back. However, I added, staggering the airlifts meant we would have only enough food for twenty-one dogs for the final phase of the trip. The team nodded in agreement. But, Paul cautioned, before it could be confirmed, he would have to work out a flight schedule with

Bradley Air, which, in turn, would have to coordinate it with the media personnel who held contracts with us to be on those flights.

The meeting was then opened for airing grievances. Cheese was the first issue. At Drep Camp, extra cheese had been up for grabs and my crew had grabbed some, thus embarking on the journey with a slightly greater supply than Group 2. With appetites growing monstrous, the extra one and a half ounces we added to our pemmican stew each night was no longer an incidental matter. It was time now to find an equitable way of distributing it, lest we face another incident like the one over the soup mix. Tensions had been raised over our gas supply. Several team members claimed that now that the temperatures had moderated a bit, we weren't being frugal enough in the use of our stoves. Resentment had been brewing on the evenings when one tent crew—occupied with sewing or equipment repairs—had left their stove running long after the other crew had shut theirs down. To eliminate this source of tension, we agreed to divvy up the supply. From now on, each tent crew would be in charge of its own fuel canisters. The crew that used more fuel now would have the colder tent toward the end of the journey.

It seemed that the expedition was about to enter a new phase. During the previous twelve days we had gained a lot of savvy about travel on the polar sea, and now, following a day of repast and reflection, we felt stronger as individuals and as a team. As Paul noted in his journal that night, "Today was the beginning of the maturing process. We've reassessed our supplies, our load, our pace, and our strategy. We've met the enemy. We know the variables. We're confident in our problem-solving abilities and, in particular, route finding. There's always a way through. As Richard always tells me, it's just a matter of time."

DAY 14

"OH MY GOD, A MAJOR DOGFIGHT!"

The first day of spring, March 21, broke cold and clear, with the sun rising at 6:00 A.M. Rested and refreshed from our festivities, we hit the trail with renewed gusto. We encountered fewer ridges but more long stretches of the topographic hell of rubble fields, areas of scattered blocks ranging in size from grapefruits to garages. A blustery wind during our layover day had dropped about four inches of new snow, which had settled in deep, soft drifts between the blocks. The general surface pattern was pan, ridge, rubble. The pans, with their surfaces scoured free of snow, would offer fast travel. But they rarely ran more than one-third of a mile before ending abruptly in a forty-foot wall of ice. Once we scaled that obstacle, we'd inevitably have to hack our way through up to a half-mile of rubble before the ice would open onto the welcome vista of another pan.

As the day wore on, the minor surgery I had done on my sled the day before—shortening it by three feet and removing the upstanders—proved to be a mixed blessing. My load was now ninety pounds lighter, but the shorter sled couldn't straddle the gaps between blocks as well as the others, and more often became mired in snowdrifts. And without the upstanders I now had to pull it rather than push it. The technique is not without precedent. It's the standard sledding system in the central Arctic. On that flat, windswept terrain, Eskimos use sleds up to eighteen feet long. With the runners slightly cambered and the load packed low and in the middle, these huge sleds are surprisingly easily to maneuver. The driver sits on the front of the sled, controlling the dogs with whip commands. To steer, he jumps from side to side, pushing the front of the sled into the turn. In rough ice, steering from the front gains you much more leverage than does yanking on upstanders on the back of a sled. But in front you risk catching a foot under the sled runners, or being pinned against an ice block.

I chalked up my effort as an experiment. Our plans called for gradually trimming all of the sleds back, and it was useful to find out how they would perform. I concluded that our payloads were simply too large yet for shortened sleds to be effective. In a few weeks it might work better. On my sled, the heavy weight was now spread over too small an area, and my uprights were sorely missed. Instead of giving a steady push from behind to break the inertia of the sled each time it stopped, I now had to walk around to the front and snap the gangline, yanking back on it to create some slack and give the dogs a running start. Well over a hundred times each day, I'd pull back on the ten-foot chain that connected my dogs to the sleds, hollering out to them, "Ready?" The dogs would hunker down and prepare to launch. Then I'd issue the sharp command, "Let's go!" and lunge forward, tugging on the line with them to help break the sled loose and generate momentum. The yanking and tugging took a heavy toll on my intestines. Soon my stomach was so sore I found it hard to stand up straight.

In midafternoon that day, Geoff and Brent dropped their loads and returned to camp to retrieve the supplies we had left. Their teams, our heaviest Eskimo dogs, proved to be workhorses the first two weeks. Stuck with the thankless job of taking up the rear, Geoff and Brent put in the longest hours each day. Backhauls wore on their morale and their dogs as they retraced a well-worn trail time and again. On most days, they dropped their initial loads on the spot where those of us in the scouting crew had left the tents for the night's camp. Their Eskimo dogs, upon seeing the tents, would think the workday was over and bark anxiously for their meals. It took a lot of persuasion by Brent and Geoff to get them to turn around and return for the shuttle. Worse yet, when they'd reach the depot, which was usually at the previous night's campsite, the dogs would think surely this was the end. Many would lie down and settle in for a night's sleep while Brent and Geoff loaded the sleds. The drivers would then have to pour out a litany of encouraging commands with as much pep as they could muster until, one by one, the dogs arose. Some of the dogs would have to be lifted to their feet. Then they would tug halfheartedly on their lines while Geoff and Brent pushed harder than ever to reach camp, meals, and warmth.

Generally, someone was left at camp to set up shop while the scouting and backhaul were under way. This offered a real advantage. By knowing that tents and water would be ready when we returned, we could thus extend our relays longer, reserving only a little energy for camp chores. Preparing a few gallons of water by melting snow and ice often took two to three hours. If that process was started earlier in the day, more hours of tent time could be reserved for sleep. Furthermore, morale was boosted tremendously when sled drivers returned to the campsite thoroughly spent and found the tents glowing with light and steam curling out of their tops from tea brewing inside.

Often we arrived nearly frozen, barely able to muster the strength to stake and feed our dogs. We all lived with the dream that someday soon our supplies would be light enough for the dogs to pull them without relays. Each night that we and our dogs returned to camp exhausted, this prospect seemed a long way off.

Late that day, Richard and I were out front, about a half-mile ahead of the teams, chopping a trail. Swinging my pickax and breathing hard in the rarefied air, my world consisted of the tinkling sound of ice being pulverized. Pausing for a minute to cool off, I watched splinters from Richard's ax flying high and sparkling in the heatless sun against a deep blue sky. Suddenly our polar serenity was broken by an explosion of barks and growls in the distance and then, Ann's voice screaming for help. "Oh my God, a major dogfight!" she shouted. We dropped our tools and ran. I knew it was my team. The brutal conditions had made them very edgy. A few scuffles had broken out, but thus far nothing serious had erupted. As we tumbled along, scampering over ice blocks toward the roar, adrenaline flowed and anger welled up in me. When we arrived, Brent and Mantell had joined Ann, who was desperately trying to pull the dogs apart. The frenzied dogs were knotted up in the tangled lines, their fur matted with saliva and blood. Amid the chaos, it was hard to assess the wounds. The many facial wounds we found were superficial. It was the leg injuries that concerned us—they were the debilitating ones.

Ann was leaning over Sam, and as I walked up to her, I noticed a tear rolling down her face. Sam was badly injured. The inside of his leg was torn up. "They jumped him," she said as I put my arms around her. "First Choochi and Yeager pulled him down and then the whole team joined in." Sam was her favorite dog. In fact, she was hoping to have him as her own after the journey. At our campsites, on days when she was feeling lonely, she would spend a moment with Sam, petting him and airing her feelings. He was a great source of strength for her.

But he was the odd dog out on my team, a very strong unit that accepts only dogs born in my kennel or introduced to the team as puppies. A male introduced as an adult is forever an outsider. If that male is aggressive and tries to dominate, immediate trouble ensues. The other males, regardless of their positions in the team hierarchy, will lie in wait for a chance to nail him. If the introduced male is not aggressive, he may be tolerated after a time.

Sam joined our team during our training expedition across the Beaufort Sea in the spring of 1985. One morning in late April, as we neared the Canada-Alaska border, we happened upon a military radar station, one of dozens of DEW Line bases spaced

100 miles apart along the North American coastline to monitor polar airspace for Soviet aircraft and missiles. As we pulled up to the barracks, a dog came out from behind the buildings to investigate our two teams. The station staff said the dog, whom they had named Sam, had just showed up one day months before. Despite his wild and elusive nature, they had taken a liking to him, feeding him leftovers every day, but found that he never allowed them to get close enough to pet him.

I watched him for a while as he curiously sniffed our sleds and looked over our teams, which, infuriated by his presumptuousness, broke into growls and barks. Something about Sam's dignity appealed to me. Though he kept a respectable distance from my team, he showed no cockiness or fear. Rather, I somehow sensed that he wanted to join them. After a brief visit at the station, we continued on our journey. An hour up the coast, I looked back and saw Sam sprinting after us, leaving the food and comforts of the station to follow us into the unknown. For the next few days he stayed with us, maintaining his distance and never allowing us to catch him.

Richard took a keen interest in him and worked patiently at winning his trust. The usual method for catching a loose dog is to starve it down for several days, and then, when it lets down its guard at feeding time, jump it. Instead, Richard opted to befriend Sam and wait for him to express a willingness to join us. On the third day it happened. "I got him!" Richard yelled with joy, and we all gathered around to welcome the new member of the team. With his long legs and nose, handsome features, and silky, silvery gray and white coat, he appeared to be of Mackenzie River stock. As we slipped a harness over his head, he lifted his front paws in position for the shoulder loops. He was obviously a seasoned veteran of another team, and during the final 500-mile leg of our journey to Barrow, he proved to be a powerful, determined sled dog. It was probably just my imagination, but I had a strong sense that he had joined our team so that he could go to the Pole with us.

Sam was one of the highest-spirited dogs I'd ever seen. Though my dogs were in top shape after pulling continuously for five months, he kept up with them on the twelve-hour days. His boundless energy was balanced by an aura of gentleness; he was kind and friendly with us, and showed no aggression toward the other dogs. But he was also very "street wise" and seemed to have the savvy to stand up to a fight. Though my dogs never challenged him, he always kept an eye on them and respected their territory. He knew the consequences of being introduced into a new team.

During the months of training, my dogs' reservations about Sam had surfaced from time to time in minor scuffles. But now, on Day 14 of our polar journey, the tensions of the past two weeks on the trail were vented on Sam. During that melee, my dogs were instinctually bent on killing the outsider and taking a few nips at each other in the process. Even little Chester was thirsty for blood. As quickly as we pulled them apart, they jumped right back in to attack. Our curses and threats were unheeded. Nor did they feel the kicks and punches we were dishing out to get their attention and spare them from mutilating and killing each other.

In my rage after the fight was subdued, I stomped up and down like a madman and vowed to send all of my dogs out on the first pickup flight. Grabbing Choochi, the instigator, I screamed at the top of my lungs into his face. I could feel the pressure in my jugular vein as my anger peaked. Soon I sat down exhausted and sipped tea from a thermos to unwind. I knew it was in part my fault. My dogs are a one-person team. Anytime I turn them over to another driver, they are inclined to take advantage of the situation. As my sledding partner, Ann had gained their respect to a degree. Looking at Sam licking his wounds as he lay there crippled in the snow, I knew I would now have to take more responsibility for my dogs and stay with them more often.

All of us had been hoping that Sam would be among the dogs to reach the Pole. But, with deep wounds on the inside of his thighs, it was obvious he would be lifted out on the first flight. As we carried on that afternoon, I gazed at the pitiful sight of that proud dog hobbling along bowlegged behind the sled, and felt infuriated that my team had dashed his shot at the Pole.

After twelve hours on the trail that day, we had gained six miles. That evening we initiated a new rhythm. From now on we would allow twelve hours between the time we entered our tents after a day's work and when we exited them after breakfast the next morning. Thus we would have eight hours of sleep time and two for each of our meals. With round-the-clock sunlight, our workday now had no fixed limit. We would simply push on as long as the weather and all our energy levels allowed.

THE THIRD WEEK

A
STORM
STRIKES

DAY 15

"THE OUTSIDE WORLD DOESN'T EXIST FOR ME NOW."

Our second week on the trail opened with our first ten-mile day. Ice conditions were the best we had yet seen. Ridges were no longer aligned in waves at right angles to our route, but rather occurred in random patterns. We encountered more and more open spaces. Our only serious hindrance was the coarse, gravelly corn snow that covered the pans to a depth of about a half-foot. The weather cooperated as well—clear, calm, and only −38 degrees. It was the first day most of us felt heat from the sun against our cheeks.

Only one incident marred the bliss of a day of steady progress. That morning, Mitt Grabber, whom Geoff called "the main outlaw of my outlaw band of dogs," slipped McKerrow's grip while being harnessed up. Then, ecstatic over his freedom, he took a spin around the other teams to show off. Geoff was exasperated. This was the same dog that had gotten loose and caused us so much concern in Eureka. To have him running loose, bothering other dogs out here on the trail, would be a serious problem. We'd have a complete disaster on our hands if Mitt Grabber, now very hungry, took to ravaging our supplies at night. Furthermore, he was Geoff's lead dog, as well as his strongest and most spirited. With his rust red coat, fiendish face, and defiant spirit, he was eighty-five pounds of blessing and curse. "He is the one I like the best and hate the worst," Geoff noted in his diary. "He hates for me to touch him and even if I go up to help him when a line is tangled around his leg he fights me all the way."

Now that he was loose, he enjoyed taunting Geoff as we traveled on that morning. "Every time I stop to untangle a line," he noted, "Grabber dances around in front of me. Grabber is one up on me and he is letting me know it. I am getting more and more pissed off and if I carried a pistol I'd probably shoot him."

Later in the day, Geoff pulled up behind Brent's team, which was tangled in a scuffle. Searching around for Mitt Grabber, Geoff spotted him in the middle of the brawl. He ran up and took a flying leap on the writhing ball of dogs, tackling Mitt Grabber to the ground. "Now he was pissed off," Geoff noted. "Free one moment and slave the next." He sulked along the rest of the morning, letting his line go slack and just barely staying ahead of the other dogs. Later, Geoff found a solution for that. He shortened Grabber's line, moving him to the back of the pack. "Now the only way he can keep away from me is to keep that line taut. Also, he has an urge to be with his pack, so he is always trying to catch up. Grabber worked his ass off the rest of the day and I ended up one up on him."

As we traveled, I reflected upon how the leadership roles had been developing between Paul and me during this journey. Co-leadership was essential to cover the mammoth organizational responsibilities; one person simply could not have handled it. McKerrow aptly described our dual leadership system as "push-pull." During the first week, with my health slipping, I had little energy. Fortunately, Paul was brimming with adrenaline and led the charge. Later, as he wound down, I carried the ball. We set the pace, serving as cheerleaders. But our responsibilities also included the crucial tasks of the trip. Paul covered navigation and looked after our radio communication with the base camp. I covered our logistics and strategies for rations and relays.

As navigator, Paul would take a sun shot with the sextant every day or so and then, in the tent that evening, use the readings to fix a position on his charts. As long as the sun was out, maintaining a northern bearing gave us few problems. We all set our watches to local time, and thus the sun was due south at noon. For each hour before or after noon, we would add or subtract 15 degrees from the sun's bearing to find north. With his sextant, Paul would track our progress and determine whether we were straying from the seventy-fifth meridian, the line of longitude between Drep Camp and the Pole.

The sextant is basically a fancy protractor used to measure the sun's angular height above the horizon. This measurement is factored with the exact time of day into a series of charts and equations. The figures that result are used to graph a line on a chart. If a second line is graphed from a sighting taken hours later, the intersection of the two represents a position fix on the chart. Sextants have been the standard instrument of ocean navigation for hundreds of years. In recent decades, electronic systems that determine position fixes through radio signals relayed to land stations or satellites have all but replaced sextants. As a safety measure we carried a beacon that would allow a satellite to track us and thereby transmit position fixes to our base camp in the event of radio communication failure or an emergency. But throughout the journey we would rely on Paul's manual navigation by sextant to guide us to the Pole.

Reliance on a traditional system was in keeping with the spirit of our journey, as a deliberate throwback to the days of the early explorers. Use of the sextant also offered a practical advantage. We felt it would be much less prone to breakdowns on rough sled rides in frigid temperatures than would a delicate electronic instrument.

The sun sightings proved to be time-consuming and painful events. To gauge the sun's height with precision, Paul would stand motionless for long minutes with his eye glued to the viewfinder, and his fingers, sheathed only in light gloves to maximize dexterity, working the delicate thumb wheel that adjusted the arc. Several sightings needed to be taken and averaged to ensure accuracy. Between readings, Paul would painstakingly rub away the thick layer of frost that accumulated from his breath on the glass and brass fittings, and then run wildly in circles, windmilling his arms, to bring life back to stiffening limbs.

Readings were entered in a booklet. While dinner was cooking, we all compared our "guesstimates" of our progress while waiting for the results of his calculations. More often than not, our calculations based on dead reckoning proved to be a bit more optimistic than those based on the sextant readings.

With cold and frost hampering the quality of his sun sightings, Paul was not entirely confident of the accuracy of the position fixes he had charted to this point. On two occasions he had found that expansion and contraction from temperature changes had loosened critical parts of the instruments, throwing his readings way off. Knowing this, the rest of us at times greeted his reports with skepticism. This only added to the aggravation of the job. Time would tell whether we would find the spot from which the sun can be seen moving in a perfect spiral around the horizon. Throughout the journey he shouldered the gnawing anxiety that our goal of pinpointing the Pole without outside support rested entirely on him.

In the weeks to follow, he would come to know all the quirks of using that delicate instrument in extreme weather, and gain confidence in his position fixes. Fortunately, we could still see the mountains of Ellesmere, though they had shrunk from towering peaks to mere ripples on the southern horizon as we moved steadily out to sea. By noting the alignment of certain peaks, we were able to gauge a northward bearing along the seventy-fifth meridian. And through dead reckoning, by averaging each team member's estimate of a day's mileage, we had been able thus far to gauge progress within a mile or two of accuracy without relying on the sextant each day.

My main leadership responsibility was to look after our travel strategy, as well as to inventory and mete out food and fuel. I adjusted dog-food rations periodically according to conditions and supplies. In the morning, after discussing it with the team, I would lay out the strategy for the day and a projected plan for the next few days, though this was always open for debate. These responsibilities kept my head buzzing with figures day and night. In the middle of the night I would often awaken wrestling with alternate relay plans or dog-food rations or sled loads, or projecting how to stretch supplies if the trip went beyond Day 50, or Day 60. The success of our expedition depended upon these calculations. To feed, for example, even an extra quarter-pound of pemmican to the dogs now would put us dozens of pounds short on Day 50. That could mean sending back a team member or, much worse, running completely out of food fifty miles from the Pole. These decisions about rations had to be rigidly enforced, which sometimes led to minor conflicts. I flushed with anger one day, for example, when Brent told me he had fed his dogs twenty pounds of pemmican instead of ten. "Why not?" he said, confused at my anger. "We have so much."

On days like this one, when a break in ice conditions offered steady progress, we all shared moments of exhilaration. The first few weeks we had experienced an interesting mix of desperate feelings about the magnitude and seeming impossibility of what we had taken on, and the joy of breaking through pack ice to a clear northern horizon and seeing the "possible" once again. I fought the temptation to project weeks down the trail with thoughts of either discouragement or optimism. The journey was proving to be a metaphor for life; goals are reached by focusing on one step at a time.

"The days get gradually better, a little warmer, a little more sun, a little easier traveling, and a more organized and simplified travel system," I noted in my journal that evening. "My thoughts lie mostly in the trip. The outside world doesn't exist for me now. I don't think about the beginning or the end of this trip but stay pretty much in the slogging day-to-day present."

DAY 16

"THIS IS ABOUT AS MISERABLE AND FRUSTRATED AS A PERSON CAN BE."

When we awoke, it was balmy and overcast—conditions that typically preceded a storm. We expected it. While Paul and I were setting our forward depot the preceding evening, I noticed wispy cirrus clouds racing in from the west. These hinted that our first big blow might be on its way. Thus we had carefully marked our cache by planting a ski with a gunnysack lashed to it as a flag on a prominent pinnacle of ice nearby.

A light south breeze washed over us as we sledded toward the cache that morning. The advancing spring season was pushing the first warm, moist low pressure cell north to challenge the stable cold high pressure system that hangs over the Pole most of the year. Just after we passed the cache, the winds started to pick up and shift toward the north. The polar high had accepted the challenge and was racing south to clash with the warmth. Visibility dropped to less than 100 yards. Paul and Ann relentlessly blazed a trail through the near-whiteout conditions. Spirits started to flag.

McKerrow had done further damage to his inflamed ribs that day in trying to right an overturned sled, and was hobbling along with Sam behind the sleds, "like two old wounded soldiers," he noted. "Sam, you old bloke," he said, mustering up words of encouragement, "you're going to make it to the top. You just wait and see."

Geoff, bringing up the rear, was short two dogs. He had loaned one to Brent, whose team was underpowered since three were still recovering from sore feet, and he had lost Mitt Grabber again while untangling lines. Out of sight and earshot of the

other teams, he grunted along with a 650-pound load. Sometimes
he would have to yank a half-dozen times on his line, while
shouting "Ite! Ite!" to his eight-dog team, before his sled would
lurch ahead. "I wish now that I was anywhere in the world but
where I am," he commented. "This is about as miserable and
frustrated as a person can be." In addition to his frustrations
with his uncooperative dog team, Geoff was suffering from what
he called "rear-end mentality" since his slow progress always
kept him to the rear of the pack. As the saying goes, "Unless
you're the lead dog, the scenery never changes." Languishing in
the back, following a well-worn trail dabbled with brown streaks
of dogshit, he was anxious to be out on the cutting edge, breaking
virgin ground.

After a few hours of travel in the whiteout, we gave up and
made camp. The weather had now completely deteriorated—we
were being pummeled by blasts of wind and driven snow—but
our day was not over. We still had two sledloads of supplies a
few miles back at our cache, which would surely be lost to the
shifting ice if we waited until after the storm to retrieve them.
Mantell and I, having weathered many harrowing experiences
together, opted to go back. We relied entirely upon our lead dog
to pick up the scent of our trail, which was being quickly
obliterated by drifts. "Chester the Nose" has led me through
countless blizzards and could, I believe, follow the track of an
ant across the Gobi Desert.

But as we rumbled along, riding our empty sleds, I couldn't
help but wonder, What if we lost the trail? I flashed back to a
similar experience I had with Mantell while traveling through
near-whiteout conditions in the Canadian Barrens in 1982. That
day, leaving Mantell to handle our one sled, I had skied well
ahead to chart a route that would avoid the deepest of the
snowdrifts. From time to time I had looked back to check the
team's progress. They were plodding along, following my ski
tracks, black dots moving through the skim-milk haze of drifting
snow. I set my bearing according to the spot on my cheek that
was deeply chilled by the northwest wind as we headed due
north. Navigation by pain, I called it. My hood and face were
slowly becoming encased in ice from the moisture I exhaled. The
wind made my right eye water, and the lids froze shut. Slogging
northward with tunnel vision, I rarely looked about me because
any extraneous movements would open gaps in my clothing,
where exposed flesh might be cauterized by the wind in seconds.

A ridge just ahead offered a vista, so I anxiously worked my way to the top and turned around to check on Mantell's progress. He and the team were nowhere to be seen. Thinking he was down in a trough in the rolling terrain, I climbed to a higher point, but still could see no trace of him. I frantically set out retracing my ski tracks. They were quickly vanishing under the drifting snow. Soon the tracks were obliterated and all I could discern was an occasional hole punched in the snow by my poles. The wind increased, and visibility dropped to a few hundred yards. I was now on my hands and knees, searching for the telltale holes in the snow. My mind fixed on the sled with its load of food, fuel, tents, and sleeping bags. A chill ran through my body, alerting me to the gravity of the situation. What if I had to wait out this blow, dressed as I was in only a thin ski suit? Could I survive the night? I envisioned myself huddled in a tiny snow cave, shivering, pondering my past and my future. For a moment, curiosity replaced panic. What insights would I gain in this desperate situation? What price would I pay for them?

As I crawled along, I was overcome by a sense of humility, helplessness, and reverence. Would my mind retain the power of this experience, I wondered, so that my life would be richer for it? I lost track of time, ignored the cold, and concentrated on the tiny holes from my ski poles that were becoming increasingly indistinct. Suddenly I came face to face with Chester, sitting upright in the snow. Behind him was the rest of the team, and Mantell shoveling the sled out of a snowdrift. We exchanged brief greetings. Perhaps later that evening, I thought, when I was warm and relaxed in our tent, I could relate to Mantell the profound experience I had just had.

A sudden shiver brought me back to the present, to our journey to the Pole. Were Mantell and I about to have a similar "profound experience" on this backhaul, I wondered. In the fading gray light, the blurred outline of our cache suddenly appeared. Heat and comfort returned as Mantell and I wrestled heavy bags of dog food onto our sleds. Snow was falling heavily as we headed upwind on our return trip. Large flakes were driven into our noses and mouths, producing a suffocating, claustrophobic sensation. The wind-driven snow stung my face and collected on my eyelashes, freezing them shut. Mantell, the dogs, and I were enervated by the power of the storm. All reference to space and time vanished. In this whiteout we felt like we were traveling on an endless conveyor belt through a universe of cotton.

Chester was a hound on the hunt, his nose doing double time, a vacuum cleaner sucking up fragments of scent imperceptible to humans. An hour later we topped a ridge and watched our camp slowly take form as we approached it through the hazy light. Warm sounds of jet stoves and the friendly laughter of our teammates spilled out of the tents and greeted us. A festive spirit prevailed. The storm represented an unscheduled holiday; we were about to have some time off.

We secured the stakeout lines with extra care, organized all our equipment in piles that could be located easily if they became buried by drifted snow, and banked our tents with snow to prevent the wind from pulling the stakes loose. Special meals awaited us that night. Richard had hit upon a startling gourmet discovery by substituting oats for the noodles we would add to our stew. It resulted in a runny mixture we dubbed "pemmican soup," which was a welcome relief from the pasty dinner we were accustomed to eating. Since there were few opportunities for changes in flavor, a change in texture was relished. This would stave off boredom from our monotonous diet. Meanwhile, Group 2 worked up a similar concoction, but saved their cheese to add to the noodles in a separate pot. Thus they produced the first two-course meal of the trip, a precedent that would be followed by both groups. For dessert they enjoyed a supreme luxury—a can of salmon that Ann had given to McKerrow as a birthday present. He had intended to save it until later in the journey, when it would be savored with unimaginable delight, but Ann had lost her tin cup. The salmon can, McKerrow reasoned, would serve as a suitable replacement.

DAY 17

"I BET OUR FAMILIES ARE THINKING WE'RE NOT GOING TO MAKE IT."

The pulling rhythm of the wind lulled us to sleep like a lullaby. Craving rest, we discounted its dangers and welcomed this reprieve from the trail. All night long it vented its fury on our tents, gusting to at least sixty miles an hour. Only a few square yards of thin nylon separated us from annihilation. When we awoke in the morning, the flap and flutter of the tent walls confirmed that we would have a rest day. I felt like an overjoyed grade-school kid who has just heard on the radio that school has been closed because of a storm. We desperately needed this day off. Exhaustion, frostbite, and the demoralizing effect of relays had once again started to erode our group spirit. The dogs, safely buried in a silent world by mounds of drifting snow, slept peacefully.

My mind wandered and I drifted in and out of sleep as the day wore on. I thought about lying in a warm bed between sheets, and how comfortable my feet would feel. Fixed in my mind was a scene of me sitting at a table in a warm, barren room with my feet in slippers. Before me was a simple meal of rice. It was a great fantasy. Listening to the tent guy lines snap with a steady *tat-tat-tat* like a machine gun, I felt the comforting presence of loved ones back home. My mind relaxed. But suddenly I felt the weight of my icy bag pressing down upon my chest as I watched my breath rise out of the sleeping bag tunnel and mushroom out across the tent ceiling. My eyes fixed on the delicate latticework of frost that had formed around the opening of my bag. I'm in a deep, dark cave, I thought, and, fighting a wave of panic, counted my breaths as a distraction. Before I reached five, I had fallen back asleep.

After eighteen hours of rest, I felt ready to get up. The lack of snoring from my tentmates suggested that they, too, were awake. "Should we light the stove?" I hollered out, and they began to stir. For hours we sat sipping tea and repairing equipment. Mukluks were the key item in need of repair, but another equipment failure had arisen in the last few days as well. Metal zipper slides on sleeping bags and their outer covers (known as bivvy sacks)—weakened by the cold and the frost that was jammed into the nylon tracks—were splitting. To save the ones that remained, we would painstakingly thaw the tracks with our hands and delicately maneuver the slides along. Paul had found that we could scavenge slides from other less essential gear, such as packs and duffel bags, and maneuver them onto our sleeping bag tracks. The only other option, which Geoff and McKerrow now used, was to punch holes alongside the tracks and lace the bags shut with parachute cord.

As we worked, our conversation focused on how the people back home might view our progress. "I bet our families are thinking we're not going to make it," said Mantell.

Geoff agreed. "The few dozen miles of progress we made certainly won't seem like much to them when they see it on a map," he responded.

"Yeah, but they'll never know how we worked our asses for those miles," Richard added.

"It's been somewhat disappointing," I said, "but this is pretty much how far I figured we would be at this point. The folks back home may be doubting right now, but they don't understand that our pace will pick up dramatically in the coming weeks as we shed weight."

The wind rattled the tent abruptly, knocking a shower of frost down on my shoulders. I reflected on how these tight quarters represented such a dominant element of this journey. And I thought about how only a thin skin of ice, perhaps eight feet thick, separated us from the ocean depths that dropped eight thousand feet or more beneath our tent. Fortunately, it lay silent. Not a groan or a squeak was heard from the ice, though we knew it was now being set in motion by the blizzard winds.

We sat out the storm in relative comfort, feeling content and thankful for this reprieve. The sound of our gas stove and the warmth of our teacups against our hands were the extent of our world. How at peace we were—no trail schedule to keep, no rushing to lash sleds, no gnawing hunger, no pushing our guts out against monolithic sled loads. Casual quiet talk mingled with the roar of the stove and the staccato snapping of the tent fly.

During the times on the trail when we craved food, warmth, or sleep, thoughts of the outside world, of friends and loved ones, crept in. Now, with our basic survival needs met, I found it hard to conjure up thoughts of that world. But other team members were thinking of home, and it was reflected in their journal entries that day.

"I spent a lot of time thinking about Nala, Nigel, and Crystal, wondering what they are up to," wrote Brent. "It sure is going to be nice when I finally go home. Crystal is going to be chubbier than ever and Nigel and I are going to run dogs together again."

Mantell wrote, "I thought a lot about Carolyn, cheeseburgers, and the luxury of everyday life, just how lucky I am to be relatively healthy, have good friends and a family that cares about me. One of the most valuable things that you take away with you off the trail is your appreciation of life. Trips always put my life into a proper perspective."

"I wonder what my girlfriend José is up to right now," wrote Richard. "I can only rub my silver good-luck chain and guess. I don't even know what day of the week it is."

"Enjoyed a kaleidoscope of thoughts throughout the day,"

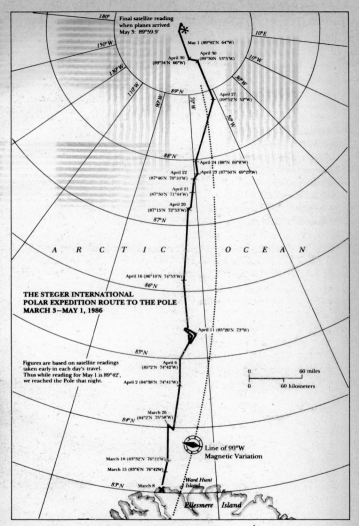

**THE STEGER INTERNATIONAL
POLAR EXPEDITION ROUTE TO THE POLE
MARCH 3–MAY 1, 1986**

Final satellite reading
when planes arrived
May 3: 89°59.9'

May 1 (89°92'N 64"W)

April 30
(89°30N 53'5"W)

April 30 (89°34'N 66"W)

April 27
(88°52'N 52"W)

April 24 (88°N 69°8'W)

April 23 (87°50'N 69°29'W)

April 22
(87°46'N 70°10'W)

April 21
(87°30'N 71°44'W)

April 20
(87°15'N 72°53'W)

April 16 (86°10'N 74°53'W)

April 11 (85°20'N 73'W)

Figures are based on satellite readings
taken early in each day's travel.
Thus while reading for May 1 is 89°42',
we reached the Pole that night.

April 6
(85°2'N 74°42'W)

April 2 (84°38'N 74°41'W)

March 26
(84°2'N 75°58'W)

Line of 90°W
Magnetic Variation

March 18 (83°32'N 76°12'W)

March 15 (83°6'N 76°42'W)

89°N   March 8

Ward Hunt
Island

Ellesmere Island

A R C T I C   O C E A N

0   60 miles
0   60 kilometers

Figures are based on satellite readings taken early in each day's
travel. Thus while reading for May 1 is 89°42', we reached
the Pole that night.

Robert E. Peary on the deck of his ship, the *Roosevelt*, during his 1905–06 expedition to the pole. Peary was the premier North Pole explorer who perfected the use of Inuit techniques in Arctic exploration. (*The Peary Collection © National Geographic Society*)

The son of a Georgia sharecropper, Matthew Henson joined Peary in 1888 as a survey assistant and later became Peary's companion on all of his major expeditions. He was a gifted linguist and skilled navigator, and among the Eskimos his sled-driving abilities were legendary. (*The Peary Collection © National Geographic Society*)

At my camp in Minnesota with two of the half-Eskimo, half-Alaskan, polar husky pups that were specially bred for the polar trip. *(Courtesy of News-Tribune & Herald, Duluth, Minn.)*

Paul Schurke (*right*) and me on the first leg of the 5,000-mile training expedition in 1985. Zap, with mouth open, and Goliath are in front. Standing behind the sled are reporter Jason Davis and his cameraman, Don Fridell. (*Minneapolis Star and Tribune*)

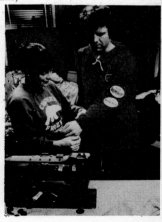

Susan Hendrickson makes final alterations on her husband Paul Schurke's Arctic clothing. Sue had the arduous job of expedition seamstress. (*Mark Wiedman*)

Brent Boddy pulls back on his ten-dog team to launch the sled while training in the pack ice at Frobisher Bay just prior to departure for the Pole. (*Will Steger/Firth Photobank*)

March 1, 1986. Sled dogs carpet the interior of the Hawker-Siddeley 748 that flew the expedition from Frobisher Bay to the Eureka weather station. (*Minneapolis Star and Tribune*)

Setting up camp on the northern shore of Ellesmere Island,
83°5′ north latitude, temperature −70 degrees, March 7,
1986. (*Will Steger/Firth Photobank*)

We chopped and pushed our way north over countless pressure ridges (*below*), (*Will Steger/Firth Photobank*) much the way Peary and Henson did in 1909 (*above*). (*The Peary Collection © National Geographic Society*)

A short reprieve of flat ice between giant pressure ridges at 84°28′. Bob Mantell hobbles next to the lead sled with frozen feet. (*Will Steger/Firth Photobank*)

At −60 degrees, the snow surfaces were as abrasive as sandpaper. Geoff Carroll wore out his mukluks on the third day. Cordura material from sled covers was used to make patches. (*Will Steger © National Geographic Society*)

A teacup served a dual purpose as a washbasin. I shaved to keep my whiskers from collecting ice and freezing to my face mask. (*Richard Weber/ Firth Photobank*)

Feeding the ravenous dogs. The dogs' food, a combination of Science Diet
Maximum Stress commercial dry food and pemmican (dried meat and fat),
was carefully metered out to the ounce. Thirty-eight hundred pounds of our
initial load consisted of dog food.

Richard Weber cuts off a six-foot length from a sled. By 84°30', enough food
had been eaten that full-length sleds were no longer necessary. Each sled
contained 175 pounds of wood, which supplemented our dwindling fuel
supply. In all, we burned two complete sleds, sent one back to a museum,
and shortened the remaining two that went to the Pole by six feet. (*Will
Steger/Firth Photobank*)

On the second week of the journey, a careening sled slammed into Bob McKerrow's chest, breaking several ribs. On April 2 he was evacuated. (*Richard Weber © National Geographic Society*)

In the hundreds of thousands of square miles of trackless polar waste, we met Jean-Louis Etienne on Day 32. He was making a solo trek to the Pole, man-hauling a 100-pound sled on skis. He was resupplied every ten days, and arrived at the North Pole on May 11. (*Jim Brandenburg © National Geographic Society*)

Twenty-one dogs were sent home on the final dog pick-up flight on April 11. Paul Schurke (*left*) and I (*center*) stand with the dogs and members of the flight crew. (*Jim Gasperini/ Firth Photobank*)

Polar explorers' techniques have not changed in 75 years. (*Will Steger/Firth Photobank*) Improvisation is paramount in reaching the Pole. Similar to Peary and Henson in 1909 (*below*), our team used small floes of ice to ferry across open leads north of 87°. (*The Peary Collection © National Geographic Society*)

We jumped across leads narrower than six feet. On a successful broad jump, Geoff Carroll leaps to the north side of a lead. (*Will Steger © National Geographic Society*)

On Day 36, in a desperate bid to make the Pole, we dropped weight from the sleds. We jettisoned two sleeping bags, parkas, and valuable camera and radio gear. (*Will Steger © National Geographic Society*)

An overhanging cornice collapsed, plunging Ann Bancroft up to her waist in icy water. Luckily the temperature was a balmy −30 degrees. Ann later commented that it was "a good day for a dunk." (*Will Steger © National Geographic Society*)

A final sextant reading at the top of the world. Schurke (*right*) and me. (*Geoff Carroll*)

The providential flat strip of ice at the Pole provided a runway for the three Twin Otters that flew the team to Resolute, Canada, en route to Minnesota, May 3, 1986. (*Jim Brandenburg © National Geographic Society*)

At the North Pole on May 3, 1986. The joy of victory.
(*Jim Gasperini/Firth Photobank*)

Our arrival home in the Twin Cities on May 5, 1986.
(*Bob Firth/Firth Photobank*)

wrote Paul, "of Susan and Bria, of Ely, of the Indian plum tree budding behind my house, of what lies ahead."

At 5:00 P.M. we enjoyed a late-afternoon snack—a pot of oatmeal—to tide us over until dinnertime. Our bodies seemed to absorb the nourishment like sponges. Then we settled back again, sewing, writing, or losing ourselves in deep thought. Hunger crept in again in a couple of hours and we made dinner. We could easily have eaten meal after meal and never felt fully satiated.

The tent fly continued to flap wildly, reminding us constantly of the fury outside. We tried to guess at the temperature. Wind-chill-factor charts bottom out at −140 degrees, Richard noted. It had certainly reached the end of the chart now. The dim gray light of the storm that filtered through the yellow tent walls, coupled with the warm meal of porridge, left me lethargic. I lay down to sleep for another few hours, awaiting our next meal.

In Tent 2, McKerrow set about preparing their meal. Reaching out the tunnel entrance to grab their bag of kitchen supplies, he found that Snickers, one of the Eskimo dogs, had been staked out too close to their tent. During the night, Snickers had eaten their wooden stirring spoons and licked the pots clean. He had surely enjoyed the feast but unfortunately had paid a dear price, for his tongue had frozen to the bottom of the pot, which was now lined with blood and bits of skin.

Hearing the dinner call, Paul exited his sled bag and entered the tent for the first time that day. His marathon twenty-two-hour nap, he told his tentmates, represented his first vacation in the two years since this expedition had consumed his life. Tucked in his sleeping bag with our whiskey flask as a urinal and a few lunch bars to nibble on, he felt completely content, he said. For an occasional drink, he would poke a hand out through a hole in his bivvy sack and grab a handful of the snow that was becoming compacted around him.

During the second night of the storm, we grew a bit impatient. After spending most of the past forty hours in our bags, our bodies no longer craved rest. Sleep served only as an escape from the long, anxious hours of waiting. Often we would lie awake listening to the wind, trying to pick up a trend in its direction that might suggest it was abating. Every now and then the gusts would seem to diminish, but then the guy lines would begin to whine with a high-pitched hum as a sixty-mile-per-hour blast roared past them. Though that sound had been a lullaby the night before, tonight it became a mournful wail. I was anxious to get moving. A one-day layover was great, but if this carried on for two, three, four, or more days, our journey would be jeopardized, for we would be cutting steadily into our supplies without making any progress. Sleep was fitful as my mind fixed on the sound of each gust, hoping that it would be the last. In desperation I stuffed cotton in my ears to keep the storm from igniting anxieties.

DAY 18

"AH, WHAT SWEET MISERY!"

On Day 18, we slept in until 10:00 A.M., lying in our ice-encrusted bags, listening to the storm. The gusts subsided, and were replaced by a strong, steady breeze from the northwest. This was a good sign, for it signified a polar high pressure system coming down from the north. An air mass such as this would bring clear weather and the bitterly cold temperatures necessary for freezing up any leads the storm had produced ahead of us. From time to time during the storm, the ice beneath us had shuddered from mounting pressure somewhere in the distance. We were desperately anxious to move beyond this zone before the ice rebounded and broke open.

By noon the clouds had begun to break. Paul shouted over to our tent, "It's a travel day." We all gave sighs of relief. We were in for a cold day, but it sure beat remaining stormbound. Anxious as we were to get moving, much extra effort was needed to build momentum after the blizzard. We felt almost drugged by dozens of hours of sleep. Our clothes, dampened by long hours in the moist tent environment, stiffened in the intense cold. The windchill cut right through to our skin. We immediately set to work shoveling out sleds, which had been buried by drifts. Digging got our blood moving and awakened our spirits. The dogs also lay buried under mounds of snow, happy to be sheltered from the wind. A few inquisitive ones popped their heads out from under their little igloos. The rest took advantage of the warmth and protection, and remained buried until harness time.

We sifted through our gear, finding that drifted snow had

compacted in every open space. We had to shake off or shovel out everything we had. Even my personal clothing bag was stuffed with snow; flakes had been driven in through a tiny gap in the zipper. We cleared space around the sleds so that they could be loaded and broken free. Harnesses and lines, caked with snow, had to be shaken off. The powdery snow melted on our gloves, encasing our hands with ice. But we were all happy to be packing up, and within an hour we were ready to begin harnessing dogs.

Dogs began to pop up from beneath the drifts, shaking the snow from their fur, waiting for yesterday's meal, which we now dished out. Their yawns and stretches attested to a good rest, though they, too, were in a stupor and walked sluggishly alongside their masters as they were brought to their traces. Our injured dog Sam couldn't be found. Knowing he had to be nearby, I began gingerly probing the drifts by my sled. To my surprise, the ground underneath me moved, and when I stepped aside, Sam pushed himself up through the crust. He had found shelter on the leeward side of my sled during the storm. Shaking himself off, he looked a little stiff, but the rest seemed to have aided his recuperation from his injuries.

The storm, we found as we examined the surface around us, had provided the break in conditions we had been waiting for. It had gathered up all of the loose snow and compacted it into concrete-hard drifts that served as ramps over the smaller ridges and gave us easy traveling over them. We decided to try moving forward without relays. We and our dogs were well rested and we had shed another 200 pounds of food and fuel while sitting out the storm. The hard, wind-packed surface was a real bonus. But with payloads now averaging 600 pounds—up a hundred pounds or so from what they had been when we were relaying—we found it took tremendous effort to make steady progress. "Ah, what sweet misery!" Paul commented in his journal. "Busting my ass behind a miserably heavy sled but delighted to be moving the whole operation along in one go." Fortunately, a day's rest had dramatically improved the dogs' strength and spirit. My dogs were pulling better than they had at any other time on this trip. Mantell's and Paul's teams also seemed to be brimming with energy. But though they could move the sleds steadily along on the flats, the slightest ripple on the surface would bring the sleds to a halt. "Every tiny drift became a mountain and a three-inch drift an Everest," wrote Brent. Countless times that day we levered our sleds with the peaveys to move them over some obstacle. To spare his ribs from further damage, McKerrow plodded along in front, scouting a route.

Often we stopped to wait for Geoff and Brent, whose sleds were moving much slower than the rest, but the cold would not allow us to linger long. We worried that they were slipping farther and farther behind. If their sleds could not keep pace with ours, we would have to resort to relays once again. That, I knew, would have a devastating effect on group morale. I pitied Geoff. Once again he was stuck in the rear with his unmanageable brutes. How could we quickly shed another 100 pounds or so from their loads, I wondered. An idea crossed my mind. "What do you think about suggesting that they drop the folding boat from Geoff's load?" I asked Paul. "That sounds like the answer," he said. Now that we were well beyond the shear zone, its value to us was questionable. Granted, we might still run into open water up ahead, but if we were to start making steady progress, it was time to start taking some gambles. Thus, with that quick exchange of words, we made the big decision to dispense with it. We scribbled a note and posted it on a trail-marking flag: "Drop the boat now! Signed, Your Leaders." That would surely pick up their spirits and their pace, we hoped.

At 8:30, with the sun setting and the temperature plummeting, we selected a campsite for the night. After staking out my dogs, I searched for other chores to do to keep warm. My group's tent was on one of the sleds that had not yet arrived. An hour later Geoff and Brent pulled into camp, minus the boat, and though limp with exhaustion, they were delighted that they did not have to resort to relays. By this time I was so thoroughly chilled I could move my fingers only with the greatest concentration and effort. The price we paid for having such a large team were the long stretches of waiting and the deep chill that they brought on. To travel alone or with one companion, as I've often done on previous expeditions, means there is no waiting, no wasted time. In contrast, with eight people and five sleds, we could only progress at the pace of the slowest team. But as our payloads steadily diminished and the sleds all began moving at a more consistent pace, we would be less prone to long delays.

As we set camp, a creamy white full moon sat directly on the horizon to the east while a tangerine sun sat on the horizon to the west. I savored the fact that we had pushed forward five miles in six hours without relays. At last things looked as if they were going in our favor. The sleds were growing lighter, surface conditions were improving, and the dogs were holding out. As winter slowly gave way to spring, we were still in good shape and spirits. In a few days, perhaps, we might find some enjoyable travel.

DAY 19

"TODAY I SAW DORSAL FINS ON WHALES, GIANT ICE CREAM CONES, STATUES OF WARRIORS AND LOTS AND LOTS OF MODERN ART."

Spirits were somber in Tent 2 the next morning. McKerrow announced in tears over breakfast that he would be going out on the first dog-pickup flight. Even in soft snow, he reported to his tentmates, every step he took jarred his injured ribs. The waves of pain were growing too great for him to bear much longer. Unable to help with the sleds, he felt he was now only a hindrance to the team's progress. It was a very lonely decision to make. There was little his tentmates could say to console him. He had invested a year of time and thousands of dollars to take part in an expedition nearly halfway around the world from his home. But fate had cast its lot, denying McKerrow his shot at the Pole.

But moods picked up as the day wore on. Day 19 proved to be our first full day without relays. In ten hours we moved ten miles. Brent found himself fascinated with the ice formations we passed. Delicately sculpted by the wind, they took shape in his mind as "dorsal fins on whales, giant ice cream cones, statues of warriors, and lots and lots of modern art," he noted. Along the way, McKerrow spotted our first sign of life, a frond of seaweed frozen in the ice. "The first piece of vegetation I've seen in this Arctic tomb," he noted. "It is the small and beautiful things like these which tug at the heartstrings and make it all worthwhile." Since the most noticeable feature of the polar sea was its desolation, finding this was truly a significant event. The surface of the Arctic Ocean is a virtual desert, nearly devoid of life. Pilots and other expedition teams have spotted an occasional polar bear, arctic fox, or seal, but we had yet even to see any tracks.

Considering the number of drifts we crossed that day, we were very pleased with our mileage. Never had we anticipated that snowdrifts would represent one of our major obstacles on this expedition. The polar sea receives only a couple of inches of precipitation a year, but as was now becoming painfully evident, much of what falls stays there and is redistributed in drifts by the wind. We encountered virtually no pressure ridges that day, yet it seemed a major accomplishment to achieve ten miles. We pressed on for hours through rubble fields buried in deep snow.

Paul's team was grinding down. He pushed, pried, and pulled frantically on his sled to keep pace with the others. I've never seen anyone work as hard as he did. Despairing that his dogs might be burning out, he seemed to be redoubling his efforts. This time, in fact, he literally pushed his guts out. While we were stopped, waiting for Geoff's sled, he slipped behind an ice block to relieve his bowels. A few minutes later, he came back shaking his head and snickering to himself. "What's up?" I asked. "Hemorrhoids," he said. "First time I've ever had those." Somehow it had struck him as funny.

Both Brent and I were continuing to suffer serious periodic bouts of diarrhea. Suspecting that it resulted from the massive doses of fat in our diet, he had given up fat and I had cut back on my pemmican. But I found that, digesting less fat, I became chilled more easily. The other team members had yet to show any problems with the diet. My tent crew ate their fill every night with no ill effects. Paul actually seemed to be gaining weight.

DAY 20

"BAD NEWS, THOSE ARE INDEED PRESSURE RIDGES."

Clear, cold weather, with a light southwest breeze and temperatures ranging between −40 and −50 degrees, continued the next day. Paul fired up the radio to let Jim know that he would have to incorporate McKerrow's departure into the plans for the airlift, which was still scheduled for April 1. That morning we drove our sleds through unobstructed country and struck a good pace. At noon Paul carefully set up the sextant and took sun sights for nearly an hour. This time he was determined to come up with a position fix with which he felt confident. His charting placed us one full degree—sixty-eight miles—north of Drep Camp. It seemed a meager amount for twenty days of travel, but considering the relays and detours, we knew we had clocked nearly twice that distance on our sleds. And considering that our pace was now picking up and we were no longer relaying, we were pleased with our progress.

But the polar sea, ever full of surprises, dashed our spirits early that afternoon, when we saw what appeared to be mirages of high walls of ice off to the north. As we continued, they loomed higher and higher on the horizon, but we were accustomed to seeing such mirages, and passed them off as mere illusions. Paul, however, out in front, yelled back, "Bad news, those are indeed pressure ridges." We sent Richard ahead on skis to investigate. He confirmed that we were entering three huge ridge systems. Back to the grind.

On the first set of ridges we worked two hours getting everything over in one load. It looked very doubtful that we would be able to continue without relays, but we all wanted to give it another try on the next ridge. Massive rubble fields buried in drifted snow lay between the ridge systems.

Wallowing through the drifts, the dogs began to burn out. But we held on to a frail thread of hope that perhaps the ice would again level out. Alas, it only got worst. We called a huddle. A few wanted to continue grunting on with full loads, but the consensus was that it was time to accept the heartbreak of relays once more. Spirits plummeted as we unloaded supplies from our sleds. We knew that more long days of relays would seriously erode group spirit. Brent, Ann, and I decided to push forward with light sleds and set up an advance depot. We each dropped 200 pounds from our loads. The other three drivers would drop 100 pounds each, move a short distance ahead, set up camp, and then return for the backhaul.

Pulling a lightened sled, my dogs ran well again. I ran ahead to scout, while Ann handled my team. I soon became thoroughly chilled, even though I was scampering over chaotic ridges with my heavy parka on. To conserve body heat, I tried to put on my face mask. The task proved nearly impossible. First I had to reach into my pocket and dig out the mask, and to do even that required running in circles and windmilling my arms to bring dexterity to my fingers. Another sprint was needed before I could fasten the mask's Velcro tabs to my hat. That required slipping my parka hood off and then, using bare fingers, lining up the tabs and pressing them into place. I was very careful, knowing that if I missed on the first try, I would have to warm up for another twenty minutes before I could make a second attempt. My hands stung and then went numb as I made the final adjustments. Finally, with the mask in place, I savored the fact that I'd taken the edge off the evening chill.

The ice conditions worsened steadily as we pushed ahead to the north. Huge green blocks of ice hinted at recent pressure activity. This fracture zone, it seemed, had been active most of the winter. At sunset we dropped our loads next to a forty-foot ridge system and headed back toward the campsite we had selected earlier in the afternoon. The dogs, anxious for rest and a meal, outpaced us as we tried to run alongside to stay warm, so I hopped on the sled, bracing myself against the windchill and gripping the slats tightly so I wouldn't be bounced off. This robbed my fingers of more heat. I sat on my feet to help warm them, but my hands and arms became increasingly stiff. I had mistakenly left my heavy beaver overmitts on Brent's sled, which was lagging far behind. How easy it would be, I thought, to give in to the cold, to let the stinging pain turn to numbness, and to allow hypothermia to slip painlessly over me. Death would come so quickly if I let it.

As my fingers stiffened, I thought of the pain that Brent and Geoff were suffering each day from their frostbitten fingers. My mind could only focus now on the pain from the encroaching cold. It seemed my whole body was at the point where my flesh would soon freeze solid. No past or future existed for me at that moment, but only the presence of the cold, trying to forge an entry into my body.

After what seemed an endless journey, I finally reached camp. Halting the sled, I dove into my tent to thaw my fingers before attending to my chores. Never before had I resorted to warming by the stove before settling my dogs in for the night. As I completed my chores, body heat returned and I was amazed at the reserves I still had left.

As we prepared for sleep that evening, I hefted my bag and found that it had gained about twenty pounds in accumulated ice. The inner layers of insulation were still somewhat dry, but the outer layers were frozen mats. We had been finding that a tremendous amount of body heat was needed to bring the bags up to a temperature at which we could sleep with minimal comfort. Some nights we shivered for three or four hours before we dozed off. Often we resorted to little make-work projects, such as slipping socks on and off fifty times inside the bags, to generate adequate warmth for sleep.

Another problem was that every night the zippers on our sleeping bags and their protective outer covers, the bivvy sacks, were frozen. With the teeth jammed with frost, the zipper heads would easily shatter unless the track was painstakingly cleaned and the zipper gently maneuvered. Many of us had broken our bivvy sack zippers during the first few days. That was an annoyance, but not a serious matter. We just pulled the covers up over us and tucked them in to try to keep frost from falling on our bags.

The sleeping bag zippers were far more crucial. Those bags were our only pockets of warmth. The prospect of trying to sleep in an open bag was a frightening one. I would thaw the frozen zipper head with my bare hands to help it slide better. It took great patience to work it free. An abrupt move could mean cold nights for the rest of the trip. In the morning we took similar care in getting out, for the zippers were caked with ice from our breaths.

All night we were plagued with cold feet. My feet were warm during the day as long as I kept moving. But my sheepskin overboots were wearing out, and with moisture accumulating in my footwear, my feet froze up whenever we stopped to make camp. By the time I entered the tent, they were numb. After "nesting up" in my sleeping bag to do my evening tent chores, my routine was to untie the mukluk laces, pull off my overboots, duffel socks, sealskin booties, and undersocks, and immediately start rubbing my toes. My tentmates did the same. The heat from our stoves was all but absorbed by the cookpot, frying pan, and snow melter around which we propped wet boot liners, mitts, and face masks. After I'd rubbed life back into one foot, I'd warm a sock with my hands and put it back on the revived foot, then attend to the other foot. The warming process for feet, socks, and duffels continued. The objective was to build up enough warmth in our feet and clothing to minimize the chill we'd suffer upon entering the icy bags after dinner.

An eight-hour night's rest was crucial to our well-being, and so the evening warming process was a key part of our routine. We went to great lengths to try to ensure sound sleep. I used all of my clothing for extra padding. To cushion my bed of ice, I placed my insulated parka under me and my duffel liners along the zipper to block drafts. I put windgear and sheepskin booties in a nylon bag under my hips and thighs for extra padding and insulation. Extra duffels were wrapped around my neck to seal cold air from entering around my shoulders. Sleeping in our clothes also eliminated the energy drain from slipping our big suits on and off.

After our meal, the rubbing and warming process continued. I would work on my caribou sleeping socks, pushing my bare hands inside them and flexing my fingers to work the ice out. Initially, the cold interior would numb my hands, but with activity the caribou fur would begin to radiate warmth. I'd slip these on my feet and massage my calves to increase circulation just before entering the bag. As I slipped into it, I could feel the weight of ice press down on me, bringing on a wave of claustrophobia. My warm feet would be plunged into the deeply chilled base of the bag. The hours spent warming them seemed to have been all in vain as they would begin to freeze again. I'd rub my feet together vigorously, as if trying to make fire from two sticks. After fifteen minutes or so, I was minimally comfortable and sleep would overtake me.

Most nights I'd awaken a few hours later with numb feet. Yanking one foot at a time up to my chest, I'd massage the toes and then rub my feet together again. When circulation returned, I'd fall back asleep. If this warming process was incomplete, or if my body's reserves had been spent by the day's effort, chills would interrupt my sleep every few hours throughout the night.

Nearly all of our evenings were spent maintaining our bodies and equipment. Though we never looked at it as such, it was a survival response. Every moment was devoted to protecting our existence. Even if we were limp with exhaustion, we knew we couldn't compromise on these tasks. If you did an incomplete job of warming your feet, you'd suffer a fitful night of chills. The next day might bring frozen feet or early burnout.

DAY 21

"FOR THE FIRST TIME I AM FEELING IT'S LIKELY WE WON'T MAKE IT."

Our spirits flagged a bit over the next few days. It was no fault of the weather. Journal entries included such comments as "beautiful day," "exceptionally nice out," and "finest weather of the trip." However, we were still in the deep freeze. The temperature hovered around −40 during the day and dropped into the fifties at night. The reason for the glowing comments was that it remained generally calm and clear. This meant good visibility, no windchill, and stable ice. The surface conditions cooperated as well. We still encountered the odd stretch of monstrous young ridges, but most of the time we traveled over pans with either widely spaced, undulating drifts—"farm country," we called it—or sharply defined drifts in a wave pattern, known to us as "trough and hummock." What more could you ask for on a trip to the Pole?

What we wanted more than anything else was an end to the relays. We had to resort to them again on Day 21, but resolved that after the dog airlift, come hell or high water, we would not relay again. We wanted desperately to travel steadily northward. Though our sleds were growing lighter, we and the dogs were growing wearier. It seemed to be a losing battle. Our muscle power was playing out at the same rate that the payloads were diminishing. Our weariness over the relays brought on despair. Geoff, the eternal optimist, sank to an all-time low, noting in his journal, "For the first time, I am feeling it's likely we won't make it."

Our troubles left some team members feeling very irritated. Richard, desperate to make progress, felt we could make better use of his abilities, and voiced his grievances to me over dinner. He said he was tired of always being stuck with "idiot work," and felt he had become the expedition "gopher boy." His main grievance was that he had joined the expedition to apply his skiing skills as a trail scout, and thus far we had never called upon them. Paul and I felt that the ice conditions were too rough and that we were moving too slowly for a scout on skis to be of much benefit. He was so frustrated that he threatened to leave with the dog pickup.

I understood how he felt. As the youngest and least experienced in my tent group, he was low man on the totem pole and often got stuck with the grunt work, such as clean-up chores. Rarely was he delegated any tasks that required much responsibility. Often I saw the frustration on his face when challenging and stimulating jobs, like scouting a lead through big ice, were delegated to someone with more experience. He might have been able to do the job equally well. He was a quick learner, very responsible, and his sharp mind and inner drive helped make up for his lack of experience. But I felt we couldn't run the risk of having him make costly mistakes while learning on the job. The polar ice is no place to trust an expedition to an apprentice.

His resentment toward me for holding him back had been brewing over the past several weeks, and he couldn't take it any longer. By voicing his frustration, he told me how he viewed his role on the expedition. During the past weeks, few of us had gained much understanding of each other's states of mind. In group meetings, Paul and I always encouraged team members to unload any tensions, but rarely did anyone speak up. I was pleased that Richard was leveling with me.

I reminded him that on our training trip across the Beaufort Sea in 1985, I had told him that we would need him as a scout, but had defined his main job description very bluntly: he would be a "grunt." But, I agreed, he had too often been left to be the "water boy" at the campsite while others went on ahead to blaze trail in the evening. I had gained confidence in his general competence. With the terrain becoming more open, his skiing ability might be put to use. I sympathized with him, realizing he needed more responsibility to feel good about his role. I volunteered to take the water boy chore for the next two evenings, and suggested he ski out in advance of the scouting crew.

THE FOURTH WEEK

OUR
FIRST
FAREWELL

DAY 22

"HELP! THE DOGS ARE IN OUR FOOD!"

The next morning, Day 22, irritations over our slow pace surfaced in Brent as well. While hacking through sharp ridges, we came upon a freshly frozen lead, a thin, shimmering ribbon of smooth young ice that cut across our route to the northwest. We always lived with the dream of finding the magic lead that would be our highway north, a road that would take us out of this ice hell. I had checked this lead out the night before, when we pushed the two loads forward, walking it for a quarter of a mile and finding that it splintered in many directions.

In the morning I led the group out across the lead and carried on another half-mile before stopping to wait for the other teams. They had gathered at the lead. I could hear Brent complaining angrily to the others that we should follow the lead, suggesting that it just might veer north. He instructed Richard to check it out. I knew that was a waste of time and the rest of us would have to wait there freezing. But I felt it was best to let him learn for himself the futility of hoping that every stretch of smooth ice might be the dream lead. If I insisted they carry on along my route, resentments would brew that might poison our collective spirit. So we lingered in the cold while Richard scouted to the west along the lead and soon returned with the report that it offered no easy route.

What made the relays particularly annoying was that they made it impossible for us to establish a regular rhythm. The scouting and backhaul crews never arrived back at camp at the same time. That meant some people had less tent time than others, and, worse yet, less sleep. So we initiated a new system.

For the next few days, until the dog pickup, our two tent groups would operate as separate units, follow a staggered schedule, and alternate the shuttle duties. With this system, each team member was assured twelve hours of tent time—four for meals and eight for sleep—and we made better use of the twenty-four-hour daylight that was now with us. That day, for example, Group 2 scouted ahead at the end of the day while my group handled the backhaul. We returned to camp first, so we took our twelve hours of tent time with plans to be on the trail a few hours before the other group the following morning. With this system, a camp would be established in late afternoon. One tent group would go forward with three sleds and the other group would go back with two. Two people, one for each tent, would remain in camp to ensure that water and a meal were ready for the returning mushers.

That day we made eight miles in twelve hours. In the evening, my crew handled the scouting so Paul's group could be first to bed. In keeping with my pledge to Richard, I remained in camp as the water boy. He went ahead on skis to blaze a trail for Mantell and Geoff. Camp duty proved to be a long, cold, four-to-five-hour endurance test, and I understood why Richard hated it. Since we were now tightly rationing fuel, the stoves could not be used for heating the tents. I hauled in the water pot, placed some ice in it, and fired up the stoves. The tent warmed to about −40, some twelve degrees warmer than it was outside. After unzipping my sleeping bag, I slipped off my wind shell, settled into my sleep gear, and crawled into the bag. In fifteen minutes the interior of my bag had thawed to the point where it was becoming damp. To pass the time, I tried to write. The pens continued to freeze up, so I kept two going in rotation, burying one in my polar suit. The ink, slow to dry, smeared on the page. I put the journal away and sat in meditative silence. In this void, time passed effortlessly. My thoughts turned to food. Hunger was proving to be a greater constant in our minds than the cold. The cold can easily be forgotten about, but not hunger. I was anxious for supper, our one payment for the day's work. For the next few hours I busied myself preparing it to perfection, knowing how wonderful it would be for the crew to return to the aroma of a steaming hot meal. As the noodle water began to steam, I held my hands over the pot lid, savoring the escaping heat and the one moment in the day when I had warm fingers.

Journal entries and tent conversations that evening described an emotionally wrenching day for many people. McKerrow and

Geoff had had a long heart-to-heart talk about friends and family. Paul wrestled with severe bouts of loneliness for his wife, Susan, and his daughter, Bria. Thoughts of them had served as a refuge for him during the first excruciating weeks of the journey, but as the days wore on, he found himself increasingly plagued with homesickness for his family. At times he would have to deliberately block them out of his mind to focus on the task at hand. He, like the other three fathers on this trip, Geoff, McKerrow, and Brent, occasionally felt a gnawing sense of irresponsibility about being away from his family. He trusted that Susan, who knew better than anyone how well we had prepared for this trip, wouldn't fret the weeks away at home. And he justified his absence from Bria by reflecting on the pride she might someday take in Dad's journey, and on the spirit of adventure he hoped it would help kindle in her.

Ann, too, had had a hard day. She handled my team in the morning while I walked just ahead of my dogs, leading them through a stretch of rough ice. At one point, while struggling with my sled, she slipped and fell flat on the ice. I went back to help. As we maneuvered the sled forward together, tears welled up in her eyes. Ann had high expectations of herself. Anytime she fell short of them, her pride was deeply injured. She dearly wanted to succeed, both for herself and for the women all over the world who were counting on her to set a new precedent about women's place in major expeditions.

I got very little sleep that night, feeling very sick from dinner. The immense amounts of fat we were ingesting, pemmican mixed with butter, were causing a severe reaction in my system. My stomach felt burning hot. At times I felt as if I were going to throw up. An acid taste lingered in my throat. All of us suffered from this reaction at some point in the trip, but it seemed to plague me the worst. Geoff was also finding himself nauseated by the fat, and no longer added butter to his stew. Brent cut back on his pemmican rations in hopes of curing his diarrhea. Now that our bodies had become acclimated to the cold, it seemed they could not handle the vast amounts of fat.

Later that night we were all shaken from our sleep by a near disaster. A growl that seemed suspicious caught my ear. I hoped it was nothing, but again I heard a rumble from outside. It was the growl of a dog protecting something. Soon a ruckus broke out. I peered out our tunnel and saw Geoff's dogs loose and ravaging our food and equipment on the sleds.

Dressed only in underwear and duffel socks, I shot out of the

tent door. Two dogs were fighting over a pair of sealskin mukluks, a couple more were tearing through a sack of butter, and
one was gnawing on the stock of our rifle. Screaming for help,
I started grabbing at dogs and pulling them back from our
precious supplies. I worked frantically, increasingly angry that
it was taking the others so long to react. If the dogs did serious
damage to our supplies, the expedition might be over. This was
no time for complacency. Finally a few others toppled out of
their tent doors, tugging on pants and boots, and helped me get
the crazed dogs under control. We surveyed the damage. Fortunately there was no serious loss, and the event served as one of
the best lessons of the trip.

DAY 23

"PERHAPS FEWER THAN A HUNDRED PEOPLE IN HISTORY HAVE WITNESSED THE SEASON'S FIRST MIDNIGHT SUN ON THE POLAR SEA."

The next morning at our team meeting we agreed that another
slip-up like this could cost us our shot at the Pole more surely
than running out of food or fuel. In a big group, it is easy to
become complacent. Team members tend to rely on the leaders
to make the first move in most situations. I insisted that we all
be on guard from now on.

For a week now I had watched McKerrow wrestle with a
decision about whether to leave the expedition and seek medical
care for his damaged ribs. At times he said he was coughing up
yellow phlegm, which suggested the possibility of damage to his
liver or lungs. He wanted desperately to carry on, but it was
apparent that he would have to leave us.

Day by day the pain had increased, and he was now barely
able to walk. He came to grips with the fact that the expedition
was over for him. After entering our lives by pure chance, he
would now be bidding us goodbye. I thought about the odd twist
of fate that had brought him to the polar sea as I watched him
hobble painfully through a difficult section of ice. It was obvious
he was in great need of compassion. The disappointment he was
bearing over having to leave was reflected in his hunched back.
In these hard times of survival, emotions are too often pent up

inside. I had watched him suffer the last few days, but had said nothing to him.

On this day I couldn't hold back my empathy for him any longer. He was walking ahead of me as a "rabbit" to keep my dogs going. When my dogs caught up with him, he stopped and turned around. A wave of pity swept over me as I looked at his frozen face. I walked up and embraced him. We both started to cry. Tears poured off his parka and hit the ground in frozen beads. "I don't want you to go out," I sobbed to him. We hugged each other in silence until the chill overtook us.

As the sorrow flowed through me, my spirit seemed to be cleansed, leaving me feeling light and almost happy at the release of this burden. I looked in McKerrow's tear-filled eyes and saw that he, too, was now relaxed. We had needed this moment of connection, reaffirming the bond of mankind amid the ice. Its hardships had isolated us. In that brief moment he and I drew strength from each other that revitalized us more than a day's rest would have done. He straightened his back as I threw an affectionate punch to his shoulder. The other sleds were coming up just behind us, so he hobbled on ahead. I gave my dogs the command to carry on.

After another twelve-hour day, we had covered only five miles. Along the way we gave a few of the dogs special treats, feeding them mukluks that were worn beyond repair. Even paper-thin moosehide had a few calories, we figured. A special treat was also in store for us later that evening. With McKerrow and Mantell tending our snow melters at camp, Paul's crew went ahead to scout while mine went back for the shuttle. While returning to camp around midnight, our eyes fixed on the sun, which straddled the horizon. "Wonder when it will set," Richard commented as we plodded along with our sled load. The orange sliver of sun grew ever thinner, stretching out like a tangerine pancake right over the North Pole. An hour passed. "You know, I think it's getting larger," I said to Richard. We both stopped and gaped in amazement at the sun, which had just treated us to our first twenty-four-hour day. "Perhaps fewer than a hundred people in history have witnessed the season's first midnight sun on the polar sea," I commented to him. We now shared something very special with the world's great explorers, such as Nansen and Peary, who were drawn north by the polar spirit.

Revitalized, I walked effortlessly back toward camp, sensing that my spirit mingled with the iridescent glow of the pack ice, the violet, green, indigo, and maroon bands along the horizon, and the heart-red half-sun sitting due north. Each expedition of my past twenty-three years, I reflected, had drawn me closer to this point, to the land unpeopled and unchanged, cold and silent, where the only forces at work were in the hands of God.

DAY 24

"I HIDE MY TEARS BEHIND A FACE MASK AND A COLD DAY."

The night was long and cold, and moods were somber in the morning. Long faces sulked about the campsite as we loaded sleds. Paul and I held a quick powwow, stepping away from the crew and walking in fast, tight circles to stay warm as we talked. We had sensed seeds of disillusionment among the team regarding our plan to reach the Pole without resupply. We were all growing weary, and though nothing could be done about the trail conditions, a little extra food and fuel would certainly help morale. Would tomorrow's airlift trigger suggestions of a resupply, Paul and I wondered. We reconfirmed our commitment to each other—we would entertain no compromises—and headed back to camp to host a pep rally. The troops gathered. Paul and I gave our standard motivational trail speech: Buck up and do your damnedest, it's the plugging away that wins the day, rah, rah, rah. But it was McKerrow who really set all of us on fire. He gave an impassioned endorsement of our chances for success, saying that though he would soon be leaving us, he knew beyond the shadow of a doubt that we would make it to the Pole according to plan.

Bolstered with renewed pride, our bent bodies straightened up a bit as we left camp that day. We needed that extra boost, because our first four miles were as hellish as anything we'd encountered since leaving Drep Camp, an absolute chaos of car-sized blocks. Mantell hobbled along in excruciating pain, a blister on his frostbitten left foot having grown to nearly three inches across. Zap hobbled alongside him, favoring his injured paw. "Stay with me, Zap," I overheard him say, "we cripples got to stick together." At one point, Mantell's sled was caught on a ridge. With healthy feet he would have been able to grunt it over without problem. But since pressure meant pain, he now had to call one of the other team members over for help, and, as he noted in his journal that night, he fought back tears of despair and helplessness. "I've considered going out on the plane," he wrote, "but then I think of all the people who have worked so hard for this expedition and, more important, the commitment I've made to myself. Do I give up when things get tough? First the Pole trip, then maybe a job, later perhaps a marriage? No, I must endure or I won't be able to live with myself." While Mantell wrestled with his reasons for continuing, McKerrow wrestled with his decision to go out. As his foot broke through the crust of snow with each step, his inflamed ribs sent waves of pain through his body. Tears flowed freely during the last few hours of the day as he took his last turn behind a dogsled, helping Brent drive his sled, the *Crystal,* which like all of our sleds was named after family members or friends associated with the expedition.

Geoff was having problems of a different sort. His ravenous renegade dogs had discovered a new trail snack—human feces. And with many of us now suffering from bouts of diarrhea, these snacks were widely distributed. The dogs would take great pains not to step on dog crap, but if they spotted human feces along the trail, a stampede would erupt. So we established a rule that latrine sites had to be well off the trail. But that did little to deter the dogs. "We'll be going smoothly down the trail," Geoff noted, "when the dogs will suddenly bolt thirty feet off to one side and have a shit riot, with nine dogs all trying to eat one morsel at the same time. Usually a fight breaks out. More often than not, Fuzzy ends up with it. But occasionally," he continued, "it works to my advantage, such as when the dogs spot something 200 yards down the trail and race down to it, pulling the sled with a huge burst of energy, only to find it's a dog turd. It keeps life interesting."

An entry in Geoff's journal a few nights before read, "Time after time we have come up against almost impossible problems, only to have them solved by the right thing happening or the right person coming along. That aspect gives me a lot of confidence." It was true that evening when we happened upon a half-mile stretch of smooth, stable ice—the longest flat pan we'd yet seen on the journey—that looked just right for an airstrip. It would be home for a day and a half while we waited for the airlift.

DAY 25

"WHEN THEIR LINES ARE UNTANGLED AND THE
DOGS SPREAD THEMSELVES OUT INTO A WIDE FAN,
RUNNING INTENTLY WITH THE SLED SLIPPING
QUIETLY ACROSS SOFT SNOW, IT IS ONE OF THE
NICEST SENSATIONS I HAVE EVER EXPERIENCED."

We indulged a bit and slept in the next morning. Though it was
−40 degrees outside, the sunshine of a clear, calm day streamed
through the yellow walls of our tents, warming them, like little
greenhouses, to nearly zero. What a pleasure it was to awake to
such comfort. With fuel restrictions tightening, we were allowing
ourselves very little heat from the stoves. When I pulled my
journal out of its plastic case, it became enveloped in fog as its
frigid surface came in contact with the damp, torpid air in the
tent. Thick vapor rolled off the pages as I wrote, looking like
something out of "The Addams Family." I noted that morning,
"I can tell how warm it is outside by how fast the ceiling frost
melts. In the early days of the trip, the heat from the stoves had
no impact on the ceiling frost. Now, with temperatures moderating slightly outside, it begins to rain as soon as the stoves are on."
   During a noon radio check, Paul learned that the airlift would
be in around midday the next day, weather permitting. He sent
a birthday message home to his father, an April Fools' Day baby,
and reported that his sun shot that morning placed us at 84°36′
north latitude, about 100 miles out. Brent and Geoff set out on
a backhaul while Paul and Mantell lopped several feet off their
sled runners and relashed the upstanders. Soon the splintered
runners were sending plumes of smoke out stovepipes projecting
from the tent walls. Inside Tent 2, Paul and McKerrow painstak-

172

ingly spliced together the movie camera's microphone wires,
which had shattered like dry spaghetti in the cold. After warming the battery pack in the teapot on the woodstove, McKerrow
headed outside and had a field day, filming everything in sight
to make up for lost time.

In my tent, Mantell warmed his injured feet and pondered his
future. The tips of four toes on his right foot were blackened with
frostbite, and a huge blister was wrapped entirely around his left
heal. With Ann's help, he drained nearly half an ounce of fluid
from it and fashioned gauze dressings to protect the damage.
Though that tender tissue would be abraded and pounded each
day as he walked on it, we were all hoping upon hope that
somehow it might heal.

Late that afternoon, Brent and Geoff returned from the backhauls. Geoff was glowing, having just enjoyed one of his first
pleasant experiences with his misfit team. They pulled well, and
since there was no rush, Geoff was able to ride along and take
in the scenery. "The dogs seemed to enjoy themselves," he noted.
"When their lines are untangled and the dogs spread themselves
out into a wide fan, running intently with the sled slipping
quietly across soft snow, it is one of the nicest sensations I have
ever experienced." Brent, on the other hand, was in a dour
mood, irritated that he and Geoff had spent half the day on the
trail while the rest of us puttered about camp. That morning we
had agreed that, come hell or high water, we would push ahead
in one load after the pickup flight. To hedge our bets on that
plan, I offered to take a light load forward and give us a head
start. But in lieu of that, Richard went out on skis after Brent
left and scouted the next five miles of trail, bringing back a report
of improving ice conditions. Brimming with frustration as he
pulled into camp, Brent shouted over to me, "Did you take a
load forward?" I shook my head. "Predictable," he mumbled,
and stormed off to shorten his sled.

His anger was understandable. He had so often been stuck
with the backhauls that he was suffering another bout of "rear-
end mentality." That would soon change, because we were determined that there would be no more backhauls. By shortening our
sleds and consuming another 300 pounds of food and fuel during
this layover, we would be in good shape to push ahead in one
load. And tomorrow we would be sending out on the airlift a few
hundred pounds of gear that was no longer needed, including
McKerrow's clothing kit and sleeping bag. A pile of extraneous
items destined for Resolute—spare battery packs, a tripod, our

sun compass, a spare tent, extra ice tools, and other items we deemed inessential—was growing alongside the tents as we sifted through the sleds.

We enjoyed our third trail party in the tents that night. The silence of the polar sea was broken by the sound of popping corn and occasional raucous laughter. Paul and company prepared a humorous and slightly irreverent set of tapes to send out with the media crew. But as the night wore on, activities in their tent became increasingly subdued. Brent crawled into his bag, but the other three sat up, slouched against each other, feeding the stove and keeping a quiet, pensive vigil throughout McKerrow's last night on the trail. At 7:00 A.M. Paul checked in with Resolute by radio. The weather was good and the plane's ETA was set for 1:00 P.M. The radio operator for the Ran Fiennes crew, the British exploring team based at Ward Hunt Island, intercepted the message and mentioned to Paul that they were finding open water along the coast. Spring was advancing northward.

DAY 26

"THAT WAS THE MOST DANGEROUS LANDING I'VE EVER MADE IN MY TWENTY YEARS OF EXPERIENCE."

The polar sea witnessed its first rummage sale that day, as McKerrow spread out his personal gear on the snow and invited team members to file by and take what they needed. With our deep concern over weight, little was taken—a pair of wristlets and wool socks and some down booties. Paul crawled into his sled bag for some privacy while he taped a long love message for Susan and Bria that would go home on the plane.

As we waited, the woodstoves continued to blaze in our tents; smoke from the burning sled runners drifted lazily up into the deep blue polar sky while mitts and socks dried on strings stretched inside the tents. Milling about piles of gear, team members busied themselves sorting and inventorying supplies, as well as shortening the sleds and chopping the lopped-off sections of runners into bits for the woodstove. Our forty-nine sled dogs dozed peacefully in the calm, clear weather. Seven of them, the injured and spent, including Zap, would be heading home with

McKerrow. Sam was not among them. He'd been improving steadily, and we decided to hang on to him until at least the second dog pickup and see how it went. I just had this feeling that he was meant to go to the Pole, and couldn't bear to part with him. In the tents, sleeping bags dripped overhead while the stove tenders stitched worn mukluks. The pleasure of this reprieve from the exhaustion of the trail took the edge off our regret over McKerrow's departure.

Paul's noontime sun shot placed us at 84°36', a little short of our goal, but no serious problem. Though we had progressed only about 100 miles northward, we had clocked nearly three times that distance on our sleds, with the detours and relays factored in. We had traveled the equivalent of more than three degrees of latitude—fairly respectable mileage, considering the conditions.

It appeared we were entering a new ice zone, one with smoother surface conditions. Now that the relays were behind us, we felt we should start to pick up steam. Our total payload was now less than 2,500 pounds, nearly one-third of what we had started with. Two more sleds, Paul's and Brent's, were shortened by four feet. We all realized that leads, bad weather, and rough ice might await us, but at least we could now make steady mileage when conditions were tolerable. Tucked away in our sleds were five pairs of skis and poles. The extreme cold and rough ice of the first twenty-five days had continued to render them entirely useless.

At noon in Tent 2, static crackled over the radio and we heard the familiar sound of Paul's voice booming into the radio, "Bradley 69, Bradley 69. Steger Expedition here. Do you copy? Over." We all paused in our tasks, listening intently for a response from the aircraft that was headed our way. The pilot, Karl Zberg, soon responded, yelling into his microphone so that we could hear his response over the drone of his engines. They were ahead of schedule, he said, and would be arriving in a little over an hour. And, he added, since the weather looked a little fickle, their visit to our camp would have to be brief, no more than an hour.

His announcement threw us into frantic action. No more leisurely rest day. The media crew that was about to arrive had forwarded instructions that they wanted to film us breaking camp and taking off during the short time they would have on the ground—as they had at Drep Camp. We frantically wolfed down our breakfast and scrambled to finish organizing our gear and sleds. The intrusion of the outside world brought on the same stomach knots and headspins that Paul and I had experienced during our whirlwind promotional trips to the East Coast. The intense physical and mental stress we had undergone on the trail seemed healthy compared to the frenzied rush we dealt with each time we encountered the business world.

Soon we heard the drone of an airplane toward the southeast. The dogs perked up their ears at the new sound, and broke into a howl. Then it became silent again. Would they be able find us here, I wondered. Though Paul had given them our coordinates to within a couple of miles, we were mere specks amid 5 million square miles of drifting sea ice. The Twin Otter's fuel capacity allowed little time for searching. If they failed to find us and had to return for more fuel, our debt load would take another quantum leap. McKerrow set our garbage pile ablaze and heaped on gunnysacks and bits of runner plastic cut from our sleds so that it would smolder and send thick black smoke billowing skyward as a marker.

Relief swept through the crew as we heard the plane banking toward us from the northeast. Our twenty-five days of isolation were about to be broken. During our meetings in Eureka, some members had expressed concern about the intrusion these pickup flights represented, and had suggested that morale might be damaged when well-rested, well-fed people suddenly wandered among a crew undergoing enforced deprivation. One arrangement we had considered was to stake the outbound dogs some distance from camp, so that we wouldn't have to be in direct contact with the plane and its crew. Those concerns were now forgotten. We harbored no hangups about being psychologically disarmed by the presence of visitors. In fact, we were all looking forward to having some company, and spruced up our humble homes to show them off to our guests.

The plane swooped over us time and again as Karl surveyed the half-mile landing strip we had marked with gunnysacks alongside the camp. Though its surface was serrated with riffles of hard-packed drifted snow one or two feet high, it was the smoothest stretch of ocean surface we'd yet seen, and we were proud of our makeshift runway. Karl seemed less certain. The Twin Otter's powerful engines shook the ice as he made several practice runs, swooping down and nearly touching the strip. We saw nervous faces looking out the windows of the fuselage as the plane swept past us. We held our breath and the dogs hunkered down low as Karl positioned himself for his final approach. Karl cut the engines and the plane dropped delicately toward the ice.

Bam! Its skis hit the first ridge and sent the plane bounding upward. Another muffled shock was heard as it bounced again. Like a toy, the plane rocked violently back and forth as it skidded along, careening off the tops of ridges, its wingtips nearly touching the ice with each dip and its skis kicking up clouds of snow. McKerrow kept his camera rolling while our hearts skipped a beat. That plane, which moments before had symbolized security in our minds, was now representing impending disaster. We had friends on board. How would we possibly deal with a plane crash a hundred miles out to sea?

A few dozen feet short of the end of our makeshift strip, Karl miraculously got the plane under control and brought it to a halt. As the crew tumbled out, we took a deep breath, feeling immensely thankful for Karl's skills and experience as an Arctic bush pilot. His job was far more dangerous than ours. Despite the hazards we faced on the polar sea, Karl dealt with a heavier daily dose of life-and-death risks. If he had an engine problem while flying over the chaotic pack ice, there was little chance that he could safely land and be rescued.

"That was the most dangerous landing I've ever made in my twenty years of experience," Karl gasped, shaking his head and catching his breath as Paul and I walked up to greet the crew. Feeling responsible, we apologized profusely for our choice of an airstrip, and explained that by our standards it looked as flat as a paved road. The media crew was visibly shaken as well, but swarmed about us with notepads and cameras, like excited children. Shock registered on their faces as they peered into our sooty, swollen, haggard, scabbed, and oozing visages. With their rosy, clean-shaven faces, they looked like cherubs by comparison. How bad has it been? they asked, looking pityingly at us as though we were prisoners of war. Paul and I countered their concerns with an optimistic report, downplaying the grim details so that the folks back home wouldn't have cause for concern. Soon they began wandering around our campsite, filming everything in sight and cornering team members one by one, hoping, no doubt, to get the real scoop. But it was all done in a friendly atmosphere. These journalists, Sharon, Jason, Don, and Mike, had been covering our project for so long that it almost seemed they were part of our support crew. Indeed, that day they were. While gathering information for their stories, they offered hugs and words of encouragement. We were thankful for their visit, knowing that within a day they would have reports of our well-being in the hands of friends and loved ones. In fact, I viewed the interviews as a means of communicating with my family. But countless other well-wishers would be touched by this coverage as well. The information and pictures the reporters gathered during their one-hour visit would transform our isolated polar world into one shared by millions of followers. People all over North America were about to live this day vicariously. The images they saw in the newspaper and on television would stimulate a host of feelings—curiosity, compassion, intrigue, ambition, and even disgust. I marveled at the power that this visit represented, realizing that it set our polar expedition apart from all previous ones in terms of its impact on people.

Meanwhile, McKerrow, awaiting his turn to be interviewed, braced himself against the emotional upheaval that it might cause. He'd hold strong, he thought, make a few brief comments, and head for the plane. But as Jason approached him the tears rolled down his cheek, freezing in a row like glistening pearls along his chin. Jason captured on film the emotional anguish of a man about to say goodbye to friends and a project that had consumed him for more than a year. We gathered for a final team photograph, and stepped up one by one to hug McKerrow. Ann clung to him in a long embrace. In her loneliness as the odd one out on this team, she had found refuge in McKerrow's warmth and sensitivity. We would all miss his gentle soul, his entertaining banter, and the source of philosophical strength that he had come to represent for all of us. Though the polar sea had bested him physically, his spirit still came out on top. The only team member with whom he hadn't forged a strong bond was Richard. They approached each other tentatively, then wrapped arms in an awkward hug. "I somehow got the feeling that McKerrow doesn't really care for me," Richard commented in his journal that evening. "Perhaps it's because our philosophies of life are so far apart." Richard, the analyzer, and McKerrow, the socializer, had found their personalities clashing from time to time. McKerrow, too, felt uncomfortable and regretted later that they had not been able to overcome that edge of estrangement.

The seven dogs earmarked for departure were put on short leashes and walked to the plane. Like wounded soldiers marching off the field of battle, McKerrow and Zap hobbled along together and climbed aboard. Off in the distance, Karl and his copilot scouted out a better landing strip for the takeoff, and lopped off the tops of snowdrifts with shovels. With misty eyes, we harnessed up our teams and prepared to depart so that the plane could circle overhead for aerial shots of our convoy.

McKerrow's departure left us with more determination than ever to reach the Pole.

The drone of the Twin Otter's engine once again filled the air as it prepared to take off. Though we couldn't see the plane—a huge ridge system blocked it from our view—we shared the anxiety of those on board as Karl taxied back and forth across a small pan, checking for bumps and dips in the drifts of snow that might thwart his takeoff. Their nerves were still rattled from the rough landing. Now, I'm sure, they were all sharing a prayer as Karl prepared to attempt a takeoff on a very short, undulating strip. As the engines roared in a crescendo, we paused in our tasks and looked back, gripped with anxiety. We lingered, waiting to catch sight of the plane clearing the ridges that surrounded the makeshift runway. Finally it shot up, scrambling for altitude. "Thank God!" I muttered, sighing with relief. "They're airborne!" The needle on the tachometer, McKerrow told us later, was dancing wildly in the red danger zone when the plane finally lifted off the ground.

With one of our team members and seven of our dogs among the passengers, I felt that part of my heart was heading south with that plane. I felt a wrenching sense of separation as I watched the tiny white aircraft climb into the deep blue polar sky. The huge void in our hearts left by McKerrow's absence would never be filled. The outbound dogs, all of whom had found a place in our hearts, would also be missed. I was particularly disappointed that Zap, our lovable team mascot, would not be sharing the rest of the journey with us.

As we levered our sleds forward, the plane circled overhead. Our rendezvous with the media was not quite over yet. Before departing, Don, the cameraman, had instructed us to head out in tight formation, keeping all five sleds close together. Karl, in turn, had agreed to make several passes directly overhead so that Don could get aerial shots of our caravan, an important clip for KSTP's documentary film. Even in the best conditions, sledding together in a train was no mean task. Each team pulled at its own pace. And while some sleds were struggling across ridges, others were sprinting across pans. On most days of our trip, the front and back sleds were separated by hundreds of yards. Our "choreography" on this day proved to be no better than it had been on the others. Try as we might, the sleds were soon separated by wide gaps. Meanwhile, the plane would bank and then swoop down over us time and again with its wings nearly clipping the tops of the ridges. I felt as if I had just stepped onto a World War

II movie set; our entourage was a German military train being strafed by Allied fighter pilots. A deafening concussion rocked my dogs, sending them darting for cover, as the plane swept down upon us. My lead dog Chester hit the ground and curled up in a tight ball while the others scrambled, creating a tight knot of tangled lines. It may have made for some interesting film footage, but it wasn't the shot Don was looking for. As I untangled my dogs, the plane circled around to the north, preparing for a second pass. I delayed, waiting for the other sleds to catch up.

During our months of training, we had become so accustomed to visits by the media that accommodating their needs seemed entirely natural to us, almost like an instinct. Given the extreme conditions and the brevity of their visits, it wasn't reasonable to expect that they could get the material they needed with strictly candid shots. In fact, at their request we had set up photo sessions for them in Frobisher and Drep, little maneuvers on the ice that were tailored to offer the movie cameramen and still photographers the proper lighting angles and action. And even here now, a hundred miles out on the polar sea, frostbitten and fatigued, we were striving to accommodate their needs on cue. But we weren't just being nice guys. We knew that good film clips and photos would make for better documentation of this journey.

As the plane banked for a second pass, I signaled to Brent, who was waiting with his team in front of me, to head out. I delayed a moment before giving Chester the command to follow, so that my team wouldn't bunch up with his. Paul's sled was coming up from behind, but it appeared that the other two were still stuck on a pressure ridge. This time the plane swept so low I thought it was about to land. I braced myself in anticipation of the roar, but my dogs, who now realized the sound held no threat, pranced along as if performing in a Walt Disney movie. But again Don's mission was not accomplished, because the two back teams were still out of camera range.

For the plane's third pass, we managed to have three of our sleds, Brent's, Paul's, and mine, in perfect Hollywood formation. But the other two lagged behind. Oh, well, nothing's perfect, I thought. As the cameras rolled, I thought about my family at home, who would be watching this footage on television within a day or two. My little nieces and nephews would be pointing excitedly at the screen, shouting, "Look! There's Uncle Willie! And look, there's Chester! And Tim's there, too!" Thinking about that link to loved ones that the plane represented, I felt a sudden longing for the love and warmth of the outside world.

The plane made a rapid ascent as it passed over Mantell's and Geoff's sleds, and banked toward the south. "That's it!" Paul shouted. "We're alone again." The back sleds soon caught up, and we traveled on in a string of five. As I listened to the plane trailing off toward home, my mind fixed on the mental anguish McKerrow must have been suffering, the pain of the separation from the team, the hollowness of having to return to the base, and the heartbreak of defeat. I was overcome with pity. I envisioned him sitting on the plane next to Zap, sipping tea and chatting politely with a reporter to mask the pain inside. In a few minutes the drone of the plane faded into silence, and McKerrow's presence became a memory. We were now seven people and forty-two dogs struggling to reach the top, our determination fortified by McKerrow's absence. The visit moments before suddenly seemed surrealistic. As Geoff noted that evening, "The plane coming in seems like a strange dream. Very unreal. We have had such an isolated community for so long that it was hard to accept this interruption from the outside."

DAY 27

"THE TEAMS AHEAD LOOKED AS THOUGH THEY WERE WALKING THROUGH WALLS OF FIRE."

The ice conditions we encountered the next day, April 3, were markedly better than anything we had seen before. "Prairie" pans stretched for nearly a mile in width, and the ridges between them were worn down and smoothed over by drifts and erosion. Richard scouted miles ahead on skis. Brent broke trail with his team while I followed close behind. The other three sleds formed the rear guard, with Ann helping out wherever she was needed, which generally was in back, with Geoff. We readjusted loads time and again, trying to balance out the paces of the five teams. Paul's sled had the heaviest load, so I gave him Mongo, my Eskimo powerhouse, to add to his team. As a result, I had only eight dogs, including Sam, who was pulling well again, but was a bit stiff.

My dogs, like me, were drawing energy from the lengthening hours of daylight. And now, with Brent's team in the lead, they were especially excited and pulled with vigor. Chester found it impossible to relax whenever there were dogs in front of him. Whenever I stopped my sled, he would cry and beg with his barks for me to let the team carry on. That little dog continually amazed me. He was a pure, gentle spirit. Chester could outpull any other dog, regardless of size. His energy was virtually without end. Time and again I found myself inspired by his example. All my dogs continued to do well, and their spirits remained high. When they had mercilessly attacked Sam weeks before, I had considered sending the whole bunch out on the first flight. I was now certain they had shaped up.

I am extremely demanding of my dogs. My anger flares when they are not putting out a hundred percent, and I punish them sternly when they fight among themselves. But between us flows mutual respect. Love and affection were the essential ingredients in training them to be loyal, hardworking sled dogs. But it starts with a good puppyhood. As pups, most of my dogs enjoyed the playful company of children. The more carefree they are as pups, the more stable and persevering they will be as adults. Physical training for my dogs begins at seven months. Their first runs with the team are brief. As soon as they show any signs of tiring, they are taken out of harness and encouraged to run alongside or behind the sled. Gradually, more and more expectations are placed on the young dogs. Sled dogs instinctively crave to pull. If they are left tied on a chain when young, the pent-up energy can make them neurotic. Training releases puppies' excess energy and makes for stable adult dogs. In fact, the worst punishment that can be meted out to disobedient dogs is to leave them behind for the day when the others are being harnessed up for a run.

The training focus for the first year is on stabilizing the young dogs. Through constant attention and affection from people, they grow confident of human care. On training runs, they learn that they have a functional role in their canine family; association with the team at an early age gives the dogs a sense of social purpose. Closely related to wolves, they have the instincts of a pack animal and depend on being part of a group structure. After their first winter season, the dogs are conditioned to know that their lives center on pulling sleds. Intensive training during their first winter season as adults also establishes a solid muscle structure that is maintained throughout their lives. Dogs, like people, require a steady training regimen to keep them in top physical condition. As the winter progresses, I steadily lengthen the workday. In March, when the days are long, they are often on the trail up to twelve hours, freighting heavy loads of supplies on the three-mile track from the end of the nearest road to my cabin.

Whenever possible, I have my second-year dogs do an "apprenticeship" expedition of a few thousand miles. My rule of thumb is that only dogs with 10,000 miles of trail experience are candidates for major expeditions such as the North Pole journey. There is no training substitute for expedition experience. Through those thousands of miles, the dogs develop a trail sense. That includes losing their fear of traveling on thin ice, learning to sleep warm during blizzards, and learning how to maintain their paws. A "trail moxie" develops in each dog as it learns the tricks of the trade for staying warm and dry, conserving energy, and keeping its lines untangled. Another key feature of this apprenticeship is the relationship that builds between my dogs and me. When I am traveling solo with them, our survival is closely intertwined. They understand that. The interdependency develops a lasting relationship, one that is based on trust, respect, and affection.

The value of that relationship was clearly evident now as we neared the end of our first month on the trail. During the past twenty-five days, we'd accomplished one and a half degrees of latitude, 100 miles of forward progress. More significantly, we had crossed a huge barrier: we had survived our immersion into ungodly cold temperatures, torturous pack ice, darkness, blizzards, and ruthless winds. The initial challenges of the polar sea had turned back most polar expeditions, including all attempts since Peary's to reach the Pole without resupply. We had come to terms with them, and the worst were, we hoped, behind us.

Our key challenge, the cold, had taken a heavy toll on everyone. Yet I found that my long-suffering team members rarely used such words as "brutal" or "grueling" to describe the past three weeks. They accepted the hardships without complaint. However, the blistered and blackened flesh on their faces, fingers, and toes clearly told of what they had endured. This group's uncomplaining, positive demeanor was probably its greatest strength. And our greatest success was that we had maintained strong group unity. After persevering for weeks, our group of people and dogs now stood on the threshold of spring in harmony. This unity had enabled us to overcome the worst physical barriers nature could place in our path. By pouring everything we had into this effort, we had not only survived, but had made steady progress. Equally important, the dogs gave 100 percent every day. They, however, gave out of their loyalty to us, not out of any sense of striving toward a goal. Theirs was an example of pure selflessness.

During our last thirty miles, the lay of the "land" had definitely improved. We still had to fight our way over ridges, but the pans were getting larger and less obstructed with deep snow. Things were finally starting to go as planned. I had anticipated an upswing after the first 100 miles or so; those better days, it seemed, were now upon us. How refreshing it was to feel optimistic again! Maybe the expedition would now carry on according to the script.

That day we traveled well into the nighttime hours, using the sun to chart our course northward. Navigating by the sun proved to be very simple on the polar sea. Since the sun was now up around the clock, it served as a twenty-four-hour direction indicator. At local noon, the sun was due south. At midnight it was directly over the North Pole. At 6:00 A.M. and 6:00 P.M. it was due east and west, respectively. And it moved fifteen degrees for each hour in between. That meant that while traveling along at 11:00 P.M. that evening, we merely had to plot a course fifteen degrees to the right of the sun. The trick of plotting a course according to the sun lies in determining local noontime, which varies with each degree of longitude. Only Paul's sextant readings could tell us how closely we were following the seventy-fifth meridian, the one along which we had embarked on leaving Drep Camp. It marks the boundary of Eastern Standard Time, according to which our watches had been set. So far, Paul's reading indicated that despite the ice drift and detours, we were still close enough to the seventy-fifth that no adjustments were needed.

The temperature dropped to −50 degrees that evening as we traveled northward into the sun. Thick clouds of steam enveloped each team of dogs. Geoff and Mantell had fallen far to the back, and though we couldn't discern their dogs or sleds, we could trace their progress by a big ball of fog that hung directly over them. In the frigid air, you could hear them conversing a half-mile away as distinctly as if they were right next to us—an amazing phenomenon. Occasionally the commands from the drivers to their dogs could be heard clearly for distances of two miles or more. One time when I was leading I heard the dogs panting behind me and stepped aside to let that team pass. When nothing happened, I turned around and found that they were nearly a half-mile back. The squeaks and groans of your own sled runners would drown out all distant sounds. But upon stopping, you could hear the activities of all the dogs and drivers.

As midnight approached and the sun's pastel tones intensified, the clouds in which we were enveloped blazed orange. In the rear, Geoff and Mantell were treated to an amazing scene, watching the four teams silhouetted against the oval tangerine disk of the low-lying sun. Geoff found it to be "fantastically beautiful and eerie, the perfect scene for a sci-fi movie. The teams ahead looked as if they were walking through walls of fire." Many people had suggested we'd find the scenery on the way to the Pole monotonous and boring. The otherworldly panoramas we were encountering were proving them wrong time and again. Indeed, we often felt ourselves to be aliens on our own planet. Tonight's spectacle enraptured all of us. It reminded me of the overwhelming sense of awe I had felt when, as a boy of eight, I witnessed my first eclipse of the sun.

That evening I noted in my journal: "Now that we are nearing 85 degrees, there are times of open spaces, carefree walking, and even time to look at the sun and the immediate surroundings. There's time now between sessions of toil to enjoy the beauty and, yes, there's even time for an occasional quick daydream. But these are abruptly interrupted by the reality of another pressure zone. How far will it be through this one, I wonder? Will it be a short haul or a hellish struggle that will stop us cold and rob us of our goal?

"I continue to grind north, but the sled is stuck again. Pry, push, grunt, curse, and then it is loose. The dogs pull for another couple of minutes, until another ridge stops them. Encouragement is mixed with disappointment, with encouragement usually winning out. Each day now is a little easier than . . . in the past. A string of five teams is stretched out across the ice for a mile. Some sleds are stuck and some are moving smoothly. The air is filled with the sound of commands and curses, the metallic groan of steel pry bars being levered against Styrofoam snow, and the grating squeak of sled runners inching along. Some dogs are barking. One that is being reprimanded by its driver for not pulling is crying. The trademark of each driver is the commands they use: Paul, 'Hup, hup, hup, G'dogs. let's go!'; Mantell, 'Gee-up there, critter, gee-up. Okay, ready-e-e-e, go ahead!' "

DAY 28

"OUR DOGS ARE STILL GRINDING DOWN FASTER
THAN THE SLEDS ARE LIGHTENING UP."

I crawled into Paul's tent with our chart of the Arctic Ocean and
laid it out across Ann's sleeping bag. Paul's crew gathered
around, glowing with excitement, as if a map of some hidden
treasure were being unveiled before us. With my weathered and
blackened index finger, I traced our progress from Drep Camp
to 85 degrees. It spanned two inches on the chart. We had five
more inches yet to go to reach the spot where all the radiating
lines on that empty blue chart—like the target in a game of
darts—converged on one point, the world's bull's-eye. The chart
suggested we'd covered less than a third of the distance. "And
that," I pointed out to the group huddled around me, "is how
the folks back home are viewing our progress." On a recent radio
check, Paul had heard that skepticism was mounting among our
followers. Even the media, we learned, were intimating that our
dream might indeed be impossible. But, Paul and I underscored,
that was no reason for discouragement. It was true, as the press
was now reporting, that we had used up about half of our supplies. But what the skeptics didn't understand was that those two
inches represented some of the coldest and most rugged terrain
on the planet. Nor did they understand that, given the relays, we
had virtually traversed those two inches three times. We had
actually covered six inches; in that respect we were over halfway
there, in terms of total mileage. We had crossed the 100-mile
barrier of overwhelming conditions. The temperature and the
terrain were now moderating. And, most important, we were
traveling much lighter. Barring some unforeseen obstacle, there

186

would be no more relays. From here on in, every move we made would be northward.

"If these conditions hold up, we should soon be averaging twenty miles a day," Brent added optimistically. Paul did some quick calculations in his journal and pointed out that we would have to average at least that to reach the Pole before running out of food.

"That might mean some severe rationing," I added. "Are you prepared to make that sacrifice?"

They nodded unanimously. Brent, who was still harboring some resentment over inequities in fuel consumption between the two tents early on, said, "Look, trimming back on rations is no problem, but our fuel supply is what's going to make or break this trip. No fuel, no water."

Paul and I agreed, saying it was imperative that we continue to be spartan in our use of the stoves. But, I added, the factor that would tip the balance between success or failure was not fuel but the spirit of the dogs. We were treading a fine line with them; they were growing weary, their food was being rationed, and our loads were still a bit heavy.

"In other words," Paul said, "our dogs are still grinding down faster than the sleds are lightening up. We've just got to turn the corner on that problem real soon."

Statistically, we could expect consistently better ice conditions north of 86 degrees. That was where we'd enter the section of ice influenced by the Transpolar Drift Stream, the wide band of current that sweeps across the top of the world from the Bering Strait to the Greenland Sea. Thus far, we'd been traveling over huge backwater eddies of that massive slow stream, on ice influenced by largely random and erratic forces. Within the steady Transpolar Drift, the ice is subject to less buckling and heaving. Most polar expeditions have reported finding increasingly fewer ridges as they got farther north. But satellite studies suggest that in certain years that may not be the case. Like the jet streams of the upper atmosphere, the Transpolar Stream apparently alters course a bit, resulting in massive ridges all the way to the top. Thus we still faced an element of chance. Would 1986 be a good year or a bad year for sea ice as we neared the Pole, we wondered.

That morning we clipped along at a steady pace, a string of five sleds within a few hundred yards of each other. We encountered our biggest pans yet, some over a mile across, with only small ridges separating them from their neighbors. "Farm country," we called it, neat little pastures separated by tidy hedge-rows. We cruised along pleasantly, but then, in the early after-noon, the polar sea, as unpredictable and inconsistent as ever, had a surprise in store for us. We were abruptly stopped by a twenty-foot wall of ice, beyond which loomed row after row of ice ramparts. Richard and Paul climbed among the piled blocks, looking for a gap that might be made passable with some chop-ping. "It looks real bad," Richard shouted back to us. "We may be in for our first portage," he added, hinting that we might have to unload the sleds and carry the supplies across like polar Sherpas. I followed him as he moved along the wall toward the west. Suddenly he disappeared among the blocks. Following his tracks, I found he had entered a perfect ice canyon that led right through the ramparts to smoother ice a hundred yards beyond. "This is my definition of luck," I yelled to the rest of the team as I waved for them to join us.

A few minutes later, Paul caught up with us as we sledded through the gap and reported that among the blocks he had seen fresh arctic fox tracks, our first sign of wildlife on the polar sea. The news excited us. It was nice to know we were sharing this desolate place with other living beings. But did that also mean there were bears in the vicinity, we wondered. Scavenging left-over food, foxes will often follow bears as they hunt seals that come to breathe in the cracks in the ice. As a precaution, we pulled our rifles out and placed them on top of our loads. But for Brent, who was keen on hunting, the prospect of running into bears registered as a chance for securing fresh meat. I wondered how we would reconcile taking game with our goal of no resup-ply. Fortunately, we never had to deal with that issue, since the fox tracks were to be the one and only sign of animal life we saw on the journey.

Ironically, that same day, we had another encounter with living beings—a small plane passed overhead, flying fairly low. We recognized it as the tourist plane Jim had told us to watch for on a recent radio check. The charter flight was carrying a group of tourists on a day trip to the Pole, where they would enjoy a quick toast of champagne and then hurry back to Reso-lute. We waved to them, wondering what their thoughts might be as they peered down at us, little specks of red in a vast sea of white.

As the day wore on, our dogs began to grind down. Their tongues were nearly dragging on the snow. We slogged our way along for ten hours, making fifteen miles—our best mileage to date—but they were fading. The future looked grim. The dogs on half-rations, the twenty-one that were destined to go out on the next flight, were barely moving at all. I wondered how we were going to get another week's worth of power out of them. Brent and Geoff, whose teams were hit hardest by the burnout, dropped far to the rear. Our plan for a twelve-hour day was aborted. While the others set camp, I went back to give Geoff and Brent a hand. Muscling his sled forward while his dogs staggered along, barely able to stand, Brent was thoroughly discouraged and nearly in tears. My heart went out to him. It's devastating to have your dogs burn out on you when you still have hundreds of miles to go. As we slaved along, very little was said. We were lost in thought, pondering the fact that though we finally had good weather and ice conditions, we couldn't make the miles. It was like finally reaching the freeway entrance ramp after driving for miles over rutted dirt roads, only to have your engine die. This inauspicious introduction to 85 degrees north was fitting for a degree of latitude that was to test us physically, emotionally, and spiritually.

We knew we had no choice but to take the next day off. What a shame not to be able to travel with this calm, clear, −40 weather! With spring heading northward, each day was extremely valuable. The intense cold that we had relied on to keep our traveling surface intact was now steadily diminishing. Very soon, perhaps after the next storm, the warm south winds of spring would set the ice in motion. Running out of time now became as great a concern to us as running out of food or fuel. We could soon expect to encounter splintered ice and open leads.

THE BIZARRE ENCOUNTER

DAY 29

"THIS HAS TO BE THE MOST DESOLATE PLACE ON
EARTH, NO SOUND, NO SMELL, NOTHING LIVING, NO
MOVEMENT."

We woke up feeling rested and raring to go, but impatiently
waited out a pristinely calm, clear day while our dogs recharged,
snoozing in the sun whose heat we were finally beginning to feel.
I noted in my journal that this marked the longest I had ever
been out without resupply; my journey with Mantell across the
Barrens had been twenty-eight days. It was tempting to try to
push on. After all, tomorrow might bring a blizzard. But I knew
better than to push our luck with the dogs. I had been in a similar
situation during a solo expedition on the Mackenzie River. My
dogs were burning out and, completely out of food, I had fifty
miles to go in −60 weather to reach the nearest village. I considered pushing on, but I thought of the advice the Indians had
given me of the regenerative powers of sleep: If you are caught
on the trail without food, stop and sleep before you try carrying
on. I made a fire, relaxed, and slept for twenty-four hours
straight. The next day the dogs and I felt fresh, and continued
on empty stomachs with little difficulty all the way to the village.
  I hoped this rest day would refresh the dogs as well as that one
had. I spent time with each one that morning, patting them and
telling them what a great job they had been doing. Affection, I
knew, was as important as a day of rest for regenerating their
spirits. Even though it was a −40-degree day, most of them felt
toasty warm, especially the darker-coated ones. Chester's thick
black coat, a highly effective trap for the sun's heat, almost felt
hot. I spent a long time talking to Sam, the one dog on the line

who stood up to greet me as I approached. He had healed so well in the last couple of weeks that I had placed a wager with Ann that he was going to make it to the Pole. His indomitable spirit had brought him back to health and would carry him through. "Keep it up, Sam, I know you're going to make it now," I told him, and from his steady gaze I sensed that he understood what I was saying to him. What great companions these dogs are, I thought, just like members of my family.

We spent most of the day sleeping. For some, it was a long, cold, restless nap. "I don't like rest days," Richard noted tersely in his journal. "It's too hard to stay warm." Just before supper the dog drivers met in my tent to make a final determination regarding which twenty-one dogs would be going to the Pole. We agreed to take a second rest stop in three days as a hedge against another bout of burnout. Afterwards, a few of us stepped out for a walk. I ventured out well beyond camp, and it was the first time I was able to concentrate on the stark and beautiful desolation of this place. I was also struck by the silence. As I focused on it, I began hearing a strange, dull, rhythmic pounding. Was the ice being squeezed, I wondered. There was no sign of movement. And I couldn't imagine the dogs or team members making a noise like that. Then it dawned on me—I was hearing my own heartbeat.

Geoff had a similar sensation on his walk and recorded in his journal that night, "When I got away from camp, I was struck by the absolute silence. This has to be the most desolate place on earth, no sound, no smell, nothing living, no movement. As far from everything as a person can possibly be. All that exists here are the sharp edges of the ice and the gentle curves of the drifts. This is the only real untouched wilderness I have ever been in."

Meanwhile, in Resolute that day, McKerrow was preparing to head home. His ribs were well on their way to recovery. Since he was airlifted out, he'd been barraged with phone interviews from journalists all over the world. Rumors had spread that our chances for success were growing slim, and the question all of them pressed on McKerrow was, "Do you *really* think they'll make it?" As he noted in his journal, he was now faced with a challenge almost as big as the one he had dealt with on the ice, as he attempted to convince them that we would make it, that their gloomy prognoses were unfounded. He found that even some of our staunchest supporters had given up hope, and he gave them each a powerful version of the pep talk he had given us the day before he left.

DAY 30

"SAY, I HEAR YOU'RE THE OTHER CANADIAN ON THIS JOURNEY."

The fine weather continued on Day 30, and we got up early. We were greeted by anxious dogs as we climbed out of the tents. Chester, the barometer of my team's spirit, jumped up and down when he saw me, doing a little twirling dance and twisting his head up into the air. The other dogs were bobbing their tails in agreement with Chester's antics. Optimism filled the air as we loaded our sleds, and when we launched them, the dogs charged forward at a near sprint. Stumbling along behind my sled to keep pace with the dogs, I shouted over to Paul, "What a pleasant problem this is!" He, too, could barely keep up with his team. With well-rested dogs, a musher could easily clip off forty to sixty miles a day in these conditions, I thought to myself. I reflected on Peary's claims. His strategy of expending the energy of four units of men and dogs to break trail ensured that he and his fifth unit were still fairly fresh when they headed out on their own, past 88 degrees. That was just the edge that would be needed to make big miles near the Pole. What I had learned from the journals of the early explorers and satellite photographs of sea ice suggested that that was the case. Now we were experiencing it firsthand.

Upon our request just before leaving Frobisher Bay, a Washington, D.C.–based Arctic Ocean consulting firm gave us their prognosis for ice conditions that winter. An unusually windy fall and early winter, they reported, had set the ice in rapid motion. Though the winds had subsided by January, the forecasters told us that we would encounter an unusually disturbed surface, with numerous leads and ridges. Their analysis suggested that the first seventy miles would be severely buckled in monstrous ridges, and that a zone of high pressure would extend out past 86 degrees. Given this gloomy prognosis, we had been prepared to deploy three or more team members as a full-time "road con-

struction crew" during the first few weeks. However, as bad as
the first one hundred miles of ice were for us, we found ourselves
doing less chopping than expected. The snowdrifts proved to be
a surprisingly taxing obstacle. But the most ponderous burden
that plagued us had nothing to do with the Arctic Ocean: it was
the payload weights on our sleds. As I considered this, I again
reflected on Peary's journey. The payload weights on each of his
nineteen sleds never exceeded 600 pounds—and averaged about
a third the weight of our sleds when we left Drep Camp. Thus
his strategy offered a better chance for achieving 40-mile-plus
days than did ours.

Our plan, like Peary's, called for a final "dash." By sending
dogs and men back on a weekly basis, he steadily whittled his
team down to five companions and twenty-six dogs. Traveling
light and lean, this assault team traveled on alone from 88 degrees, 140 miles short of the Pole. We planned to begin our
"dash" after the next dog pickup, which was tentatively scheduled for April 9, when we expected to be nearing 86 degrees.
From that point on, our plan called for making steady twelve-
hour, twenty-mile-plus days, and reaching the Pole by the end
of April. It was a two-part equation: dogs and time. The twenty-
one dogs destined for the Pole would have to be maintained in
relatively good form. If their reserves were spent now, the dash
would falter. And if we ran short of time, if we failed to stay
ahead of the advancing spring weather, we would run out of ice.
Thus, we calculated, we would have to average fifteen miles a day
now to position ourselves for the dash.

That afternoon the temperature warmed up to a balmy −30
degrees. We had just entered a zone of freshly broken ice when
Brent, who was breaking trail out front, shouted back to us that
he was stopped by an open lead. We all pulled up to the edge of
it and gazed at the lane of bronze-colored water that stretched
across our route. It was a narrow gap—no more than a dozen
feet across—but it was slowly widening. What made the scene
even more sobering was a suspiciously strong wind that was
building from the south. Richard headed east and I went west
to search for a closure where we might cross, but no passage
could be found. Meanwhile, Paul initiated a bridge-building project by rolling huge blocks of ice into the lead and jamming them
against each other. Having given up our reconnaissance efforts,
the rest of us joined in, heaping block upon block until we had
a huge, floating mass of rubble that was wedged tightly in place
between the sides of the lead. Feeling like kids playing in a big

rain puddle, we welcomed this pleasant change of pace from the boring routine of pushing sleds. Our bodies warmed as we pried and rolled immense chunks of ice into the chasm until a substantial mound spanned the gap. Then we carefully aligned Brent's sled in position for crossing. We were excited; this was high adventure. We were also very nervous because a slight miscalculation in alignment could send the sled sliding into the ocean. The dogs, sensing the danger, gingerly stepped from one chunk to another as Brent guided them to the other side and positioned them for pulling the sled across. Then on cue he launched his team while we lunged against the sled to send it sailing over the bridge. Seeing it veer slightly to the left, Geoff heaved into the side to give it a last split-second correction. The backs of its runners dipped down in the water as it shot up and over a bank of gravelly ice on the far side. Then, in quick succession, the other sleds were sent across. We applauded ourselves for this successful lead-crossing strategy, and enjoyed a sense of unity.

This was one of the first challenges we had encountered on the expedition that had demanded perfect coordination as a team. It helped break up a trip that, as Geoff noted, "had been a rare blend of boredom and misery as far as recreational activities go." In his journal, Brent had noted his analysis of how a typical day's time was spent: "20 percent walking beside sled, 15 percent pushing moderately, 10 percent pushing hard, 10 percent snap and pull, 20 percent stopped, 5 percent running, 10 percent helping others' sleds over ridges, and 10 percent chopping ice." The tasks of this journey generally kept us isolated in small groups—as sledding partners, trail choppers, tent crews, or scouting parties. That did little to build a sense of teamwork. It also meant we were alone with our thoughts most of the time. One rarely visited with other team members during the day. In fact, yesterday Richard had happened upon Brent and, slapping him on the shoulder, said jokingly, "Say, I hear you're the other Canadian on this journey."

Thus, challenges like this lead were useful for enhancing camaraderie. By the time we had our sleds organized on the far side of the lead, the wind was gusting wildly, whipping up clouds of snow. Though there were telltale cirrus clouds in the sky to suggest a blizzard, I didn't trust this sudden change in weather. On the polar sea, a south wind always means trouble. The pan just beyond the lead was firm, multi-year ice. We decided to set camp there, since it would offer an island of refuge if the wind broke up the ice around us. Anticipating a storm, we added extra

guy lines to the tent and stockpiled old ice alongside the tent
doors as a water supply. The searing windchills reminded us of
how we'd been blessed with calm weather during the past ten
days. Noting in his journal that evening that this day marked the
end of our first month on the sea ice, Richard said aptly, "Not
one of us would have missed this, but I don't know who would
want to do it again." In the tent next door, Paul was receiving
a garbled radio message from Jim. "Two teeth" were the only
words he could make out. Finally, in a flush of joy it dawned on
him that it was a message Susan had relayed from home, inform-
ing him that his daughter was now sporting her first teeth.

All through the night, the tent fly fluttered rhythmically and
the taut guy lines hummed. These sounds didn't represent the
soothing lullaby they had during our first storm, because we
knew we could not afford another travel delay. Wondering how
long this one might last, I thought about the five-day blow that
had thwarted Ralph Plaisted's first attempt to reach the pole by
snowmobile in 1967. A week-long storm now would finish off our
expedition as well. Like Chinese water torture, the snapping of
the tent fly started to drive me crazy. I packed my ears with
cotton to muffle the noise.

DAY 31

"OH, TO BE IN RED WING AGAIN!"

The wind had not abated when we arose the next morning. "Are
you alive out there?" I yelled to Mantell, who was huddled in
his sled. A few minutes later he shouted, "Coming in!" over the
roar of the wind. This was our cue for Richard to untie the
side-entry tunnel, and for me to move Mantell's dog-food bucket
in position for his chair. "Some wind," he gasped as he dove in
across our sleeping bags, a billowing cloud of steam and snow
following behind him. He reached outside and pulled in his bag.
From the way he winced as he sat down, I could tell the night
had been hard on him. He wasn't about to spend this nasty day
in his sled. Then, wildly shaking his hands to revive circulation,
he gave us the condition report: "Cold as hell, windchill must be

—140, but there's no cloud cover." We were relieved; the sunshine meant this would just be a windstorm. They rarely lasted more than thirty-six hours.

We fixed a hasty breakfast, careful to conserve fuel, then crawled back in our bags. "Sleep marathons" were what Geoff called these storms. To kill time, I focused my thoughts on my favorite holiday—Thanksgiving—the one that for me embodies the essence of human existence: peace, love, friendship, warmth, and plenty of food. I learned later that Paul's mind was fixed on the same holiday that morning. He passed the hours staring at a big piece of pumpkin pie heaped with mounds of whipped cream. The nice thing about holidays is that they are portable— you carry in your heart the warm sense of family bonding they engender. All I needed to do was curl up in my bag and conjure up those feelings, and the polar sea no longer felt so remote.

Later I began mulling over the numbers game again: gallons, pounds, people, dogs, distance, and days. The fuel pinch was tightening. At our present rate of consumption we would just make it to May 1. I calculated that by utilizing every burnable item we had—sled wood, gunnysacks, plastic bags, boxes, and ropes—we might be able to carry on to May 15. If we had to carry on that long, we would face very slim pickings in food as well. How would group morale hold up under those conditions? Except for Mantell and me, none of us had experienced severe rationing before. An extreme challenge like this would either cement us together and bolster our resolve for reaching the Pole or shatter us in splintered groups scrambling for survival.

As I thought about our chances of carrying on into mid-May, the ice beneath our tent rumbled like a freight train. The notion of extending our timetable instantly vanished. The forces that launch the annual ice breakup were being revved. The lead we crossed the day before was to be the first of many. But worrying would do me no good, so I focused my mind on the sounds of the wind and the gentle snoring of my tentmates.

That evening, as we huddled around the cookpot, waiting for tea water to boil, I studied the grizzled faces and hands around me. The ends of all five fingers on Geoff's right hand and three on his left were black and swollen—the result of endlessly having to untangle knotted traces with ungloved hands. His fingertips had split from frequent refreezing, and glistened with a salve he had put on to prevent infection. Mantell's index fingers showed similar damage. Richard's face was windburned but his digits were intact—his fetish for meticulous grooming had paid off. My tentmates told me I was the hands-down winner of the "Ugly Face" contest; Brent's comment of a few days before was that it looked as though I had stuck my face in a sizzling frying pan. The flesh of my cheeks, chin, forehead, nose, and even of the area around my eyes had been flash-frozen during the first weeks of the journey and was now caked with mottled yellow scabs. But I was not concerned; the healing process was well under way. Facial tissue is highly vasculated and responds quickly to such damage. On all of my Arctic journeys I've come back with a new complexion. In fact, one doctor told me that facial frostbite has an impact similar to a facelift, though I don't recommend Arctic journeys as a substitute for cosmetic surgery.

My fingers were frost "burned," a condition in which the skin dries out and cracks but the flesh below remains healthy. This was the result of frequently ungloving my hand to wield my camera. Paul had a similar condition from working with the sextant. My toes, though they had not been frozen, were numb from being constantly chilled. I had experienced this sensation before. It seems they can only take so much cold before the nerves go into hibernation, as if to say, "That's all the pain we're going to report for this winter." After I traveled across Alaska in 1985, it took three weeks of California sun to bring them back to life.

The injury we found most serious was the frostbite damage on Mantell's feet. They were in serious trouble. Three toes on his right foot and four on his left were blackened, swollen, and festering. We looked on with pity as, gritting his teeth and grimacing in pain, he swabbed them with an alcohol pad to curb infection. The huge blister on his right heel, which had recently refrozen again, was marbly white. Mantell's feet were a victim of the inadequate soles on our moosehide mukluks. When his had worn through during the first week, he had switched to sealskin kamiks, a boot system designed for wet conditions rather than extremely cold, dry ones. In the mornings he'd slip on cumbersome sheepskin overbooties for added warmth. One afternoon the cold caught him unawares, slipping through his thin footwear and freezing his feet. Once frostbitten, flesh is much more susceptible to refreezing; the cell walls are weakened. Thus, though Mantell now wrapped his feet with extra care every day, he faced a losing battle. The prescription for health was heat and rest, and this journey offered precious little of either. Furthermore, the damage was aggravated every day as he walked on the injured tissue. He wrestled with excruciating pain.

The pressure in his swollen heel sent stabbing pains up his leg with each step he took. He said it felt as if hot needles were being thrust into his calf muscle. I wondered how much longer he could take it, and I worried about gangrene. It seemed there was little chance his feet would heal on the trail. All we could do was hope.

Thus far, he had been unflinching in his determination to reach the Pole. That night, though, I noticed he was in an exceptionally somber mood. His face reflected deep sadness. I asked him how he was doing. With tears welling in his eyes, he told us he had decided to go out on the next dog-pickup flight. A heavy silence settled over the rest of us as we tried to empathize with the intense mental anguish Mantell was suffering. I dearly wanted him to be at the Pole with me. After all, he had been my tentmate on the night of the blizzard four years before during which this expedition was conceived. Since then, he had poured immense amounts of time and energy into helping prepare for it. Hoping that he could somehow still carry on with us, I encouraged him to postpone the decision—to hang back on the workload for the next few days and give his body a chance to regenerate. Maybe things would turn around. Only time would tell. He agreed to apply a heavy dose of "positive mental attitude" and try to stick it out with us.

DAY 32

"SKI TRACKS!"

"It's a travel day, rise and shine!" Paul was shouting as he shook our tent the next morning. It was clear and breezy but bitterly cold, the usual conditions that follow an Arctic storm. We were soon digging out equipment that had been buried under mounds of snow. The cold invigorated us as it cut through clothing dampened by our long session in moist sleeping bags. Brent was painstakingly untangling his knotted traces. As the cold crept in while he unraveled each knot, his movements became steadily faster. Then he would suddenly drop the rope and bolt off at a sprint, running in wide circles and windmilling his arms. After a minute or two, he abruptly stopped and picked up where he had left off. His behavior was pure reflex, just part of our way of life on the polar sea.

During one of our sprints that morning, Richard and I ran a ways back up our trail, curious to see what the winds had done to the lead we had crossed. The gap was now several hundred yards wide. The huge ridge we had encountered just before crossing it was now just a barely discernible bump on the horizon. How terribly fragile this landscape is, I thought. "We're damn lucky we crossed that before the storm hit," Richard commented. I agreed, but I was glad to see that a two-inch skin of fresh ice pavement covered the gap. That meant that though the temperatures were moderating, the cold was still sufficient to repair the damage of these storms. Nonetheless, the rest of our journey would be a real gamble. We were in for some high adventure. After a month of misery and monotonous slogging, I was looking forward to it.

We traveled fast that morning on the freshly wind-packed surface. Richard was well ahead, scouting, when we suddenly saw him stop and get down on hands and knees. "Ski tracks!" he shouted as we approached. We were all stunned, but knew immediately whose they were: Jean-Louis Etienne, the French explorer Ann and McKerrow had met in Eureka. We knew he had departed Ward Hunt Island on his solo attempt to reach the Pole about the same time we left Drep Camp. It was a monumental undertaking, and most of us had guessed that he had given up by now. Though we were somewhat chagrined that he had overtaken us, we were amazed and impressed that he was still on the move. And more than anything, we were stunned at the bizarre coincidence of having encountered his trail amid the trackless expanse of the polar sea.

We wondered if we might run into him. Richard attempted to follow his route, but soon lost the tracks in snow drifts. Four hours later, plodding along with my team out front, I heard a noise in the ridges to my right. Suddenly my dogs lunged in that direction. Looking up, I gaped in amazement as I watched a man in a bright blue jacket step out from behind a pinnacle of ice. He welcomed us with outstretched arms. Here we were, the only two expeditions on the Arctic Ocean, and we happened to meet. Pondering the odds of that happening, I shook my head in disbelief. Ever since McKerrow and Ann had told me about Jean-Louis, I had looked forward to meeting him. But I had never imagined that we would meet under these circumstances.

Surely, I thought, this proves that like energies attract. I felt as if I were greeting an old friend after a long separation. The other team members gathered around, each embracing Jean-Louis and glowing with amazement.

He led us back behind the ridge to a tidy little camp. His home was a tiny, one-person tunnel tent. Neatly organized inside were a sleeping bag, a Primus stove, a cookpot, and a plastic bag containing his evening rations. Trailing out the door was his antenna wire, stretched across the tops of wide, stubby mountaineering skis planted in the snow nearby. Then he showed us his small toboggan—a two-by-seven-foot Kevlar shell—that he towed with a waistband and two slender poles as he traveled along each day. As he pulled back its nylon covering, we saw inside seven color-coded plastic bags, each containing a day's rations. Stuffed along the front were seven bright red fuel bottles. We marveled at the beautiful simplicity of his travel system, compared with our complicated operation. Every other week he was resupplied by air. Thus, his sled never had more than about a hundred pounds in payload.

Jean-Louis was only lightly dressed—he'd been huddled in his bag when he heard the commotion from our teams—so we took a quick group photo and made plans to rendezvous along the trail the next day. We carried on a couple of miles before setting camp. Our spirits were soaring.

DAY 33

"IT'S SO GOOD TO HAVE SOMETHING DIFFERENT TO EAT."

The next morning I awoke to the singsong sound of my name being repeated over and over. "Will, Will, Will, Will, where are you?" I realized it was Jean-Louis, milling about our campsite, trying to determine which tent I was in. "Good morning!" I shouted. "Please come in." We all sat up and hurriedly began assembling our stove. What a rare treat it was to have a visitor stop by for tea! In honor of our special guest, we allowed the stoves to burn extra long and warm the tent a bit as he came in. In answer to our queries, he told us he was a doctor from Paris who had given up his practice to become an adventurer. Though he had many mountaineering and backpacking expeditions to his credit, his goal was to be the first person to ski alone to the North Pole. An attempt he had made the year before was thwarted only twenty miles out by badly broken ice conditions. His daily rhythm was to travel seven hours, achieving about as many miles. He carried a small beacon from which a satellite tracked his coordinates. Through nightly radio contact with his base manager, Michel, in Resolute, he was kept abreast of his progress.

Later he paid a visit to the other tent, where Paul's crew asked him about his diet. Their mouths watered as he told them that his menu included freeze-dried entrees such as lobster, as well as fruits, nuts, and chocolate bars. The regular airlifts allowed him the luxury of foods that were not as concentrated in calories as ours. In my tent, minutes later, we heard a burst of laughter. "While Jean-Louis was telling us of his wondrous diet," Paul recorded later in his journal, "we were finishing up our umpteenth pot of saltless, sugarless oatmeal. I scraped the last bits of cold, pasty porridge from the bottom of the pot and was about to flip it out the door for the dogs. Jean-Louis grabbed my hand and said, 'Aren't you going to eat that?' I shook my head. He took the spoon, gulped down the porridge, then leaned back and said in his strong French accent, 'It's so good to have something different to eat.' So much for freeze-dried lobster, we thought."

Our jovial new friend went on his way as we loaded our sleds. We expected to overtake him later in the morning. He was looking forward to following our route so that he wouldn't have to break a trail. I watched him plod along over freshly jumbled ice just north of our campsite. His was a tedious job. Trudging at a snail's pace, wielding skis and poles and with a sled lurching along at his heels, he looked like a big blue insect.

Our route took us over young, windswept ice studded with table-sized blocks that protruded a few feet above the surface and looked like giant snowflakes. As we maneuvered our sleds through this obstacle course, we could on occasion see through the clear, thin surface ice to the black sea water below. This was very fragile country; a wind would quickly churn this into a maelstrom of ice and water. Miles ahead along the northern horizon, Paul and I noticed a dark smudge. We hoped our eyes were deceiving us, but as we traveled on, we knew we were looking at sea smoke—the telltale sign of a large system of open leads. This phenomenon results when moisture rises from cracks in the sea ice and condenses as a thick vapor. This lead system, we knew, was the result of the recent windstorm. The piper was being paid. We wondered if we were about to meet our match. Though we had learned to hack our way through pressure ridges of any size and slog our way through endless mounds of drifted snow, we simply couldn't walk on water.

We decided to veer toward the northeast, where the trail of sea smoke seemed to thin out a bit. Within a few miles we began crossing small cracks. As we pushed on, we entered a shatter zone where the cracks became larger and more frequent and crossed at all angles. We were able to thread a trail through this maze by going around the ends of the widest cracks. These maneuvers required deft coordination as a team; each of us ran back and forth among the sleds, jockeying them around fissures and coaxing timid dogs to leap the cracks. It felt great to be operating as the finely tuned machine that we had set out to be during training. The dogs rose to the challenge as well. Though they were initially frightened by the splintered ice, they seemed to catch on to the sport of weaving a way through it, and their noses keyed in on the new smell of open water.

The cracks grew wider and more numerous. When will this maze trap us? I wondered. At 4:00 P.M. we found ourselves on the brink of a thirty-foot-wide gap covered in wafer-thin ice. Brent and Richard scouted to the east and west and found that the lead stretched on for miles. The ice around us creaked and groaned like a haunted house as we considered our next move. We had only one option: we would have to wait and hope that the lead would refreeze or close. It was sufficiently cold——45 degrees—for the lead to firm up adequately within a day's time. And fortunately, with our second dog-pickup flight slated for the next day, we could make good use of this delay. However, a suspicious two-foot gap of open water in the middle of the partially refrozen lead suggested that it might be opening wider. If so, we could only hope that at some section of the jagged-edged lead, the ice might twist and crunch together, forming a bridge.

Paul's sextant shot placed us at 85°22′, 310 miles from the North Pole and one degree of latitude north of our first pickup flight. The pan on which we were camped was far smoother than the bone-jarring mogul field we had offered Karl before. Though it was a bit short, we assumed it would serve as a tolerable airstrip. We set camp on a pan alongside the lead, joking about our beachfront view. Despite the delay, we were in good spirits, looking forward to enjoying the woodstoves and anxious to reorganize our teams and sleds for the next phase of the journey. We would be trimming back to just three sleds pulled by seven dogs each; of the other two, the *Indre* would serve as fuel for the layover day, and the *Gaile* would be sent out as a museum piece. Soon the air was filled with the sound of bow saws and axes as the *Indre* was transformed into piles of splintered wood. The name plate was saved; it would go out on the flight as a gift for our support staff member for whom the sled was named.

The news on the radio that evening was disheartening; a storm had closed the airport in Resolute. No flights tomorrow, Jim informed us but perhaps the next day. "Here we sit," I wrote, "another one of the countless moments of waiting on this trip. Our hourglass is now more than half-full." The rest would do us good, but we worried about the twenty-one dogs that were to be airlifted out. In keeping with our rationing schedule, they had not eaten in two days, and now the feast of meat scraps Jim had collected was to be denied them for yet another day. Most of the dogs going out were Geoff's. These Eskimo dogs are accustomed to a feast-and-famine cycle—life in the Arctic demands this—so we knew they would be fine. But their voracious appetites represented a threat. Waiting for a morsel of food, they eyed every move we made and lunged violently against their stakeout lines when we fed the other dogs. We would have to sleep lightly during this layover. If any of these dogs broke loose from their lines during the night, they would wreak havoc with our sled loads.

Jean-Louis joined us at our camp that evening, setting up his little blue tunnel tent a hundred yards away from us. He stopped by my tent for a cup of tea and another pleasant visit. I told him I wanted to cross Antarctica by dogsled. His eyes lit up. He had considered a similar expedition, but had no access to dogs. Well, we'd need a doctor on our team, I said. Perhaps we could work together. We brainstormed about plans, and I jotted down his phone number in Paris, saying I would call him that summer.

DAY 34

"MY EYES ITCHED AND BURNED SO BAD FROM THE SMOKE, I OPTED TO EAT OUTSIDE."

In the morning, Jean-Louis decided to carry on. Another day's travel time, he said, was more important to him than having a marked trail to follow by waiting for us. The lead had remained stable during the night. The ice was now an inch thick—just enough to support a person on skis, but not a dogsled. We watched nervously as he crossed. The thin, pliable ice deflected slightly with each gingerly movement of his skis. We waved goodbye to the blue figure that slowly disappeared among the ridges on the far side of the lead, and marveled at the courage it took to travel in this dangerous territory alone.

With the ample piles of firewood from the discarded sled, we attempted to dry our sleeping bags. The effort proved futile. The volume of accumulated frost was now so great—some bags weighed nearly fifty pounds—that the minimal heat from the stoves merely redistributed the moisture rather than driving it from the bags. We were able to wring nearly a gallon of water from each, but when we took them away from the heat, the remaining moisture froze in blocks where it had collected, creating cold spots that plagued us each night. Fortunately, the heat was sufficient to dry mittens, socks, and mukluks.

Burning the sled parts became a mixed blessing that evening. The shifting wind caused downdrafts that blew smoke into our tents, and the caustic fumes of burning plastic and sled-runner glues tortured our eyes and lungs. Over dinner, Richard suffered a severe allergic reaction—his eyes felt as if they were on fire—so he finished his meal outside.

With the lead nearby, I was on guard all evening, concerned that the ice on which we were camped might shatter. At one point a loud crack boomed under the tent, and I bolted for the door. Things seemed to settle down and I crawled back in, but a while later I heard another loud boom. My body tensed, my heart pounded, and I prepared to exit again, but then I realized it was Brent splitting wood for his stove.

Waiting for word on flight plans, Paul kept a lonely vigil on the radio well into the night, one of many nights on the trip during which radio duties cost him precious sleep. At 2:00 A.M. Jim reported that Karl was en route. ETA was 11:00 A.M. A few hours later I woke to the sound of the dogs padding on the snow. I looked out the door and was astonished to find that my dogs were loose, milling about my sled with plump bellies and satisfied looks. Chester was dozing peacefully on top of my sled load. Bits of cardboard were scattered about. I shot out of the tent and surveyed the damage. They had quietly consumed a twenty-pound box of pemmican. It was my fault. I had mistakenly left the rope that secured the end of their stake-out cable within reach of the dogs. It had been chewed through. Fortunately, my dogs were still on full rations and thus had been relatively well-behaved throughout the escapade. The damage was minimal. I would make up for it by not feeding the culprits for a few days. If it had been Geoff's dangerously ravenous dogs, our supplies would have been ripped to shreds.

With the dogs resecured, I took a moment to survey the stunning beauty of this early spring morning. Sunlight filtering through the sea smoke that drifted lazily above the lead cast our campsite in deep tangerine hues. Through the haze, the pastel-tipped snowdrifts looked like meringue. The silence and soft colors were mesmerizing. I hesitated in returning to my tent until the cold sent a chill through me.

DAY 35

"TELL THEM WE'RE EVEN MORE HELLBENT TO
REACH THE POLE THAN WE WERE THE LAST TIME
YOU SAW US."

In the morning, Brent and I rounded up the dogs from each team
that would be heading home. Twenty-one were to go and twenty-
one were to stay. But when we gathered up all the dogs that had
been taken off rations, we counted twenty-two. We were stunned.
These selections had been based on thorough observation of each
dog's performance and frequent discussions over the past few
weeks. How could we have miscounted? It was a serious mistake,
because it meant we had only twenty well-fed candidates for our
remaining three sleds—two teams of seven and one of six, a
serious imbalance. I scanned the dogs that were going out, pondering a solution. My eyes fixed on Slidre, the one dog from my
team among them, and his rotund belly. "Slidre," I said, "your
thievery last night just bought you a ticket to the North Pole."
  I laughed as I thought of the bizarre twist of fate that had
befallen Slidre. Never had I intended for the shy and retiring dog
to go to the Pole. Though well-built and strong, he was the least
spirited dog on my team, somewhat lacking in ambition. I'd
picked him up, a little white puppy with dark markings, in
Eureka when Mantell and I passed through there on a dogsled
trip in 1982. His mellow, agreeable personality won my heart
and we became good friends. Slidre's parents were part of a pack
of half-wild Canadian Eskimo dogs that the staff at Eureka kept
around to keep polar bears away from the weather station. Their
lineage included some Arctic wolf blood. Thus, Slidre was directly related to the wolves that had ravaged our supplies on the

runway in Eureka the day of our first shuttle flight to Drep Camp. Once in a while his wolf instincts were evident, as in an episode in Frobisher at the beginning of our training. I had him there as an alternate in the event of injuries to any of the ten dogs I had slated to take to the Pole, my "A" squad. His taste for blood had made him the aggressor in the dogfight in which Goliath, one of my favorite dogs, was killed. I didn't begrudge Slidre that incident; I knew he was just responding to instinct. Hank was to take Goliath's place, but when Hank went AWOL as we were leaving on March 1, Slidre got the nod. Now he was getting the nod again to be among the dogs that were likely to reach the Pole.

The plane arrived at 11:00 A.M. sharp. Karl circled our camp twice and then off to the southeast. From his aerial perspective he spotted a better ice strip than we had, and landed a mile away, hidden from our view by pressure ridges. With several of the twenty-one outbound dogs harnessed to the *Gaile,* and the rest on short bits of discarded rope fashioned into leashes, we hurried toward the billowing cloud of snow that had been kicked up by his engines. Five people, including our base manager, Jim Gasperini, Karl and his copilot, and two media representatives, *National Geographic* photographer Jim Brandenburg and his colleague Lynn Peterson, greeted us with warm hugs. Gasperini pulled Paul and me aside and asked in a hushed tone, "Now tell me, how are you guys really doing?" His sympathetic look reflected the skepticism that was mounting back home.

"Tell them we're even more hellbent to reach the Pole than we were the last time you saw us," Paul responded with firm confidence.

"We're going to make it, Jim. Don't worry," I added.

He nodded, knowing that somehow he'd have to sell that sense of assurance to the media crew in Resolute. He went on to report a litany of business matters: more problems with various media contracts, conflicts over the cost-sharing plan for additional flights, and logistic difficulties in returning the outbound dogs to their homes. More headaches and more debts were what all this meant to Paul and me. We scrambled for a solution to each problem. The business side and the trail side of the expedition were two different worlds, and we had to think for both.

Meanwhile, Karl transferred fuel from two fifty-five-gallon drums into his plane's tanks while our teammates loaded the sled and tied dogs in place. Excited by the new smells, the famished dogs nipped at everything in sight, hoping to hit upon a morsel of food. One wolfed down a pair of mitts left lying in the snow, while another grabbed Lynn's tape recorder from under a seat on the plane. Tape was scattered across the plane floor like confetti by the time she got to it. After a flurry of photos and handshakes, the plane doors closed and in a flash they were gone.

We returned to camp, where Richard, who had been baby-sitting the other dogs, was waiting, and then held a quick huddle to organize our departure. "I have an idea," said Brent. He suggested we check the two drums Karl had left behind on the ice, to see if there was any fuel left in them.

"Wouldn't that be cheating?" Geoff asked.

"No one would ever know," Brent responded.

"And besides," Richard added, "it's not really a resupply, just something we found on the ice."

Paul glanced at me and asked, "What do you think?"

I was stunned. I knew our fuel shortage had remained a major concern among the team, but I wasn't aware that it had become so grave an issue that they would be willing to break our own rules over it. "Listen," I said, "the goals we set for ourselves are more important than the fuel in those tanks. And besides, I personally don't feel our fuel shortage has reached crisis propor- tions. As the weather warms, we'll be needing a lot less fuel than you think."

This episode, like the crisis of conscience we underwent fol- lowing Ann and Mantell's retrieval of additional supplies from Drep Camp on Day 4, tested our commitment to a goal that was to make this North Pole journey unique from others since Peary's: we would rely solely on the supplies we brought with us. And since this rule was self-imposed, the integrity of the expedi- tion had as much to do with how it hung on our consciences in years to come as with how the media portrayed it. If we bent the rules, we would only be defeating ourselves. Furthermore, if we accepted so much as a scrap of paper from outside, doubts might be raised among observers about our adherence to the plan.

The issue came up in subtle ways. For example, when we were having severe problems with a plug on our movie camera a few weeks before, a service technician suggested sending a replace- ment part out on the first dog-pickup flight. As important as that camera was to us, we declined the offer. We would find a way to fix it ourselves or go without. And during our visits with Jean-Louis, I insisted that we accept not even so much as a cup of coffee from his rations. Paul squeezed a bit of levity out of that edict by playing a practical joke on me. The night Jean-Louis camped with us, Paul's tent crew invited him in for popcorn. Geoff joined the gathering in Paul's tent as well. After Jean-Louis retired, Paul suggested to Geoff that he slip back to his tent and nonchalantly mention to me that the popcorn had been traded for some of Jean-Louis's freeze-dried lobster. Geoff followed through, and I bit. Upon hearing of the alleged swap, I exploded with rage and, pouring out obscenities, was headed toward the door when Geoff caught me and clued me in on the gag.

That day, April 11, was to herald a new phase of the expedition, one that's well-illustrated by the spaceflight analogy. Like a rocketship that has escaped earth's atmosphere, we had now surmounted the worst of the brutally cold weather and the pack ice. By sending out our twenty-one most exhausted dogs, we were, in essence, jettisoning spent booster rockets. Each of our three remaining sleds, the *Bria,* the *Crystal,* and the *O'Donnell,* was now twelve feet long, three-fourths of its original length. Dubbed the "zip ships," they each now carried 600 pounds in payload. Thus we now had a third of the weight and slightly less than half the number of "engines" we had on leaving Drep Camp. The spaceflight analogy ends there, because the remaining twenty-one dogs did not represent "fresh fuel." Though they had been kept on full rations and had just enjoyed a day's rest, their reserves were severely diminished.

Apprehensions mounted as we harnessed up our three seven-dog teams. Because the supplies carried by the *Indre* and the *Gaile* had been redistributed, the remaining sleds now carried 150 additional pounds and would be pulled by smaller teams. The one compensating factor was that two people could now be stationed full-time on each sled. We all hoped that Mantell would take advantage of the seventh slot and go easy on his injured heel.

The lead in front of our campsite now had a coating of fresh ice a few inches thick. Brent, our resident expert on young ice, tiptoed out on it, probing with a harpoon, and gave us the high sign to come forward. We levered the sleds forward and eased them down onto the forty-foot-wide highway. The dogs dug their claws into the velvety brine crust that carpeted the fresh sea ice, and, after we helped them build momentum, pulled the sleds along at a good clip. The lead veered north for a short way, so Brent led us along the edge to take advantage of the easy travel. Then, when it swung east, he searched for a safe spot to cross its weakened center portion. A seam generally forms down the center of refrozen leads, where the ice either overlaps or pulls apart a foot or more from residual motion that comes after the initial shifting that formed the lead subsides. He found a section with an overlap, and we lined up the sleds to shoot them across, one by one. The thin, pliable ice deflected a bit as each sled rumbled over the center. The drivers stepped lightly, distributing most of their weight on the sled, to avoid punching through the ice.

We continued northward on old pans interspersed with eroded ridges. The area was covered in a deep mantle of what we called "freeze-dried corn snow," in which the flakes have been consolidated by the Arctic's cold, dry winds into a latticework of ice crystals. It has the texture of very coarse sand, and is about as difficult as sand to push sleds through. The friction was tremendous. The dogs pulled mightily while we pushed like pistons against the upstanders. As each of the three dog teams started grinding to a halt and dropping to the rear, Paul and I frantically switched team members around, hoping to strike a better distribution of power. Ann, the smallest member of our crew, got bumped three times, replaced by someone who had more bulk to thrust against a stuck sled. Among the array of intense emotions we were all experiencing, she now added anger to her list. Much to her credit, she was determined to be considered an equal player in good times or bad.

We carried on for a few hours, moving only a few hundred yards. Suddenly the handwriting was on the wall: we would never reach the Pole. From the distraught looks on my teammates' faces, I knew they had come to the same horrifying conclusion. We were doomed. Paul and I, grunting along together behind the *Bria,* pondered our situation. We agreed without a doubt that this expedition's only chance for success now lay in trimming back to just a couple of people and our very best dogs, so that the remaining rations could be stretched well into May or possibly June. To us, it seemed the only chance. We had no other options. But how would we break the news to the others? And how would we make the awful decision as to who would go and who would stay? Paul and I assumed the team would find this proposal abhorrent, and we feared serious dissension would break out if we brought it up now. At team meetings in Ely and Frobisher, we had discussed this very scenario. Paul and I had made it clear then that if we hit dire straits, one or more members might be asked to go out. Furthermore, if it came down to choosing just two candidates, he and I reserved the right to fill those slots. They had all acknowledged this months before. But now that they had invested weeks of excruciating work and hardship on the trail, would they still agree to it? Would they let go of their dreams of standing at the Pole, of tasting the fruits of their labor? If the group split in factions over this scheme, the hostilities that would develop in our state of mental strain would doom us more surely than our heavy loads. What if it erupted in a mutiny? What a horrible scene that would be. To end this trip on a note of bitterness would be far worse than failing to reach the Pole.

"The only way they'll accept this proposal," I said to Paul, "is if they come to realize of their own accord that it's the only option."

Paul agreed. "We'd best just carry on for a few days till everyone is utterly fried, and then ask for suggestions," he said.

I looked back. Neither of the other sleds was moving. Geoff was trudging toward us, shrouded in thick frost that had condensed on his clothing from perspiration. "We'd like to have a meeting," he said, panting heavily. "We can't go on like this any longer."

Paul and I nodded. We levered the sleds to an open spot and set up the tents. Then, with long faces and heavy hearts, we all packed tightly into Paul's tent. It felt as though we were attending a wake. We knew that this "summit conference," as we called it, would be a pivotal event; we had both of our pocket tape recorders running.

"The reality hit hard today," Paul said as he opened the meeting. "It's apparent that more of this grind is not going to get us to the Pole. We need an immediate and a long-range plan that will assure that we reach the Pole without resupply."

To Paul's surprise and my own, Brent immediately forwarded the proposal that we had been contemplating. He suggested setting aside enough rations for three people and one dog team to make a final dash. "The way things are shaping up," he said, "we're going to get stuck doing that anyway. We might as well plan for it. Those going out can push themselves into the ground for the next few weeks, and then two or three people can go on with one tent, two sleeping bags, three gallons of gas, and a hundred pounds of pemmican—making a quick pace with ten dogs." Mantell and Geoff nodded in agreement. I glanced at Paul, realizing we had misjudged the team. They had come to the same conclusion we had.

"Let's make the rounds here," Paul said, asking each of us to state what we thought our best bet was for reaching the Pole.

Geoff went first. "Personally, I wouldn't mind getting a resupply if it meant that everyone could get to the Pole. But that's not the consensus of the group. Our best chance is to somehow trim more weight and travel as fast and far as we can. Then, if we start getting close and have only a few supplies left, we send just two people on. I'm willing to be one of the 'retro rockets.' "

"I guess I feel the same way," said Mantell. "Originally the 'unsupported' part was real important to me, because it is the biggest challenge. But when I dig down real deep inside and ask myself whether I would want to get there unsupported or not at all, it's real touchy. But I guess I could live with the fact that I may not get there personally."

Brent was next. "To me, the bottom line is that the expedition has to be successful. If I'm an instrument in making that happen—even if it's just Will crawling on his hands and knees to get there—then I'll be happy."

"What are your thoughts, Richard?" Paul asked.

"It would be pretty hard to go back. I'm here to go to the Pole," he said firmly.

Then it was Ann's turn. "I don't know, really, how I feel. I've said from day one that if it meant getting people there, I'd be willing to go out. Each day, though, that gets a little harder to swallow. I feel almost as strongly as Richard does. But on the other hand I agree with Brent. It will do the expedition as a whole no good if someone doesn't make it. No one looks at second best."

"Can I say one more thing?" Richard added. "Deep down inside me, if we don't all get there, I'll feel this wasn't unsupported. To me, pulling people out is using air support backwards, sort of a 'reverse resupply.' Instead of that, let's take some gambles. Let's chuck all of our personal gear, except maybe an extra pair of socks, and drop a tent and get down to cooking on only one stove. We could also eat a lot less and stretch our food further."

The group looked toward me, knowing it was my turn to speak. "The reality of this expedition changed for me today," I said somberly. "I realized that it's impossible to accomplish what we set out to do. Unless we're lucky, we're simply not all going to make it, and that's very hard for me to accept. Though there's a chance we could carry on as planned, I feel that to be safe we have to have a plan for sending a few people and a certain number of dogs on at the end. We have to figure out the supplies needed for that, set them aside, and then work as a group with what's left." I pointed out that we also had a financial consideration. The only way we could afford an additional flight to send out more dogs and people was to share one of Jean-Louis's resupply charters. His next one was about two weeks away. Whatever plan we came up with would have to be targeted for that date, I said.

"Why don't we figure out what we'd need for this final assault team," said Brent, "and then figure out what we've got left in our sleds."

Ideas now started flying as we sought to forge a plan. Discussion about the makeup of the final assault team was tabled; it was simply too difficult an issue for us to reckon with in our exhausted state. Rather, we focused on more neutral issues—our dogs and sleds. We considered our diet; perhaps we could rely on cheese as our main protein and turn over our own pemmican rations to the dogs. We considered ways of shedding more weight. We felt that with close scrutiny we could find ways to trim weight from the sled loads. Jettisoning a tent and its equipment was one idea; that would save forty pounds. But it would place us at great risk if we encountered a severe blizzard, so we discarded the notion. Another idea concerned our sleeping bags. We all knew they were the silent killers. Some of them now contained more than fifty pounds of ice. We realized we could save a hundred or more pounds if we threw the heaviest ones out. By zipping the others together in pairs, we could sleep three people in two bags. It seemed like an acceptable notion, but we agreed that we would have to test that system for a night before discarding the bags, to see if we could tolerate such tight quarters.

We set a goal: each sled was to be 100 pounds lighter before leaving the campsite. We would give the dogs a day's rest and feed them well. In fact, we agreed to give each dog three pounds of pemmican for the next few nights. That move was a big gamble. It would cut heavily into our remaining supply, but we felt it was the only means of bringing the dogs back up to full steam. We would also shed more than 100 pounds of weight from the sleds. We agreed to do some soul-searching that night and make lists of every item we could possibly jettison. When we assembled again in the morning, we would compare our lists and get to work reorganizing our loads.

We adjourned the summit conference with a sense of relief.

Despite the misgivings some team members harbored about the assault-team proposal, our spirits were boosted by this sharing of ideas and the sense that we were now taking firmer control over a desperate situation. The discussion left us with a glimmer of hope that with a bit of luck—a long, northbound frozen lead, perhaps—we could still get all seven people to the Pole. Fate would tell between now and Jean-Louis's next charter flight. In the meantime, it was imperative that we prepare to deploy a final assault team. As disagreeable as that option was, we firmly felt that it still represented our only clear shot at success, and we were pleased that the proposal seemed to have been accepted relatively painlessly by everyone.

THE SIXTH WEEK

DESPERATION CAMP

DAY 36

"I HAVE THE PLAN!"

After breakfast the next morning, we rendezvoused in Paul's tent for round two. Out came the lists of items to be jettisoned. We had agreed to drop nearly 300 pounds. I felt it was time to broach the assault-team proposal. We had to come to grips with factors that had been left unresolved. I wondered how people's feelings had changed about it overnight. Testing the waters, I asked, "Do you consider the assault-team option to be the final plan, or is it just a contingency? Is it Plan A or Plan B?"

"I have the plan," said Richard with surprising firmness, thumping his diary for emphasis. "I think we're giving up too easily. This trip has been much tougher than I thought, but we still have a lot left in us. We're still fat and sassy, and if I have to get on a plane heading out feeling the way I do now, I'll be very ashamed. . . ." His words trailed off as his eyes welled with tears. From his diary he pulled out a page riddled with computations, and when he had regained his composure, he outlined a twenty-day man-haul plan that would put all seven of us, assisted by a few dogs, at the Pole. It would require cutting our own rations in half—to about a pound each per day—but he insisted that with the right mix of food items we could do it.

His impassioned plea riveted our attention. But a pathetic picture formed in my mind as I envisioned seven people on starvation rations pulling heavy sleds. Dozens of early explorers had died in their tracks doing just that. A man-haul might be a heroic gesture for keeping our crew intact, but I felt certain that with that scenario we'd be calling in an evacuation flight long before we neared the Pole. He underscored that his proposed

distribution of our rations for the next few weeks would not
preclude the assault-team plan, if that was deemed necessary.
But I realized then, struck by the tone of absolute conviction in
his voice, that no matter what happened in the next few weeks,
Richard was not willingly going to give up his chance to reach
the Pole; he would never volunteer to be a "retro rocket," as
Geoff, Brent, and Mantell had. I admired his tenacity. But both
Paul and I worried whether Richard would stir up opposition
among the others regarding the assault-team plan over the next
couple of weeks. When it came time to make pivotal decisions,
would we find ourselves saddled with a lack of consensus? As
leaders, we could make unpopular decisions and bark out orders,
but what would be the upshot of that? What backlash might we
face if angry, bitter team members were sent home against their
will? The press would jump on their stories, prying out of them
every inflamed diatribe they could. The integrity of this expedition might be left in a shambles, whether or not we reached the
Pole. And more important, given that scenario, how would we
feel about each other a month from now, or a year? Would the
friendships we had formed over the months spent building this
dream turn to bitterness and hatred? Would memories of this
expedition haunt us like a nightmare?

Mulling over these thoughts, I said a silent prayer: "O God,
please get us all to the Pole." A few team members expressed
some interest in Richard's proposal, but the group deferred to
Paul and me. We chose the middle ground. We didn't reject his
idea, but insisted that we put food in the "bank" for an assault
team. The consensus was that two people would be most efficient. That, of course, meant Paul and me. To assuage their fears
that we were co-opting them, we offered to set aside rations for
three people. I would set aside sixteen days' rations for two
people and six dogs in one bag and rations for a third person in
another bag, and carefully protect these deep inside my sled load.
I emphasized that putting this food in the "bank" did not mean
that the assault team plan was a certainty; it just meant we would
be ready to deploy either a two- or three-person team if we had
to.

They all found this plan agreeable. The troubling question
was, if we went with three people, who would the third choice
be? No decision would be made on that, we said, until the time
came. We pointed out that many factors would be considered. We all agreed that representation was a key one. Geoff
and Mantell represented Alaska. They stood to be the first from

the North Star State to reach the Pole. Brent represented Canada's Northwest Territories, which had assisted tremendously with this project. On the other hand, Richard was also a Canadian and a far better skier; his speed might be needed. And in terms of this expedition's historical significance, Ann might be the best choice; she would be the first woman to trek to the Pole.

Paul and I knew that the decision would be the most difficult one we would ever have to make. It would take some time. Fortunately, the group empathized. They realized that it offered a built-in incentive for everyone to put out a hundred percent for the next few weeks.

Mantell pointed out that to choose someone now might leave the rest demoralized. "How are you going to feel?" he said. "You're having a shitty day, working your ass off, and you know you're not the one going to the Pole. It could play on your psyche all the time."

"Yes," said Paul, "we could make a decision now, but if all seven of us don't work our butts off to get the final team to the launching pad, it means nothing."

"And some people are going to be in better shape than others by then," Brent added. "Let's not get locked into a decision at this point."

"Whatever decision we make," I said, "I don't want to see our friendships split over this. For me, this would be the ultimate heartbreak. We have to work for each other, instead of against each other."

We outlined assignments for the afternoon. Richard and Geoff would ski forward to give us a prognosis for the next day, Brent would fix up a stew for the dogs, and the rest of us would comb through supplies, pulling out the items we had agreed to jettison. We were about to adjourn the meeting when Mantell, who had been deep in thought, looked up and said, "I hate to introduce a down note, but if it could be arranged, I would consider going out soon. I'm not really ready to give up, but I'm not sure my feet will make it to the Pole. I know I can't ski thirty miles a day." By sending him and his gear out, he figured we'd take a hundred pounds from our load. "I'm pretty confused right now about what my goals are," he continued hesitantly, "but I want the expedition to succeed, and if my leaving will help, then I'll do that." Our understanding of the gravity of Mantell's decision was reflected in the long silence that followed.

While the others set about their chores, Paul and I took a long walk with Mantell, hoping to get a clear sense of his real feelings.

We considered the health risk he faced if he carried on. His feet hadn't gotten any worse in the past week, but they hadn't improved, either. Only rest and warmth would bring healing. He acknowledged that. He'd been able to bear the pain of trudging a few miles a day, he said, but once we started clipping off twenty or more miles a day—and he expected us to do so soon—he knew he would severely aggravate the damage and very likely face losing several toes. But he feared that being evacuated would leave him with a sense of shame and failure. We assured him that none of us considered it a failure, and that his friends and family wouldn't, either. He expressed concerns that arranging another flight would put us more deeply in debt. The money was the least of our concerns, we countered; his feelings came first. He thought for a moment, and then said that more than anything he wanted to do what was best for the expedition. At this point that meant going out as soon as possible, he concluded. His voice was choked with sorrow, but I think he was relieved. Making that decision had been a long, agonizing process for him. Now it was over. Paul would get on the radio and check on flights. Jean-Louis was due for one right about this time; perhaps Mantell could catch a ride on that plane. It was a bittersweet moment for Paul and me. Though deeply saddened at the thought of Mantell's departure, we were glad that his burden of pain would soon be lifted.

When we returned to camp, we found the "purge" well under way. A pile of jettisoned items was growing alongside the tents. Mantell pulled out the burnable and created a blaze for heating the oats and noodles for the dogs. Paul and I set about reorganizing our sled loads. Meanwhile, on scouting detail, Richard and Geoff encountered a quarter-mile-wide lead, sheathed in a thin skin of ice and oriented toward the northeast, a few miles north of our camp. In attempting to cross it to continue northward, Geoff found this day-old ice to be very rubbery, and had a brush with disaster. His diary recounts the incident: "At one point the back ends of my skis broke through [the ice] while we were out in the middle [of the lead]. My first reaction was to hesitate, but then I skied forward quickly and onto a slightly thicker area. I was terrified. How horrible it would be to go through the ice with skis on. You'd just be helpless. A nasty way to die. I became much more cautious after that."

That lead, they reported upon returning to camp, would be safe to travel on the next day. They were hopeful that it might bring us some fast miles, but in any case, they had found the snow and ice conditions north of camp to be good. Spirits were cheery in our tents that evening. We had met our goal of shedding 300 pounds, that is, as long as our experiment with sleeping three people in two bags proved successful that night. Geoff paid a visit to Tent 2, where a discussion ensued about an odd phenomenon we had all been experiencing. Throughout the expedition, most of us had found that the capacity of our bladders had apparently diminished. We were urinating small amounts numerous times each day. And some of us were hit by the urge as we slept. Paul was careful to take his pee bottle—our plastic whiskey flask—to bed with him every night. Geoff, tapping his vast knowledge of biology, explained that this was a mammalian response to winter weather known as "cold diuresis." Decreasing temperatures trigger a diuretic response, in which body fluids are voided frequently. It is nature's way of drying out skin and hair in winter, to increase their insulation value when evaporation is minimal. Paul's crew listened intently while heating up their noodle water for dinner. Explaining that he, too, had what he called "a leaky peter," Geoff said the urge had just hit him and asked if he could use the tent's piss can. Brent passed it over to him. Geoff squatted in position, but before he got everything aligned, a squirt slipped out and cut a graceful arc across the tent into the cookpot. The group looked on dumbfounded, then burst into laughter. "Ah, well," chuckled Paul, "we needed a change of flavor."

DAY 37

"NO LONGER DID OUR SLEDS GET HUNG UP ON
EVERY SNOWFLAKE THAT WAS OUT OF LINE."

Our experiment that night with the new sleeping system was deemed a success. Each tent group paired its driest left- and right-hand zippered bags, and we snuggled in like three peas in pod. Though we slept fitfully, we felt rested and knew that within a few days we'd be thoroughly adjusted to this system. Until Mantell left us, we would hang on to one additional bag for the seventh person. During a radio check over breakfast, Paul learned that Jean-Louis had a flight scheduled for April 16, four days away. That would be Mantell's ride home.

With a day's rest and bellies full of food, the dogs were nearly as vigorous as they had been the day we left Drep Camp. They squealed and howled ambitiously as we strapped our sleds. Our loads looked manageable. This day would, I knew, represent a turning point for the expedition. We had finally struck a compatible match between weight and power.

The lead that Geoff and Richard had encountered the day before was amply frozen. In fact, it had closed considerably overnight. As we crossed it, the center seam was slowly overlapping, emitting a high-pitched squeak. We stopped for a moment to record the eerie sounds while Ann, who had taken over McKerrow's duties with the movie camera, filmed the motion. We traveled at a steady two-mile-an-hour gait until 7:00 P.M., stopping for the night while the dogs were still fresh, lest we burn them out again. Our thirty-seventh day had been a glorious one. Some eighteen miles of sea ice had passed under our sleds. As Brent commented, "No longer did our sleds get hung up on every snowflake that was out of line."

In his journal that evening, Geoff aptly compared sea ice and geology. "When large pans of ice are moving, it is like continental drift, plate tectonics," he wrote. "The formation of pressure ridges resembles continental plates pushing together and thrusting up mountain ranges. These ice mountains then melt and erode and look like miniature Appalachians rather than Rockies, though the process takes a few seasons rather than eons." Then, reversing the perspective, he added, "People may think of the land they live on as being very solid. Actually, like ice on water, terra firma is only a thin crust riding on a sea of molten rock."

There had been little talk that day about the man-haul versus the assault-team plan. We were just glad to be making miles. But that night, thoughts about those plans kept me awake. It had been a positive day, spirits were high, and I was sure everyone felt that our prospects were good. But we would need ten consecutive days like this to get close enough to the Pole for me to feel reasonably assured that we could make it as a group of six. Would we be able to go ten days straight and then be ready immediately to begin a 150-mile man-haul? Or would they be ready to call it quits, to hop on that plane knowing that after a day of rest, warm showers, and food, they would have to face the empty feeling of missing out on a shot at the top? The choice would be dictated by the travel conditions we encountered over the next ten days. I took comfort in the notion that it was out of my hands and finally fell asleep.

DAY 38

"IT WAS A GOOD DAY FOR A DUNK BECAUSE THERE WAS NO WIND."

The next morning, Paul's tent crew was raring to go at an early hour. A difficult sewing repair job delayed me in our tent, and my crew fell twenty minutes behind the others in pack-up chores. Paul angrily pulled me aside when I crawled out of the tent. "Are you trying to run down the clock on this crew?" he said pointedly. "C'mon, we've got to set the pace if we're going to have any chance of getting them all there." His allegation stung. I certainly wasn't purposely killing time, I responded, but after a night of reflection, my sorrowful gut feeling was that we simply would not get them there. My sense of urgency had lapsed. Feeling bad for overreacting, Paul apologized for launching that barb. To clear the air, we sledded together and had a close talk, sharing feelings about this journey and about loved ones back home. Paul told me that his key source of drive lay in thoughts of his older brother Mark, who had been killed in a car accident five months before. Mark had had a vibrant personality and an incomparable zest for living. Paul noted that the demands of the expedition obliged us to operate at capacity—mentally, physically, emotionally, and spiritually—day in and day out. "Like life in fast forward," he said. In a way, he felt it offered him a chance to live for both himself and his brother—if only for a short time. As we trudged along, he explained that he had discovered that a vast, untapped reservoir of vitality existed within all of us. He had come to the conclusion that the beauty of projects as big as this one was that they offered a chance for experiencing one's full potential. I smiled, knowing that he had articulated the revelation that had drawn me northward time and again.

Geoff enjoyed a pleasant break that afternoon; for the first time he put skis on and went ahead to scout. It was perfect therapy for rear-end mentality, he said. But he had a tricky assignment; the ice conditions progressively worsened, slipping from "rolling prairies," as we called the wide pans, into tight "hedgerowed pastures." Upon encountering each successive ridge, he would stop and methodically contemplate the next move as if he were playing a giant game of checkers, wondering which square of ice we should move onto next.

Late in the afternoon he was stymied by an open gap a couple of yards wide. He went east while Paul skied west along it, looking for a spot where we might cross. A quarter-mile away, Paul found that the lead narrowed to a few feet. He signaled Ann to bring the first team toward him, and then went back to help muscle the sled over a bank of snow along the lead. As they neared the brink, Ann went out front to coax the skittish dogs into leaping the gap. Then she suddenly dropped out of sight. The cornice of snow on which she stood gave way, and she plunged waist-deep into the ocean. Reflexively she flung her arms wide to bridge the gap and spare herself a complete dunking, then wriggled up onto the edge of the far side. Paul hurried the team across on a safer spot a few yards down, and then began tearing through the sled to find dry clothes.

Within minutes, Ann had changed pants and socks and was back on the trail, working hard to regenerate lost heat. Though it was −30 degrees, "it was a good day for a dunk," Ann quipped later, "because there was no wind." She was calm and collected throughout the incident, so much so that the rest of us barely made mention of it in our diaries. It had registered in our minds as just another minor episode in a day on the trail. Nonetheless, Ann felt its impact for a long time. In fact, she said later that it was two days before she felt warm again. In the tent that evening, she found herself so stiffened by the deep chill that she needed help from Brent in taking off her mukluks and wind gear. When news of Ann's dunking reached the media through Paul's next radio check, it became one of the most widely reported episodes of our journey. Ironically, in seven journals—even Ann's—it received scant comment. We took it in stride as just another day in the life of a polar journey.

That night, for the second time, we were stopped by a lead, one that was 100 feet or so across, and covered by paper-thin ice. We hoped for a cold night so that it would be firm enough to cross in the morning.

DAY 39

"AN AWESOME TIME."

Brent went out scouting early the next day, April 15, and found a firm section for our traverse. The center seam was very rubbery, though safe. Ann trained the movie camera on that spot as each sled rumbled over it, depressing the ice as if it were a water bed. It was our third day since leaving "Desperation Camp," and a critical one for the dogs. Their performance today would suggest the trend in their spirits over the next few weeks. After clocking thirty miles in two days, I was now cautiously optimistic, though my mathematics said it still looked nearly impossible to stretch things far enough to get us all to the Pole. But other team members were exuberant, particularly Ann and Richard. The team members with the least experience in expedition logistics, they were less troubled by the dismal picture the numbers painted. With youthful naïveté, they overlooked that. Their notion for overcoming the challenge was to throw themselves at it all the harder. Ann noted in her journal that she was no longer pacing herself. Paul and I were delighted that we no longer had to shoulder the cheerleader role. We now had several enthusiasts who would help in that capacity. Efficiency was now highly fashionable. Camp was broken or set in as little as half an hour. Mantell was charged with enthusiasm as well, though he was still resigned to going out on Jean-Louis's flight the next day, and had been phasing in Richard to take over as musher for his team.

That afternoon our spirits got a huge boost when we hit our first "wild card," a firmly frozen lead that was headed our way. Actually it tended northwest, but we stayed on it for six hours, knowing that by clipping along at four miles per hour we were gaining on the Pole faster than if we had trudged along due north over pans and ridges. Richard calculated that, given this lead's bearing, we gained one mile north for each mile and three quarters of travel. It felt great to be on skis. The five pairs of Epoke 900s that we had were in big demand; we rotated them among us. The ice had a thick, velvety covering of frost formations known as "salt flowers." A lacy growth of condensed moisture anchored to salt crystals on the surface, these look like miniature white maple leaves or fern fronds. They shimmered with the slightest breeze, acting as prisms that set the surface aglow, twinkling in every color of the spectrum. "A carpet of Christmas lights," Paul called them.

We came to the end of the lead late in the day, and camped on a large pan. Paul's sun shot said we were just above 86 degrees, meaning that we were twenty-four miles closer to the Pole than we had been that morning. "An awesome day," Richard noted; "we really rushed toward the Pole." In the tent that day, Mantell divvied up his spare clothing among team members in need. And he distributed his remaining stash of personal rations—some boxes of pilot biscuits. Having something crisp to eat after weeks of mush was pure ecstasy.

Our three-in-a-bag system became increasingly comfortable. Warmed by three rather than one source of heat each night, we spent much less time shivering when we climbed in. Nonetheless, the middle person slept the least soundly. Unless extra clothes were tucked tightly between us, frigid air would sweep down both sides of that person. In Tent Two, Ann, being the shortest, was sandwiched between Brent and Paul, appropriately the two married men in our crew. We joked about whether the people following our journey through media coverage would look askance at that formation. Geoff's response: "At forty below, even the thought of sex is repulsive."

The sardine-tin quarters led to some interesting adaptations. After just a few nights we had learned to roll over like dominoes, without disturbing anyone. But it was taking a bit longer to get used to everyone's sleeping quirks—we had cooers, moaners, and scratchers. Geoff and Brent were our two heavyweight snorers. The rest of us would "race" to sleep in hopes of reaching dreamland before the rasping started. Ann found herself snuggling close to Brent each night. His side of the bag was drier and less aromatic. Only two or three team members had turned ripe as a result of our lack of bathing for two months, and Paul was one of them. He was a marked man; his pee bottle had leaked and marinated part of his polar suit.

The night before, our tight sleeping quarters had resulted in a rude awakening for Ann. Tent Two's alarm had gone off at midnight, the prescribed time for briefly switching on our SAR-SAT beacon, which would give Jean-Louis's resupply pilot a backup set of coordinates for tomorrow's flight, on which Mantell would be leaving. This small orange box gave us no information, but it would provide our base camp with a means of locating us in the event of an emergency. Ann slept with it tucked alongside her to warm the batteries. When the alarm sounded, Brent sat upright and began reaching and tugging near Ann. Paul was soon awakened by Ann's insistent questioning: "Brent, what are you doing? What's going on here? Hey, why are you doing that?"

Paul, assuming that Ann was in a half-stupor and didn't realize Brent was merely trying to reach the SARSAT, encouraged him. "Go ahead, Brent, don't worry, Ann's not quite awake yet," he said.

"Yes, I am!" she hollered back, annoyed as Brent intensified his efforts. "Brent's the one in a stupor. He's trying to pull my face off!" Half asleep, Brent had been absentmindedly tugging on the sleeping hood Ann pulled tightly over her face each night, confusing it with the beacon.

DAY 40

"I CAN'T STAND THE SUSPENSE OF THE NEXT TEN DAYS."

The cloud cover changed dramatically on the morning of Day 40, another sign of advancing spring. For the first time in the journey, the sun was darting in and out among pillowy cumulus clouds. The cloud cover previously had been either fog, haze, or stratus clouds. As wave after wave of shadow swept across the surface, the snow and ice took on a new, gentler, less threatening quality. It seemed almost park-like.

Paul led us across a freshly frozen lead that meandered through the pans like a creek. It was quite thin, but we had become increasingly cavalier about such hazards. Fortunately, we had had just enough close calls to keep us on our toes when we needed to be. We had one this morning. The back of my sled, the *Bria,* punched through a narrow strip of wafer-thin ice hidden by drifted snow. I shouted for help as the back of the sled began sliding into the sea. Geoff ran up and gave it the herculean thrust needed to get it back on safe ice.

We made easy miles in pleasant country all morning. But just after noon, reality struck again. Ahead loomed a wall of pack ice nearly as big and brutal as the Great Wall through which we had entered the pack ice at Drep Camp. We knew we'd find no landing strips once we entered that maze, so we parked on a pan along the edge of the wall and waited for Jean-Louis's plane. It arrived at 3:30, carrying *National Geographic* photographer Jim Brandenburg and a KSTP television camerawoman. Once again it was time for the "dog and pony show," and we obligingly maneuvered our sleds through a small clump of rubble ice near the plane while they shot film.

Paul and I cornered Jean-Louis's business manager, who was also on board. We explained that we anticipated needing to share his next flight, scheduled for April 26, to send out more dogs and, quite possibly, people. Yes, he replied, something could be arranged, and he offered us hot coffee from his thermos. We declined, though the aroma was absolutely beguiling, and explained that we could accept nothing that had come in on the plane. He stared at us in quizzical disbelief. "My, but you're committed to your plan," he said. "We sure are," I responded, and then walked over to help Mantell load his things on the plane.

His departure seemed unreal. Our minds were numb to it, or perhaps we blocked it out. There was a round of hugs, but the grieving had taken place on the trail and in the tents as each of us prepared to lose another teammate. Yesterday it had struck me hard, as intensely as the death of a close friend. Ann had been in a somber mood the past few days. Before the trip, a friend had advised her to reach out and form a close relationship with two team members. The two she had selected were now gone. The trip was becoming increasingly lonely for her.

Since making his decision at Desperation Camp, Mantell had not faltered. Today, in an instant, he entered the world of warm feet, where the healing process would have a chance. Though the physical struggles would end, he would face many lingering mental ones as he reconciled his involvement in the expedition and its impact on him. I knew he would face that challenge with the same patience and steady determination with which we had tackled every obstacle along the trail.

We learned later that the flight made one more stop—to pick up Ran Fiennes and company a hundred miles out from shore, about half as far as we were. They had experimented with a system for man-hauling sleds to the Pole. Ran, like Mantell, had succumbed to severely frostbitten feet.

The intense pack ice stretched for two miles. We camped on a smooth pan just beyond it, having made twelve miles. For Paul and me, our stint in the big rubble was a very sobering experience. It reminded us that the polar sea is indeed unpredictable, but it left Ann and Richard undaunted. They no longer considered the assault-team plan a viable option—no matter what surprises the polar sea might have in store for us. Unknown to Paul and me, Geoff and Brent had been swayed as well. They knew, however, that if Paul and I deemed it necessary, we would insist on that plan, and they felt anxious about who if anyone might carry on to the Pole. Richard noted in his diary, "I can't stand the suspense of the next ten days!"

Some of them seemed to be lobbying us subtly, dropping occasional hints as to why one or another would be the best candidate. The issue continued to trouble Paul and me as well, and was the subject of hours of soul-searching. The symbolism factor, the constituency that each team member represented, was our primary consideration. Logistically, having a third person on the assault team offered no advantage; two people could travel more efficiently. Thus the skills of a third person were of minor concern. No clear choice had yet emerged in our minds. The tension was creating a discernible rift between us and the others. Over dinner that evening, Paul felt estranged from his tentmates. Relations were a little uneasy in my tent as well. The moment was ripe for open dissension. The thought frightened me. After mulling it over long and hard, I came to the conclusion that, since the issue was pulling the team apart, the best move would be to drop the third slot. That would help relieve tensions and, more important, it might just get us all to the Pole; the thirty-two-pound bag of rations reserved for that person could be used to beef up our dogs' meals for the next week or so. And that, I reasoned, might just be the edge we'd need to keep them well maintained, so that, come April 26, we could dispense with the fourth flight and keep on going.

DAY 41

"WE'VE HIT THE WILD CARD!"

As we prepared to launch our sleds in the morning, I called a meeting to present this proposal. It was time to take another big gamble, I said. Why hang on to food for a person whose role would be largely symbolic, when we can feed it to the dogs and boost the odds that we'll all make it? The proposal backfired. As Paul noted in his diary, "the shit hit the fan." Rather than offering relief, the notion of dropping the third slot left them all feeling as if we were pulling the rug out from under them. Brent and Ann were angry. Richard was incensed. Even the soft-spoken, easygoing Geoff was agitated, telling us that he was now "desperate" to get to the Pole. Richard, as usual, didn't mince words. "The plan stinks," he said emphatically. "No way will I get on that plane." Then he dropped the bomb, contending that the proposal was merely a thinly disguised "Steger-Schurke plot" for putting just two people on the Pole. He insisted that we dump the assault-team plan and pull all of the reserve rations "out of the bank."

Defending the proposal, Paul told them we would do everything we could to get all of us to the Pole. But we weren't about to go for bust with all six of us. He pointed out that although they had all invested a tremendous amount of time and effort in this project and had much to gain if we succeeded, they didn't have a lot at stake if we failed. Unlike us, they would not be held accountable by the press or our creditors. Paul and I had our careers on the line, as well as our financial futures. If we didn't reach the Pole, we'd face nearly $100,000 in debts, with no residuals—no book, no lectures, no film—to pay them off.

We talked it out at length and decided to hang tight for another day or so before making changes. We did agree to turn over all our own pemmican rations to the dogs. Brent, a diehard meat-eater, found that decision unsettling. "I should have known that these granola heads would want to try going to the North Pole on noodles and oats," he quipped in his journal.

Heavy drifts and a succession of old eroded ridges gnawed at our pace that day. Richard experimented with man-hauling, slipping a spare harness over his head and falling in step with the dogs. Out in front, scouting, Geoff became increasingly frustrated as we seemed to get deeper and deeper into a maze of intersecting ridges. Late in the afternoon he veered steadily east of north for no discernible reason. We all knew that sometimes a scout just follows a hunch when hemmed in by ridges. Nonetheless, we all tended to be "backseat drivers" from time to time, second-guessing the scout's choice of alleyways. And as we watched Geoff head off track, the comments started to fly. He climbed a huge pinnacle of ice, scanned the horizon, and began frantically waving his arms, signaling Paul and me to join him. We scrambled atop the forty-foot lookout. We could hardly believe our eyes. Just a little farther to the east was a huge refrozen lead that stretched northward endlessly.

"We've hit the wild card!" Paul shouted. "That looks as wide and long as the Amazon River."

The others, too, came to have a look and join the celebration, howling with glee.

"Now, how'd you know this was over here to the east?" I asked Geoff.

"I don't know, I just felt it," he said, shrugging his shoulders. This wasn't the first time we'd sensed that Providence was working with us. It seemed that our prayers and those of our supporters back home were always answered at critical moments.

We hurried the sleds onto the foot-thick highway of smooth ice and rumbled northward at a swift gait, four to five miles per hour. Most of us jogged along, some skied, a couple were even able to catch a ride from time to time. "My screaming feet rejoiced," Ann commented in her journal. Richard and Paul, strutting their stuff on skis, would spin an occasional donut on sections of glare ice. Several miles along, we were stymied by a twelve-foot-wide rift of open water. We reconnoitered in both directions and found a spot where it narrowed to eight feet. With a long jump, Richard vaulted the crack. I pulled my team up to the brink, tied a long lead to Chester's harness, and pitched the end to Richard. My dogs were petrified, but we knew that a short swim on a balmy −15-degree day would do them no harm. As I eased the sled forward, Richard pulled the team along. One by one the dogs, hitched along a central gangline, would plop into the water and begin frantically flailing their legs. Anxious to escape this hazard once they were up on the far side, they each gave a quick shake and pulled more powerfully than I'd ever seen them do before. With the dual bursts of power from front and back, the sled planed across the water without deflecting down more than a few inches.

Mantell's team, which was now being driven by Richard most of the time, was brought across in the same way. But Brent's team, with its fan hitch, required a different technique. He brought his sled up to the edge, thus giving each dog twenty or more feet of slack line. The braver ones willingly hopped in and swam the gap. But a few needed extra encouragement—in the form of a toss. Cradling them in his arms, Brent heaved them forward toward someone waiting to help them up on the far side. Chocolate, our bravest, most spirited Eskimo dog, was always keen to leap cracks. He vaulted headlong for the far side, but his skittish fellow team members cowered back, snaring his line. With his jump cut short, he plunged into the drink and swam back for another try.

Ann was the last to cross. She eyed the water nervously, mindful of her recent dunking and skeptical about whether she would make the distance with her short leg span. Brent and Geoff, with arms outstretched, braced themselves along the edge to catch her if she fell short. After several practice runs, she bolted for the crack and hurled herself across. Thrusting her clenched fists upward like an Olympic medal winner, she danced about and laughed. We all savored her victory.

We encountered a few more similar gaps as we moved along, but they only served to hone our skill in what was becoming a sport for us—the "polar crack-jumping competition." At ten that evening we hit a huge island of old ice. It appeared to pinch off the lead, but we couldn't be sure without some scouting. I suggested we camp on this stable floe.

Some of the team members, reveling in our fast pace, were keen to continue on well into the night. "Who knows what kind of weather tomorrow will bring?" Geoff argued.

"Wait a minute," I said. "Let's not push our luck with the dogs." We had clocked twenty miles that day. "By resting them now, they'll be fresh."

In the tents that evening, the day's victories were tempered a bit by wounds festering from the morning's heated meeting. Between Paul and me and our tentmates, the "us/them" mentality prevailed. Richard's barbed accusation had stung deeply. It would take a while to forgive and forget his contention that there was a "Steger-Schurke plot." "Yesterday I felt like Ann and Brent were shutting me out," Paul wrote. "Well, tonight I'm shutting them out." Ann noted, "Will and Paul give me the feeling that I'm going out in eight days." No doubt the tensions were in part attributable to tent fever, the irritations that develop from rubbing shoulders in tight quarters every night for weeks. In my tent, we were having a running spat over the serving up of our pemmican. It seemed to me that the cook was always getting the lion's share. "Preposterous!" was Richard's response in his diary. To eliminate cause for suspicion, we now dished out our own portions. Despite these tensions, the day had left me cautiously optimistic about our chances of getting everyone to the Pole. With a few more days like this one, I thought, we will turn the corner toward success.

Our tent felt a bit lonely after Mantell's departure, just as Paul's had after McKerrow left. The comforting bulge of the Science Diet dog-food can that Mantell would prop up as his stool between my sleeping bag and the tent wall was conspicuously absent. Having traveled thousands of miles with me on previous expeditions, he had come to be my sounding board for ideas about trail strategy; it was a bit unnerving to reckon with the fact that we would have to carry on without his quiet wisdom. Nonetheless, we enjoyed having a little extra elbow room in our tight quarters. And by adding his rations to ours, we knew we could now stretch out our time on the trail a few extra days, which might give us a better chance of reaching the Pole.

Most often, we tried not to think about the loss of two team members. To minimize mental anguish, we tended to block out our emotions on the trail. When Mantell departed, most of us stifled our intense feelings of sorrow, pretending that they didn't exist. That response seemed almost instinctive. But his absence strengthened our determination to reach our goal, giving us a second wind and an added purpose for this journey. My sadness over the departure of the man with whom I had conceived the expedition was to hit hardest in a few weeks, when we stood at our goal. Later, when he would greet us upon our return to Minnesota, I'd find it difficult to talk with him, to express the pain I felt that destiny had prevented him from accomplishing a dream we had shared. Yes, he'd tell me, of course it hurt not to have been standing there with us, but he felt no regrets. The experience had been a positive one for him. He had approached it with an open mind, knowing it held no guarantees, and had learned much about himself in the process. He viewed success as a process and not as a destination. Thus, through his contributions to the project, he'd accomplished much in which he took great pride.

DAY 42

"SOMETHING CLICKED: WE ARE ALL GOING TO THE POLE."

The morning brought another dose of "reality therapy." We awoke to an ominous scene, a thick whiteout. Our only hope for traveling through the skim-milk haze was if the lead continued due north beyond the island, providing a discernible trail. Paul and Richard set out on skis to scout. The rest of us nervously awaited their report, knowing that an unplanned layover day would put the assault-team plan back in the forefront. They returned a few hours later with glorious news: the highway continued north, and the sun was steadily burning through the heavy, low-lying clouds. At that moment, something clicked: We were all going to the Pole. In an instant our petty feuds were dropped, replaced by a wondrously refreshing sense of team unity. Ceremoniously pulling the reserve rations "out of the bank," we did a quick inventory and set up a new feeding schedule for ourselves and the dogs. We were playing for keeps. The team would no longer have to harbor anxieties over when and how the decision might be made to send some of them back.

Day 42 seemed like pure magic. We had fast, downright joyous travel. On top of that, the weather cleared. Under clear, calm skies with −20-degree temperatures, we clocked over thirty miles. The lead carried on for fifteen miles, but the wind-packed snow on the smooth pans that followed made for equally good travel. That lead, it seemed, had brought us into a zone of older, smoother, more stable ice. It was noticeably different from what we had seen at 85 degrees. The surface was no longer covered with coarse, grating, dehydrated snow.

Later that day we hit another frozen lead, stretching nearly five miles northward, and then more smooth surface. During the last three hours of the day, the dogs kept the sleds clipping along as fast as we could ski. We now felt ourselves firmly planted on the map, back on the road to success. The key was that the equation between our steady drop in payload weight and the work capacity of our dogs had evened out. They were no longer taxed beyond their abilities. Thus they could carry on day after day for twelve or more hours at a stretch without needing long rests and constant help from us. For the first time, the sleds were riding over every obstacle without stopping.

While planning the expedition, I felt this would be the key to the strategy, that the sled loads would eventually taper off and the dogs would steadily pick up the pace. I had envisioned that we would hit this point at about 86 degrees. But as we neared the end of the eighty-fifth degree a week earlier, our severe payload problems and the devastating reality of soft snow, leads, and rough ice had all suggested that the plan was mistaken. For a time, I had indeed given up any hope of getting all of us to the Pole. Our unsupported attempt had suddenly seemed impossible. This led to the scene at Desperation Camp, where we jettisoned 300 pounds of precious gear. And it did something else, something that Paul and I hadn't been able to do: it planted a burning desire in each of the other members to be among those who would reach the Pole. They now had a sense of ownership in the expedition. We all knew that as leaders, Paul and I had our tickets paid for. Barring health problems, we would be on the final dash. If we opted for three persons, that meant only one ticket was left. We were riding such a delicate edge between success and failure that only our strong human spirit would get us to the top. Lucky breaks and strong dogs would no longer do it.

That evening I noted in my journal, "The spirit that now resides with our team is fantastic. It seems the dogs have generated some of it; they ran excited all day. The end is finally over the horizon. The doldrums of the first forty-two days and the crisis on Day 36 [Desperation Camp] are now behind us. The hard times revealed character good and bad in all of us, and forged character for the positive."

On this day, Paul and I traveled together and talked business. For the first time we allowed ourselves to project beyond the Pole. We entertained thoughts of success and wondered how we would respond to it. Climbing a ridge to scout, Paul was mesmerized by a spectacular vista. "A hazy sun shone through huge plates of baby blue sea ice that dotted the landscape in every direction. Like a cathedral lined with stained glass windows," he wrote.

THE SEVENTH WEEK

THE FINAL
DASH

DAY 43

"DON'T YOU THINK THIS IS A BIT PREMATURE?"

Conditions remained favorable the next day. Geoff noted, "The trip is actually quite enjoyable now. I wouldn't trade some moments of the last couple of days for anything I've ever done." We made twenty miles before the dogs began to play out. The last two hours found us in rough ice, but with lightened sleds the ridges were now much easier to negotiate.

Diarrhea drained much of my strength again that morning. I was weak all day, and toward the end I began hallucinating from exhaustion. I felt thankful to have managed to march another full day despite the weakness and agonizing stomach cramps. I can usually push a ten-hour march regardless of my condition, but if I had felt this bad earlier in the trip, with the worst weather, it would have been devastating. Fortunately, the dogs now required little assistance from us to keep the sleds moving. We just had to slog along behind the sleds. Many of the team members were now on skis, but I found skiing more painful than walking. In these situations I felt obliged to continue setting an example for the group, despite the pain I was in. That compounded my stress. "I will be very glad to be free again," I commented in my journal, "and out from under the scrupulous microscope of group expectations."

When Paul's sun shot placed us inside of 87 degrees that day, we were ecstatic; it meant we had crossed a degree of latitude in three days. At that rate, with three degrees to go, we expected to reach the pole in just over a week, barring another setback. During a lengthy radio check that evening, Paul made the fateful announcement: "No third plane. I repeat, no third plane. We're all going for the Pole." He told Jim Gasperini that the weather had suddenly turned "warm"—for the last three days, temperatures had hovered around −15 degrees—but that we had seen minimal sign of ice movement so far. And he added that since we were putting in longer and longer days, he would have time for perhaps only one more radio check. From now on we would turn our satellite beacon every day at noon, rather than every four days. Thus the media could track our progress during stretches of silence. "Call it our 'countdown to the Pole,' and have the media track it on a daily basis," Paul suggested to Jim. Our signal for indicating that we thought we had reached the Pole would be to turn the beacon on at midnight, he added.

"Don't you think this countdown is a little premature?" Jim responded. "Uh, I mean you have a few hundred miles to go yet. Maybe we should wait a few days before suggesting that you're nearing the end."

Paul's tent crew was taken aback by this comment. Why didn't Jim share our optimism? Did he know something we didn't? Jim was privy to polar ice and weather information provided by satellites and pilots. But to share any of that information with us was ruled out as representing a form of "support."

Moments later, a new but familiar voice joined this radio conversation. Paul recognized it as that of Hans Weber, Richard's father. An Arctic scientist, he had just arrived at an ice research station and had intercepted Paul's transmission. Paul's crew excitedly called Richard over to their tent to talk with his dad. Hans commented that we would soon be crossing the Lomonosov Ridge, a huge underwater mountain range that bisects the central Arctic Ocean. Some researchers contend that the ridge seems to impact surface currents. In certain years the ice in the area above the ridge has been particularly badly broken. Hans commented that we should be careful in this area; there might be some trouble there. As he began to elaborate, Jim, listening in from his Resolute base, interrupted the conversation. "I'm sorry, but I don't think it's appropriate to be passing this information on to them," he told Hans. What information? Was this a second veiled warning of trouble ahead? We signed off for the night with our enthusiasm dampened a bit. We wouldn't find out the bizarre significance of his radio message until several days later.

DAY 44

"SURE ENOUGH, THE NEXT MORNING, WE HIT A
SERIES OF SPLINTERED LEADS AND WARM, MISTY
WEATHER. IT ALMOST FELT DRIZZLY OUT."

As we traveled on the next morning, the curious exchanges over
the radio seemed to take on added significance. Sure enough, we
soon hit a zone of badly splintered ice. Time and again we had
to detour or backtrack to find a way northward through the
maze of cracks. The sky was clear, but a very heavy mist hung
over the ice, adding to our sober moods. For the past three days
we had basked in optimism, starting to think and plan for the
end. The ominous, fog-enshrouded, bronze-colored leads that
threaded among the baby blue ice hinted that the pack might be
yielding to the longer, warmer days of spring. "In my delirious
fatigue from little sleep," Paul wrote, "I imagined them as ser-
pents hissing steam, slithering out across the ice, attempting to
stop us cold." Indeed they could. We still had more than 150
miles to go, I reminded myself. The advancing season could
bring disaster and disappointment such as none of us had ever
experienced, radically affecting the destiny of the six people who
were chattering pleasantly about home, family, friends, and food
as we skied and walked. These leads offered a stern warning:
never preconceive—keep your thoughts in the present. For the
past few days we'd been tempted to think that nothing could stop
us now. The ridges we encountered were just minor inconve-
niences. And the dogs were holding up well, a little tired and
hungry, but we felt they could carry on for a few days until we
reached 88 degrees, where we would rest them. We'd been pushing forward with ample momentum. Late that day we were

stopped by a small lead and opted to set camp along its shore, hoping that it would close or refreeze overnight. All around us was a huge fracture zone. It seemed we had struck a pocket of very active ice.

DAY 45

"AH, I CAN TASTE PIZZA."

We set a new record the next morning; we were out the tent doors and loaded, ready to go, in thirty minutes. Unfortunately, the lead along which we were camped had widened to about ten feet during the night. It took an hour to build a bridge of ice blocks over which we could cross. We traveled along on young ice under great pressure, riddled with small leads. The pans were slowly moving. The afternoon brought a grand adventure. We encountered a thirty-foot open lead that veered to the northeast. Hoping to find a point where it was pinched off so that we could cross, we traveled along the edge of it for miles, but were stopped when it swung sharply to the east. It appeared we had run out of options. But then our eyes fixed on a cake of ice fifteen feet across that was floating lazily in the lead near the turn. That, we knew, would be our answer. It seemed to have been placed there by Providence. Brent reached out and prodded it with the harpoon he carried as a probe. The block was very buoyant. Paul and Richard hopped on board and, using our snow shovel as a paddle, maneuvered it to the far side, where Richard disembarked to anchor a rope. Then, tugging on the lines, we hauled the block back and loaded one team of dogs and a sled on board. Ann and I trained our cameras on this frozen ferryboat as it shuttled back and forth, bobbing gently but amply supporting our loads. Charged with adrenaline, we all found the episode to be great fun. But the technique wasn't our brainstorm; we had learned it from Peary's accounts. We marveled at the thought that the scene we were now capturing on film was virtually identical to pictures that appear in his books.

Beyond that lead, the ice became somewhat firmer—a zone of old pans with massive ridges. With our lightened loads, we were able to negotiate these walls with little difficulty. Richard noted that before the trip "we thought the ice would get boring, but it never does." The endless variety in surface conditions never ceased to amaze us. But for me the day was filled with drudgery. Diarrhea weakened me considerably. I fought to turn my mind off to the pain of aching legs and stomach cramps. I had been able to digest only four full meals in the past nine days. Fortunately, I was sleeping soundly each night. This rest was preventing my health from totally crumbling. I was counting on the layover day at 88 degrees to recharge me. Ann, too, was having a hard time and wrote, "Maybe I've just had it. With stepping in hidden cracks up to my crotch, with these people, with cold hands, with dogs that are pooped. Maybe I'm at my breaking point."

Of our three dog teams, mine was holding out the best. The Siberians had proven their superiority over the Eskimo dogs for speed; Brent's team was being regularly outdistanced. Richard's team had been keeping up with mine, but was showing signs of winding down. Critter's spirits seemed to be flagging. On two occasions that day, he had stopped abruptly and lain down for a nap.

That evening our meal had a subtle but welcome change in flavor. Richard mixed sea water into our pemmican stew to add a bit of saltiness. Ever since depleting our meager spice kits, we had been searching for ways to vary our monotonous menu. Geoff discovered a pinch of oregano in the bottom of an empty food bag. He mixed it into his stew, took a bite, then leaned back, closing his eyes, and said, "Ah, I can taste pizza!"

DAY 46

"WE TRAVELED TO WHAT WE GUESSED WAS 88 DEGREES. PAUL WAS PRETTY EXCITED. I EVEN GOT A KISS FROM HIM."

The temperature edged down a bit the next day, to −25. Colder weather came as a relief. It would help forestall the breakup. Paul's noon sun sighting placed us at 87°49′. We stopped in the early evening, having made more than twenty miles in nine hours, at a point we guessed to be just beyond 88 degrees. As we parked our sleds, Brent let out a resounding howl, Paul planted a big kiss on Ann's frostbitten cheek, and we shared a round of backslaps and handshakes. To celebrate the victory, we divvied up an extra half-ounce of cheese to everyone. We were entering our last two degrees of latitude, the circle enclosing the Pole that historically has represented the home stretch for polar explorers. It was from this position in 1909 that Peary had launched his final dash, claiming to have hit the target six days later after five 10-to-12-hour marches. The mileage he recorded during this dash—twenty-five to forty miles during each march—is the center of the controversy that surrounds his claim. His detractors insist that to go that far in a day on sea ice is impossible. *But is it?* I wondered. During our training journey across the Beaufort Sea, we had regularly gone that far, and on our best day we had dogsledded and skied sixty-eight miles in thirteen hours. The ice conditions were better, but our payload weights were comparable to those we had now. Peary's strategy ensured that his final dash team—six people and twenty-six dogs—was relatively well rested and well fed when it left 88 degrees. At this point our crew, I'm sure, was less vigorous than his had been. We were very curious as to how we would do on our final dash. Could we maintain daily marches of two to three dozen miles during the next week?

DAY 47

"IN MY BAG WAS $200. . . . NOW IT LOOKED AS THOUGH THE CASH MIGHT HAVE A PURPOSE."

We slept late the next morning, and then my tent crew enjoyed a leisurely two-course breakfast. As Richard explained in his diary, "First we sat around with a frozen lump of peanut butter in one hand and a lump of butter in the other, and munched our way through those. Then came oatmeal." Our conversation, he added, centered on food and things we would like to do, "like sit on a porcelain toilet." I fasted, to give my bowels a chance to rest. Meanwhile, Paul attempted to get a noon sighting to confirm our position, but found his series of readings to be disturbingly inconsistent. Calculating our position as best he could, he placed us within a couple of miles of 88 degrees, but wondered whether a problem was developing with the sextant.

While the rest of us dismantled and chopped up the *O'Donnell,* Brent and Paul tightened the lashings on the *Crystal* and the *Bria,* taking special care with these North Pole–bound sleds. In midafternoon we crawled into my tent for a final team popcorn party. The camaraderie we enjoyed was the best our team had ever experienced. We could almost taste victory.

During our party, I enjoyed some bartering with my teammates. Days earlier I had come to the conclusion that carbohydrates, and sugar in particular, would solve my digestion problem. Unfortunately, being into immediate gratification, I had long ago used up my personal stash of brown sugar. But in camp yesterday I had spotted a source. While I was walking past Richard's open duffel bag, my eyes fell upon what looked like a pot of gold—a fist-sized pile of barley-sugar hard candies. The sight dazzled me; my mouth watered. I was amazed at the incredible willpower it must have taken for him to hang on to these treats for this long. Then another thought struck me. In my bag was $200. I had brought the cash and a deck of cards along in hopes of passing the hours playing blackjack during layover days. (Unknown to me, no one else had brought any money.) I had jettisoned the cards weeks before to save weight. Now it looked as though the cash might have a purpose. Perhaps I could interest Richard in it. He was a student, I reasoned, and students are always short of cash. Last night I flashed a fifty in front of him for the whole bag. "I'll think about it," he said. Now, during our party, he suddenly plopped the bag in my lap. "Deal closed," he announced with a smile. Richard and I shook hands over the best investment I had ever made. I couldn't believe my good fortune. What a bargain! I would easily have paid $100 for the candies. Now that I was on a roll, I went after other treats lingering in personal food stashes. From Ann I secured two ounces of brown sugar for ten dollars. And Geoff sold me four Shaklee Energy Bars for five dollars each. Gloating over my pile of new possessions, I felt like a rich man, as though I had won big at cards. I now held all the bargaining power in camp, though we had precious little else worth trading for. The sugar would put my plumbing back on track, and the candies would give me hours of pleasurable sucking along the trail. Furthermore, the bartering had added much mirth to our party.

Paul was up nearly all night, struggling with reception problems on the radio. This would be our last communication with

the base camp until we reached our goal or, God forbid, were
stopped by some obstacle. Jim informed us that if we reached the
top, *National Geographic* wanted to break the news first. Thus,
when we got within ten miles, we were to set off our beacon. That
would give the magazine's news bureau a few hours' time to file
the report. He also asked us what brand of champagne we
wanted to have sent along. "The best," said Paul, "the very
best."

DAY 48

"THE LEAD BEGAN TO OPEN. WE HAD DOGS ON ONE
SIDE AND THE SLED ON THE OTHER. . . ."

We launched our dash at 6:30 the morning of April 24. A few
hundred yards from camp, we crossed a huge ridge, and before
us stretched flat ice as far as we could see. Our dogs sprinted
along. We all laughed and joked as we ran behind, trying to keep
up. Though it was only —20 degrees, my fingers were still very
susceptible to the cold, and stung most of the time. The tips were
cracked and bleeding from frost damage. What I longed for most
was to be able to use my fingers without having them sting from
the cold. My feet were fine; I was having no problem keeping
them warm night or day. But I was feeling terribly weak. Though
I was now taking medication for diarrhea, my legs were so numb
with exhaustion that I hardly had any sensation from the waist
down. My body, it seemed, had begun digesting itself for nourishment. How easy this march would have been for me if I had
been in good health, I thought. The immense concentrations of
fat in our diet were doubtless the culprit. My body was rejecting
them. We should have had a larger proportion of carbohydrates,
especially for the latter half of the trip, when our bodies had
acclimated and the temperatures had risen a bit. Digestive problems troubled all the team members from time to time, but only
Brent and I had been debilitated by them. My case was by far
the most severe. Because of this plight, the journey was a much
more agonizing experience for me than for the others. But there
was a reward for this: I gained a deeper understanding of the
frailty of the human body and I felt greater empathy for people

the world over for whom hunger and ill health are daily facts of life.

Early in the afternoon, we hit a tricky gap. It was filled with ice rubble that looked deceptively firm but, like quicksand, would collapse if you applied any weight to it. "To fall into that kind of ice is one of my most dreaded nightmares," Geoff noted. "If you plunged through, you could fight your way up to the surface but you would still be under the ice." At one spot a fairly large block nearly bridged the gap. We used it as a raft, but in crossing, we had a close brush with disaster. Geoff's journal picks up the story: "Will's team went over first. We got the dogs across and were pushing the sled up onto the block when everything shifted. The lead began to open. We had dogs on one side and the sled on the other with the lines in between. Something had to give. The lines were stretched taut when the ice stopped moving. That saved us for the time being, but we suddenly had an eight-foot stretch of open water. Fortunately no one fell in, but we were pretty much committed by then, so we got the dogs all revved up, gave a big push, and sent the sled rocketing over the edge. It crashed down half on the ice and half in the water. Everything stopped for a moment, but the dogs dug in and pulled the sled onto solid ice." In twelve hours we traveled twenty-five miles that day.

DAY 49

"WE'RE GETTING A BIT CAVALIER ABOUT CROSSING THIN ICE."

The weather remained clear and balmy—around −20 degrees— with a light south breeze. Paul had more difficulties with the sextant. The readings in his noon series varied by five miles or more, but he was getting a clear indication that we were well east of the seventy-fifth meridian. We were beginning to feel the effects of the Transpolar Drift Stream. Paul corrected our course 15 degrees to the west, with hopes of getting us back on track. We camped that night within 100 miles of the North Pole, having covered thirty miles, stopping at 89°6', just inside our last degree of latitude. One more day like this, I thought, and we can start feeling confident. But, I cautioned myself, these last sixty miles could be the longest miles of our lives. We camped in a zone of badly splintered ice; it was apparent the pack was beginning to disintegrate.

THE EIGHTH WEEK

THE
POLE

DAY 50

"THE WORLD IS COLLAPSING IN UPON ITSELF. . . ."

The next day we clocked thirty-five miles in twelve hours. Paul spent much time on the sextant, hoping to get a better handle on the speed of the eastward drift. Twice he corrected our course toward the west to compensate. Our bearing was now critical. To be a little off course early on hadn't mattered much. We could correct our bearing as we went. But now we had to be securely targeted for the Pole. If we were more than a few degrees off, it would cost us extra miles. The lines of longitude were drawing tightly together, now separated by only two miles. "The world is collapsing in upon itself—centering in on its navel!" Paul wrote.

DAY 51

"EVERYONE IS GETTING SORE FEET."

This was my first day of good health in three weeks. My new diet, heavy on sweets, seemed to be working. Walking felt effortless, though most of the other team members were now plagued by sore feet. Some of the dogs were languishing badly. Dillon, one of our Eskimo dogs, collapsed. He had been one of our strongest and most consistent pullers, but was now totally spent. Brent tied him in place in one of the sleds and gave him extra rations in the evening. We traveled thirteen and a half hours, our longest day yet, and covered thirty-five miles. The last five miles we skirted the shores of a huge refrozen lead, following it until it swung east. After that night's feed, we had forty pounds of pemmican left on the sleds, about two days' supply for the dogs. We were treading a very fine line—we had to count on good ice and good weather, but the challenge increasingly exhilarated us. "This trip exemplifies adventure at its very best," Geoff noted. "We start every day heading into the unknown. We deal with whatever comes along and push on. A person climbing a mountain knows what geological features he will run into. But the ice of the polar sea gets rearranged every year and we have no idea what we will encounter."

A thick haze settled in that night as we slept. Paul got up twice to take sun shots. With confusion mounting over the drift, he was determined to make certain we were on the right bearing the next day. His calculations were alarming. They suggested the ice had been shifting eastward up to eight miles. Caught off guard in this floe, we were now near the fiftieth meridian. This unsettling news meant we would have to "swim upstream" the next day, heading more west than north, to compensate for the drift.

DAY 52

"IF WE ATTEMPTED TO MAKE THE WHOLE DISTANCE IN ONE LONG SHOT, WE WOULDN'T HAVE TO STOP OVERNIGHT AND LOSE FOUR TO EIGHT MILES WITH THE ICE DRIFT."

We departed at noon, with the weather steadily clearing. As the haze lifted, we were treated to a marvelous spectacle. Four distinct parhelia or "sun dogs," reflections of the sun's image on ice crystals in the upper atmosphere, shimmered in each quadrant around the sun—above and below and on either side of it. They were connected by a rainbow-like ring of color that seemed to shine down hope upon us. We stopped to marvel at this celestial phenomenon.

After a ten-hour march, Paul's sun sight placed us at 89°32'. Just over thirty miles to go. We were charged with adrenaline.

We should have stopped and rested the dogs, but our excitement clouded our judgment. None of us felt ready to camp. Furthermore, we knew that if we slept, we'd be placing ourselves at the mercy of the Transpolar Drift Stream and would most likely awaken farther away from the Pole. We opted to continue on as far as our energies would allow. Five hours later, at 4:00 A.M. on April 29, we stopped for a break, putting up the tents and cooking a meal. The sextant placed us at 89°42', but Paul had little confidence in that fix. The sextant readings over the past few days had conflicted badly, leading to growing anxieties among the team members. We had learned to estimate our progress fairly accurately by dead reckoning—"guesstimating" mileage—but the progress indicated by the sun sights no longer coincided with these. Paul suspected something was amiss, but held out hope that he would eventually get a reading that offered some certainty.

DAY 53

"SOMETHING'S TERRIBLY WRONG."

After our dinner we agreed to carry on once more, leaving at 7:00 A.M. Four hours later we stopped again. Plagued by concerns over the sextant, Paul opted to take a long series of readings to determine the seriousness of the problem, which seemed to have grown progressively worse. The wind had freshened a bit and the temperature had dropped into the −20s. We collapsed on the leeward side of our sleds for a rest while he set up his instrument, an agonizing process in these weather conditions. First he pulled the sextant from its wooden case, mounted it on the ball joint lashed to the uprights of the *Bria,* and swung it into position. To prepare for each reading, he'd jump up and down and windmill his arms in wide circles to bring warmth and dexterity to his fingertips. The next step was to fish out from the sleeve of his polar suit an electric wire, fed by batteries stitched inside his longjohns to keep them warm, and plug it in to illuminate the bubble level in the sextant's artificial-horizon attachment. Then, with lens paper, he'd wipe away the frost that would continually collect on the viewfinder. It was now time to bare his fingers, leaving on only his wristlets, so he could make delicate adjustments on the thumb wheel. Crouching down, he'd squint into the eyepiece. When properly aligned, three things would appear: the sun, as a tiny amber disk filtered through dark lenses; the bubble, glowing dull red; and cross hairs affixed in the center of the viewfinder. Turning a pressure valve, he'd adjust the size of the bubble until it matched the size of the sun's disk. Then he'd gently maneuver the sextant and its thumb-wheel arc adjustment until the bubble and disk were superimposed and centered perfectly on the cross hairs. In this position, the graduated arc on the side of the sextant would now tell him the exact angle of the sun above the horizon to within two-tenths of a minute of arc.

Generally, after taking several such readings, he would retire to the tent to work through the formulas and charts that would turn the readings into our position fix. But on this day he was perplexed. After each reading he paced nervously about, deep in thought. We waited patiently, huddled together to stave off the chill. After twenty minutes of effort, he walked over to us and broke the news. The position fix placed us at the same latitude as the night before. "Something's terribly wrong," he said, downcast. "Either we are well off course or the sextant is malfunctioning." Our hearts sank. All he could do, he said, was to go over the instrument part by part in hopes of discerning the problem.

Helpless to assist Paul, we set camp and crawled into our bags while he continued working with the instrument. The hours passed slowly as Paul scrambled for solutions while the rest of us tossed and turned. Ironically, for the last several days we had been sending a daily position signal from our satellite beacon to our base camp so they could track us as we neared the Pole without waiting for radio reports. Thus our base camp staff knew precisely where we were. And so did the millions of people who were following the media coverage of our progress, which was also based on these signals. But we were in the dark, and Paul was baffled.

It was a horrible dilemma. With no means to guide us, though we knew we were nearing the Pole, we might as well have been back where we started. We were virtually cast adrift on 5 million square miles of sea ice. Would we be forced to call in for help? And I worried about the delay this problem might cause. We had been carefully metering our remaining food, and would only be able to stretch it for another day or two. Barring blizzards or huge leads, we had anticipated reaching the Pole on May 1. We and our dogs might possibly be able to carry on a few more days without food, but none of us was anxious to test that theory. I was concerned that the warming trend and breeze might bring a sudden end to the ice's stability. Mantell and I had been caught in the spring breakup while sledding on sea ice to reach Ellesmere in 1982, so I had experienced the sequence of events that dismantles the surface, and knew how quickly it could occur. First the plates shift slowly, exposing more and more seams of open water. In clear weather, the warming sun will evaporate the water and set up a thick fog. After a day or so the fog burns off, but then the heat of the sun, intensifying each day, generates an even thicker fog. The pattern repeats itself, with the stretches of clear weather growing shorter and periods of heavy fog lengthening.

That cycle was now upon us. We had experienced our first period of breakup fog, the haze that had enveloped our camp two nights before. With the sun disappearing for ever greater periods, navigation would become increasingly difficult, even if the sextant could be fixed. As a last resort, we knew we could have our base camp relay to us by radio the coordinates that our emergency beacon was transmitting to them; that could serve as our navigational backup. One of our goals, however, was to determine how accurately we could locate the Pole using only traditional navigational systems. Paul and I felt that to call for help would mean we had failed in that mission. Some of the other team members, growing anxious over the accuracy of the sextant readings, suggested that it might be best to confirm our position with help from the base camp before moving any farther. Given the drift of the ice, we knew we could easily be swept well off course and miss the Pole, unless we carefully realigned our course at frequent intervals. They wondered aloud about the value of continuing to rely on the sextant, now that questions had arisen about the accuracy of the readings. As Geoff said, hoping to convince Paul and me to use the emergency beacon, "Look, the sextant navigation is your thing. All I am interested in is reaching the Pole." But we held firm. The responsibility lay on Paul's shoulders to offer them some assurance that the sextant would get us there, and I had faith that he could do it. He and I had been in many similarly tight situations over the past several years, and had always pulled through.

Suddenly the heavy silence was broken by a roar overhead. We knew instantly that this meant the *Aurora* had arrived. Days earlier, Jim had reported from the base camp that this plane, a

Canadian military jet, would be on maneuvers over the polar sea on April 29 and would fly over us if we could be located. In the midst of this moment of anxiety, we now had a gleaming silver jet making pass after pass, swooping low over our camp to get aerial photographs. Well, I thought, at least we know that our emergency beacon is giving an accurate fix on our position.

Jim had told us that the pilot would tune into our radio's frequency as he flew overhead and make a courtesy call. So Paul set the sextant aside, hurriedly strung out some antenna wire, and flipped on our transceiver. "Good morning," boomed a crisp but friendly military voice over the speaker as the pilot gave us his call sign. Paul exchanged pleasantries with him for a few minutes, masking his stress and trying to sound cheery. "How are you guys doing?" the pilot asked. Paul paused before responding, mulling over in his mind the big question: Should we ask him where we are? It was looming in a few other minds in our tents as well. "What do you think?" he yelled over to us. We all knew what he was referring to. Geoff and Richard thought he should go ahead and ask. But the decision was really his alone, because only he could assess what our chances were of pulling ourselves out of this dilemma. Encouragement came from his tent crew as well to ask the pilot for a fix. The pilot repeated the question.

"Ah, well," Paul responded slowly into the mike, "we're having a little trouble with the sextant here. What are your position coordinates?"

"I'm sorry," the pilot replied, "but your base camp manager has instructed us not to divulge that information. In fact," he continued, "we had hoped to drop you a 'care package' with some sweets and fresh fruit, but he insisted that we not do that either." We shook our heads in amazement, pondering the very thorough job Jim had done to ensure that we'd stick to our own rules. He had plugged all the gaps through which outside support might leak in to us. The pilot, sensing the tension in Paul's voice, came on the radio again, commenting, "They told us you wouldn't accept any assistance from us. However, has that situation changed?"

Paul paused a moment before responding, reconsidering this chance for outside help, and then made the fateful decision alone. "No, sir," he responded, "we'll sort things out." The pilot wished us well and signed off as we listened to the jet turn southward, heading home. We gazed at each other in disbelief. Through the bizarre coincidence of the plane's arrival at the peak of our despair, our commitment to our goals had been put to the acid test. We'd faltered momentarily, but, given the chance to reconsider, had set our sights straight again.

Paul, continuing to search for flaws in the sextant, began to suspect that the problem might lie in the bubble attachment, a sealed housing enclosing mirrors, lenses, and a floating bubble used to establish a level horizon. Using a Swiss army knife, the only tool we had left after jettisoning our repair kit three weeks earlier, he removed the access cover from the side of the attachment. He had no idea what he was looking for. He had never seen the inside of a bubble attachment, but was hoping that something out of place might seem apparent. And it did. A glint of light from a speck of frost caught his eye. Looking closer, he saw frost wedged between one of the delicate mirrors and its tiny alignment screws. Euphoria swept over him as he identified the culprit.

The oil in which the bubble floated had become so thick in the cold that the bubble was very slow to settle into position, so Paul had made a habit of removing the attachment from the sextant and carrying it in the breast pocket of his polar suit to keep it warm. Moisture from perspiration had worked its way through the silicon seal around the attachment's housing. As the water vapor that condensed on the adjustment screws froze and expanded, it pushed against the mirror. Over time, enough pressure was applied that the mirror was jogged slightly out of position, thus leading to the conflicting readings.

He felt he had solved the problem, but he couldn't be certain until he readjusted the instrument and took a series of fixes to see if the readings remained consistent. For proper adjustment of the bubble attachment, the perfect straight-line horizon of an open ocean is needed. On this journey, every horizon we had seen, including the one surrounding this campsite, was interrupted by blocks of rubble ice. He estimated the true horizon and adjusted the instrument accordingly, hoping that somehow over the next days we would hit a stretch of perfectly flat terrain where he could do a better job before it came time to pinpoint the Pole.

For hours he was in and out of the tent, taking fixes and checking them against his charts. Lying in my bag, I heard a burst of nervous laughter coming from him every now and then, and figured he was on to something. But until I had thoroughly checked out the readings, he delayed filling us in on his progress, for fear of creating false hope. Some team members were growing impatient, feeling that Paul's efforts were futile and that he was merely stirring himself into a frenzy. His tentmate Brent, annoyed that his sleep was being interrupted by the commotion, offered his heavy caribou parka to Paul in hopes that he might stay outside between readings.

Few team members really understood the massive responsibility, stress, and extra hours of work Paul had taken on as navigator and radio man. A few nights before, Richard had grumbled that Paul's all-night efforts to get a radio message through to the base camp had cost him some sleep. Nor did they empathize with the extra stress I had taken on in tracking our inventory of supplies and laying out a travel strategy each day. My only major complaint about the other six was that they didn't seem to appreciate that, as leaders, Paul's responsibilities and mine didn't end after the workday was over and camp chores were done. Many nights he and I cut deeply into our allotted hours for sleep, mulling over logistics, working through equipment problems, or coming up with some fund-raising scheme, which we relayed home by radio, to stem the tide of mounting debts. Sometimes it seemed they felt that all that counted out here was how many hours each person was leaning into the back of a sled.

As I lay in my tent, confident that Paul would soon have our navigation dilemma solved, my thoughts turned to our friendship and partnership. So many times in the course of launching this project, he and I had hit crises and had worked ourselves ragged to find solutions. Each hurdle we crossed brought more satisfaction from testing ourselves to the limit and coming out on top, ever more confident of our abilities and proud of our partnership. Turning over in my bag, I heard him do a little dance for joy outside. I knew then that we were back on track, and reflected on how heavily the demands of this journey had called upon our resourcefulness. How fortunate I was not only to have had the opportunity of this project to test myself, but to have shared the experience fully with another person. The little dance Paul did outside represented for me a triumph of the human spirit. To experience moments like these was what had drawn us out here.

The team awoke from their rest that evening to the news that Paul felt certain he had solved our navigational dilemma. Some skepticism remained, but after four hours of sleep they were all willing to place trust in the readings—which put us thirty miles from the Pole but well east of the seventy-fifth meridian—and carry on. The skepticism was understandable. Now that our supplies had dwindled to but ten pounds of dog food and fifteen pounds of people food, we had no room for error. A day's travel on the wrong bearing would cost us the Pole. I placed complete faith in Paul's ability to steer us to 90 degrees north, and let go of the tensions of the past day, confident that we would hit the target—if we weren't stopped by a lead. And, close as we were, that was still a big *if.*

DAY 54

"WE ARE ALMOST OUT OF FOOD."

We pushed off at 1:30 in the morning of April 30. With the sun maintaining a near-constant angle above the horizon, daytime and nighttime hours no longer had any bearing on our travel. I went ahead and scouted a course through the pressure ridges to the north. Within a few hours the fog had thickened into a whiteout. We now had only our compass and the sastrugi (drift patterns), both only marginally reliable, against which to set a bearing. Richard had attempted to adjust the declination of the compass against the sun that morning, but having been rushed in his efforts by an advancing cloudbank, he cautioned us against relying heavily on the compass. I set off on the bearing he gave me, checking it continually against the drift patterns incised in the snow by the prevailing winds as best I could. Throughout our journey these were aligned southwest-northeast, thus when the sun was blocked we found we could head generally northward by cutting diagonally across their peaks. But in areas where ridges deflected the wind, as I was finding along this day's route, they were less well defined and often downright confusing. Furthermore, even if they had been sharply sculpted, I knew we were taking a risk in relying on them for a bearing this near to the Pole, because "generally northward" was no longer good enough. A few degrees' error in orientation would carry us miles wide of the mark and cost us many extra hours of travel.

As the hours went by, it became increasingly apparent that Richard's compass bearing could not be reconciled with the drift patterns. As we pressed on, we grew increasingly concerned about the accuracy of our course. The clouds were moving quickly, so we clung to the desperate hope that at some point we might be able to discern the sun's disk through the clouds and check our fix. Then for a fleeting moment Brent and Paul each thought they saw a faint shadow from their dogs flicker on the snow. They couldn't be sure—it lasted but an instant and the sun itself never appeared—but it alarmed them because the position of the shadow suggested we were indeed well off course. We waited, hoping the sun might reappear, and debated our predicament, attempting to forge some consensus about our bearing.

The clouds thickened. We were too concerned with making miles to give up and set camp, but decided to catch a quick nap while we were waiting. We stretched our sleeping bags out on the ice alongside the sleds and crawled into them. Hours passed. The heavy cloud cover had moderated the temperature a bit, but the light breeze washing over us kept us from getting a sound rest. Nonetheless, the scene illustrated how well our bodies had acclimated to the cold over the weeks we'd been living in it. We were reasonably comfortable, napping in −10-degree temperatures without a tent and with our heads outside the bags.

In the evening another heavy fog rolled in, and we decided that waiting was futile. It was time to set camp. We all fell into a deep sleep and dozed so soundly that none of us heard the commotion during the night. Some of the lines had broken loose and a few of the dogs had been able to reach the sled bags and do minor damage by chewing on some of the gear inside. Fortunately, we had taken all the food into our tents for added protection.

One of the bandits was Goofy, an Eskimo dog on Brent's team that belonged to Ken MacRury, the government administrator in Frobisher Bay who had so generously looked after our needs during our training. Ken had arranged for us to get various items of Eskimo clothing, including caribou mitts and sealskin pants and boots to supplement our synthetic gear. He had even loaned Richard his own pair of dog-fur mitts. Richard cherished these and carefully stowed them in his zippered sled bag every night. That morning, Richard found the sled bag open and his mitts gone. Goofy, roaming loose during the night, had caught wind of his master's scent and searched out the source. Eating the mitts represented a link with his home.

I had seen this behavior once before, when I was dogsledding up the Mackenzie River. Snow and weather conditions were terrible, and I was nearly out of food for myself and the dogs. One of my dogs was a young male, Buffy, who had recently been separated from his sister; I had left her with a trapper. I was now using her harness on Buffy, since his had become frayed. One morning I went to hook Buffy up to the sled, but couldn't find the harness. I knew I had left it in the snow near where he was sleeping, but all that lay there now was a steel ring. Later that day the case of the missing harness was solved when Buffy left behind on the trail an undigested mound of finely ground harness material. He had eaten his one remaining link with his sister.

All of the dogs were now completely famished, but their spirits were still good. Our dog-food supply was nearly exhausted, so to keep them going we had given up our own rations of pemmican, butter, and the nut-butter bars we ate for lunch. My dogs picked up on that cue as a sign that the journey was nearing its end. They had been conditioned on previous expeditions to know that when "people food" starts coming their way, a village or food cache of some kind lies just ahead.

Some might construe the hardships and deprivations the dogs endure on journeys such as this to be cruelty or abuse. But my dogs, like me, thrive on expeditions. Their lives, like my own, are fulfilled by the challenges such expeditions offer, and the chance to exercise their spirits to the fullest. Deprivations and physical hardships are an inescapable part of long Arctic treks for people and dogs. The dogs sense when we are hungry, tired, and cold. They know that our survival is closely linked with theirs. For me, the mystique of long treks by dogsled lies in this bond.

But that bond was also the source of one of the greatest heartbreaks we suffered on the journey. It occurred that night. Critter, Mantell's lead dog, died while we slept. He was a very special dog. Mantell was very fond of this short-haired, floppy-eared dog, who had become more of a pet than a work partner. He had picked up Critter from an Alaskan trapper in 1985, when he was dogsledding from Anchorage to Inuvik to meet us for our training journey. Although he was not a husky breed—he looked more like a German shepherd—his intelligence and high spirits made him a valuable asset on Mantell's team, and before long he worked his way up to lead position.

His only flaw was that he often followed his own whims on the trail, but, crossing the Yukon mountains and the Mackenzie River delta to Inuvik, Mantell trained him to be a first-rate lead dog. Like most Arctic cross-country dog team adventures, Mantell's trek proved to be a real Jack London–style adventure in which man and dog developed a deep sense of interdependency for their survival. Strong, lasting bonds developed between Mantell and his dogs and in particular with Critter. Critter's outgoing, exuberant demeanor contrasted sharply with Mantell's shy, quiet, easygoing manner. And the attention he received from Mantell for being top dog gave him a sense of mastery over the other dogs. He seemed to flaunt the fact that he, a skinny, thin-furred dog who looked as if he should be roaming alleys in some ghetto, was lead dog on one of the finest expedition teams in the north. Critter would strut with tail held high, anointing chunks of ice and any other vertical projections in his reach with his scent as he traveled along. Mantell had to check Critter's cocky attitude constantly so he would continue to respond to commands.

Critter's spirit and personality made people fall in love with him immediately. He craved attention from people, and would go out of his way to greet you. During our training, Critter stood out among all seventy of the dogs we were working with, and won the hearts of everyone. He was marked as a real character, oblivious to the fact that he looked terribly out of place among the thick-coated Eskimo dogs that were twice his size.

Shortly before he was airlifted out, Mantell discussed with me at length whether or not he should leave Critter behind for us to use. He was an exceptionally good lead dog who would obey several voice commands and could be a real asset to us. Because Richard had worked extensively with Mantell's dogs over the past five months, Critter responded well to his commands. Thus we decided that Critter should stay on after Mantell was airlifted out, since we needed him to lead Mantell's other dogs, and Richard would be able to drive that team. We also felt we needed Critter's spirit to keep the other teams fired up. He had proven to be an effective cheerleader among the other dogs.

We all saw Mantell's affection for Critter, but none of us was aware of how closely Critter was bonded to him. On the sad day that Mantell left, we all watched him tearfully bid goodbye to his dogs. He saved his last hug for Critter, and then turned and trudged toward the plane. Critter lunged forward after him with full power, dragging the whole team and the loaded sled behind. He managed to catch up with Mantell and brush his nose against his parka as he boarded the plane.

As we traveled on that next week, Critter gave no sign that his spirits were sagging. He worked to capacity every day, responding well to Richard's commands. And Richard did an admirable job of taking over someone else's team, which is a frustrating job even under the best conditions. Fortunately, Richard picks things up very fast and had gained the upper hand on Mantell's team within a few days. He, like Ann, who often handled my team, treated his adopted team with affection and compassion and the dogs responded quickly to this. Watching him drive Mantell's team deftly over rough pack ice bolstered my pride in him as a team member.

The day after our rest stop at 88 degrees, the first sign of Critter's depression became apparent. When we consolidated from three teams to two, he was placed on my team and was no longer a lead dog. That job was reserved for Chester. Critter seemed disheartened to have been demoted to a position in the back. There he would receive no special attention, nor would he enjoy the satisfaction of leading the charge and responding to commands. Furthermore, my dogs despised him. They had picked up on his cockiness early on. Once, during our fall training, he had picked a fight with them. Now it was obvious they held a grudge. The spite my dogs held for Critter, I think, was the crushing blow for him. He probably could have handled the heartbreaks of missing Mantell and being demoted, but to feel estranged by his new teammates was too great an additional strain. Their hatred eroded his spirit, without which he would falter, no matter how strong and fit he was.

Dogs are very similar to people in this regard. Our spirit can carry us through countless seemingly impossible tasks. On previous expeditions I have been caught in survival situations, out of food in subzero weather, where my spirit carried me through. To an observer, my survival may have looked impossible under the circumstances. But spirit, our driving power, cannot easily be accounted for or explained; it can only be felt. In our dogs I saw the same phenomenon. Exhausted and nearly starving on the trail, they drew upon their spirit to keep them going. And as we neared the Pole, it was bolstered by our enthusiasm, and they seemed to thrive. In fact, Chester grew stronger by the day, despite the meager rations all the dogs were now getting.

The day before, as we had neared the end of our marathon, Critter began faltering badly, stumbling on each block of ice as he plodded along, head down, at the back of the team. We unclipped him from the team. As he hobbled along behind, I surmised that heartsickness might be the cause, but hoped that he might pull himself together after a few days without pulling. He slipped farther and farther behind. Brent's team was catching

up with him. His dogs had sensed more clearly than any of us
the seriousness of Critter's plight. They knew he was dying,
though we hadn't yet realized how fatally his spirit had been
shattered. When they caught up with him, the ravenous Eskimo
dogs out front jumped him, set to finish him off. Critter mustered
enough strength to fight back as we pulled the bloodthirsty dogs
off him. We were stunned, but knew they were simply responding to the instincts of the pack. In their eyes, a weakened animal
represents food.

We sat Critter on top of my sled load and tied him in place,
hoping that he might get some rest. But then, just before our
dinner break, we encountered a huge ridge system. Since the
sleds were prone to roll over, I untied Critter and placed him
alongside the trail. In one of the most pitiful scenes I have ever
witnessed, he tried to crawl back up on the load. Knowing I
couldn't get through the ridge with him on the sled, I reluctantly
set him back in the snow. Again he tried to crawl on. I pushed
the sled ahead and he tottered along behind as we worked the
sleds over the walls of ice. In camp that day, Critter gulped down
the extra rations we gave him. We took this as a positive sign;
if he had been seriously ill, he wouldn't have eaten. What we
didn't yet understand was that while his body was holding out,
his spirit was nearly dead.

When Ann harnessed Critter the next morning, he went into
convulsions and slipped into a coma. Paul wrapped him in a
spare parka and put him inside Brent's sled bag. When the news
caught up with me while I was ahead scouting, I walked back
to check him out. Pulling back the sled cover, I looked down
upon him as he lay there listless, gasping for air. Though it was
apparent he was dying, we all clung to hopes that he might
revive. Geoff gnawed on a block of pemmican, chewing it into
a warm paste, which he tried to feed to Critter, but he was no
longer responsive.

The physical pain we had suffered on this trip was nothing
compared to the emotional pain we bore while watching McKerrow and Mantell agonize over their decisions to turn back. And
now we were faced with the emotional turmoil of Critter's dying.
As a survival response, I turned off my feelings and we carried
on. But during the time we stopped to await the sun's return,
Critter's breathing had grown weaker. We bundled him up
tightly and laid him down alongside the sled with heavy hearts.
All we could do now was hope. I desperately wished I could tell
him, "Hang in there another thirty miles and you'll get to go

home to your master." A few hours later, in the middle of a restless sleep, I heard his dying gasps, the deep, rasping breaths that were his goodbye to Mantell and his life. Geoff and Brent buried him behind an ice block nearby. Thirty miles from the Pole we had lost a special friend. Grief over his death was compounded by thoughts of the impact this would have on Mantell, who had lost his shot at the Pole and now his trail companion.

I sought to justify Critter's death, searching for some purpose in it. Perhaps it taught a lesson about the interdependency of spirit and heart, I reflected. Without one, the other dies. Spirit, our driving force, gives meaning to our existence, and our heart connects us with one another. Critter's death served to underscore the power of the spirit and the importance of the heart in everyday survival. The Arctic has taught me that as well. By repeatedly putting me in situations in which I have to exercise heart and spirit, the Arctic has given me a glimpse of the immense potential inherent in all of us.

Like me, Paul was in a reflective mood. "I've had the opportunity to test my body," he wrote. "Now God's giving me a chance to test my soul. Perhaps we're in for a week-long whiteout during which I'll fill my journal with inspirational thoughts." The one thought that registered immediately, he added, stemmed from the book he'd been reading, Viktor Frankl's *Man's Search for Meaning*. Given our concerns over weight, it was one of the few books we had agreed to bring along, and those reading it dutifully whittled it down as we went by using its pages to start our woodstove. In the book, Frankl, an Austrian psychiatrist, recounts his experiences as a prisoner in a Nazi concentration camp and his insights about the human will to survive as he observed his fellow prisoners. The elementary truth underscored by his experiences is that no matter what challenges, setbacks, or deprivations we are subjected to, we always have the freedom to choose our attitude about any given situation. Reflecting on Frankl's discovery, Paul wrote, "With the fog closing in around us, threatening to delay our journey's end or jeopardize our chance for success, I now have an opportunity to exercise that freedom."

DAY 55

"IT WAS A GREAT FEELING TO BE SKIING ALONG, BEEPING THE MESSAGE TO OUR FRIENDS THAT WE'D MADE IT."

Early in the morning, Brent was aroused from his sleep by a shaft of light coming through a crack in the tent door. He vaulted from his bag and peered outside. "The sun's out!" he shouted with joy. How thankful we were for this reprieve from the fog. We all felt a surge of enthusiasm as a quick breakfast was made and camp was taken down. Meanwhile, Paul proceeded to take a series of sun shots. We anxiously awaited the verdict on yesterday's progress. Alas, he reported with bitter disappointment, we had veered west during our six hours of travel the day before and had gained only a few miles of northward progress. We had taken a calculated risk and failed. The price paid for traveling in a whiteout was a day's rations for ourselves and the dogs, and many hours of needless work.

We later sorted through the causes of our error, and realized where we had gone wrong. In using the sun as a sundial for determining north and setting compass declination the previous morning, Richard had confused A.M. and P.M. hours. Under the circumstances, it was a very easy mistake to make. The amount of light no longer gave any hint of whether it was day or night, and because we had just traveled twenty hours straight through the night, Richard, like the rest of us, was operating in an exhausted stupor that morning. All along our course, compass declination had proven to be 90 to 100 degrees west. The net effect of Richard's error, from taking the wrong cue from the sun and getting his compass turned around, was that we were 90 degrees off course, traveling roughly due west.

Trying to reconcile that with the sastrugi, I compounded the problem by factoring the wrong bearing from the snowdrifts. The bearing didn't seem quite right, but in the back of my mind I'd rationalized this by assuming that somehow the sastrugi were aligned differently this close to the top. But the Pole itself has no bearing on the winds. There's nothing significant about that spot in terms of polar weather or ice drift patterns. It exists only as a mathematical concept, the one spot on earth where the direction north does not exist. And as one approaches, the directions east and west become increasingly less relevant. That fact had slipped my mind that morning as I set a course; I'd overcompensated for the eastward ice drift in aligning a bearing with the sastrugi.

We had taken little notice of the sastrugi until after we crossed 88 degrees. For the final two degrees of latitude, with less obstructed ice and more well-defined drifts, we were aware of the sastrugi patterns daily. Their alignment, we realized, had remained remarkably consistent throughout our journey. And their value as navigation tools for polar travelers became increasingly apparent as I considered the error I had made on the day we traveled off course. Surely, Peary and Henson had come to understand thoroughly the value of the sastrugi over their years of travel. Though we took frequent longitude readings to fine-tune our bearing of travel, I now realized it was possible for polar travelers to carry on for days without sun sights and feel reasonably assured that they were headed roughly northward through careful observation of the drifts.

This knowledge, it seems to me, must have been part of the "sixth sense" Peary and Henson had developed through their vast experience. Having been an explorer and navigator for more than twenty years and a professional navigator for thirty-five, Peary was an exceptionally well-seasoned judge of direction and distance. Henson had worked with him during most of those years. They were both keen trail observers, intuitively factoring in signs and clues as they charted a course, and highly skilled at dead reckoning. Henson, it was said, could pace to within yards of accuracy a five-mile course in a given direction. The armchair explorer might scoff at such claims, which is understandable, because only people who have spent long stretches of time on the trail can understand our human ability to develop such skills or "trail senses."

But skills in dead reckoning alone would never be sufficient for finding the Pole. Celestial navigation is essential, though some have questioned the accuracy of manual navigation at these high latitudes. Unfortunately, Peary's sparse navigation data leaves the question of whether he located the spot wide open for debate. Even though Paul's efforts were about to prove beyond any doubt that the Pole can be virtually pinpointed with only a sextant, our expedition would shed little light on doubts cast on the adequacy of Peary's sun sightings. That issue will always be a matter of conjecture.

As far as we were concerned, however, our expedition was shedding light on the question raised about his mileage—the contention that one simply can't travel thirty-five to fifty miles a day on polar ice, as Peary claimed. Our dogs had started this journey pulling payloads that weighed nearly three times those on Peary's nineteen sleds. Surely, by the time we reached 88 degrees, our dogs were far more exhausted than Peary's were when he started his final dash from nearly the same point. Yet the average mileage for our last five marches—just under thirty-four miles—was virtually the same as what he clocked on his final dash. As did we and all other polar expeditions of this century, Peary found steadily improving ice conditions during the last few hundred miles, which nearly eliminated the need for detours. Of course, we were to be airlifted out upon reaching the Pole, whereas Peary's crew had to return to land by dogsled. Critics have a field day scoffing at his reports of returning to 88 degrees in three marches, averaging forty-five miles a day. But, I hasten to point out, he was following a well-marked trail, camping at the same igloos he had used on the way up, though skipping every other one. Only seasoned expedition dogsledders know how motivated dogs become when they suddenly have scent marks to follow, when they know they are heading home to food and rest. Mushers, too, find a reservoir of energy they didn't know they had when a long journey nears its end. In Peary's case, he and his crew had an added shot of adrenaline, knowing they were virtually running for their lives with spring advancing rapidly upon them. Thus, while the jury is still out on his navigation claims, I find his mileage claims to be plausible. Whether Peary's crew stood at the North Pole on April 6, 1909, can never be proven beyond doubt, but I believe it's possible they could have done it.

My experiences on the expedition and my research beforehand changed my views about Peary's rival, Dr. Frederick Cook.

Initially, I was ambivalent about his claims of having reached the Pole a year before Peary. But now I strongly side with the majority of Arctic researchers, who have deemed his claims invalid. Many contentions have been raised about his strategy. Mine center on his logistics and his sleds. He claims to have embarked on a 100-day journey with two Inuit companions, twenty-six dogs, and 1,200 pounds of rations. Even accounting for their reports of later consuming sixteen dogs, their rations averaged well under a couple of dozen pounds of food a day for themselves and their dogs. That would not sustain them. His sleds, as depicted in his books, were an ingenious design, but I believe their slender hickory rails and ribs and mortise-and-tenon construction were far too delicate for surviving the rugged pack ice found on the polar sea.

One other item caught my eye while surveying his books: a picture of what he claimed to be an island found a few hundred miles out to sea. Of course, no land exists there. His supporters later countered that the photo depicted a massive ice island that Cook, photographing it from a distance, mistakenly thought was land. But as I looked closely at the photo, I realized that it did in fact depict land. The topography is distinctly geologic, fingerprinting it as a rock formation rather than one of ice. Through aerial surveys, it's likely the island can be identified. When that is done, I suspect it will indicate that Cook was somewhere just west of Ellesmere, perhaps near Axel Heiberg, rather than halfway to the Pole as he claimed to be when he took that picture.

When we broke camp the morning of our last travel day, we were in somber moods over our wasted efforts of the day before. But we learned later that our misrouting had been a blessing in disguise. On a research flight just days before our sextant mishap, Bradley Air pilots had spotted a massive system of open leads dead ahead of our course. At our base camp, Jim watched with anxiety as the position fixes he was getting from our satellite beacon placed us closer and closer to these mile-wide gaps of open water. The pilots had reported to him that the only route around the leads lay miles to the west. Jim felt certain we'd be calling in heartbroken and seeking assistance when we reached this monstrous obstacle. This explained the skepticism he expressed about our "countdown to the Pole" plan during our last radio check. Our press entourage, as well, charted our progress as we approached what they assumed would be our demise and waited for our fateful radio call. But that call never came. We never saw the massive lead system the pilots had reported. As

fate would have it, the miles we had veered due west by mistake
had been the perfect detour. Jim, the press, and our followers
back home were stunned when the next blip of our beacon
showed that we had miraculously jogged west around the obstacle even before reaching it. "How did they pull that off?" was the
question on everyone's mind in Resolute that day.

At the time, of course, we knew nothing of this good fortune.
The seemingly wasted hours of travel and needless miles put on
our weary dogs left us frustrated as we packed sleds for what was
to be the last time on the morning of May 1. Our position was
89° 38', thirty miles from the Pole. As Ann noted in her journal,
"If there were a tower at the Pole, you'd be able to see it from
here." At 10:00 A.M. Paul headed out scouting on skis, belting
out old folk songs at the top of his lungs to release the intense
disappointment he felt over yesterday's routing error.

The frustrations slowly ebbed as we made steady progress.
The ice was reasonably flat, though fractured by many narrow
leads that we were able to sled across. At some point that day,
all stresses and tensions, all anxieties over weather and ice breaks
and rations and dog burnout gave way to an immense satisfaction. The burden was lifted. Six haggard bodies and weary souls
were transfigured. We stepped a little lighter. We laughed more.
We chattered excitedly about the warm beds and sumptuous
meals that lay just ahead. Marching two by two, we looked and
felt like kids on parade. Providence was shining down upon us.
We marveled at the millions of shades of blue around us, an ice
sculpture garden shimmering in myriad hues. The blues of the
ice and of the crystal-clear polar sky blended together. The
horizon was but a delicate gossamer thread of white through
the blue. It seemed no coincidence to us that in early afternoon
we happened upon just the stretch of ice Paul needed: a perfectly
flat pan with a level horizon against which he could adjust the
sextant. We encountered several minor pressure ridges that day,
but rather than curse them, we now found them to be good sport,
treating them as a series of Olympic events, the Ridge-Mushing
Competition. The sleds were rammed up and over them with as
much bravado as we could muster while an imaginary panel of
judges scored our performances.

At 10:00 P.M. we stopped for dinner, popping up the tents for
a brief layover. Paul's reading on his newly tuned sextant placed
us ten miles from the Pole. That was the magic figure we had
been waiting for. We could now set off our satellite beacon to
alert *National Geographic* to prepare to release the announce-

ment. Geoff tucked the beacon in a backpack and headed north on skis while the rest of us finished dinner. It was 11:30 P.M., EST. We wanted to be sure the position coordinates our base camp was posting from this signal were well inside the ten-mile mark before May 1, 1986, had drawn to a close. Throughout our training, that date had settled in all our minds as the most appropriate one for reaching our goal. In fact, on the blackboard in my workshop where we had listed a tentative schedule for the journey months before, the final phrase read: "Anticipated arrival at Pole—May 1." Geoff enjoyed the assignment immensely. "It was a great feeling," he wrote, "to be skiing along, beeping the message to our friends that we'd made it." At 11:45 we harnessed up the dogs and followed in his tracks. A couple of miles later we encountered the most active zone we had yet seen. The pans had pulled apart in huge ten-to-one-hundred-acre gaps or ocean lakes known as *polynias*. Temperatures edged above zero. Several team members wondered aloud if we might have to settle for being eight miles from the top. Paul led us farther west, skirting a huge chain of polynias. With the drift carrying us east or—since east and west have little relevance at this latitude—toward our right, he planned to come in to the "left" side of the Pole, so that during our next camp we would drift right over it while he took his readings. He was out of sight, scouting, when the rest of us encountered a crack along his tracks that had widened into a ten-foot lead. We were stymied. As we stood there perplexed, the ice swiftly began to move. The walls of the lead slammed shut like a drawbridge. Dazed by this fortuitous event, we hurried across before the ice shifted again.

We traveled on for hours, working our way through this maze, mesmerized by the scenery. The sun was festooned with sun dogs. The patches of open water formed calm reflecting pools. Some had a wafer-thin coating of ice, with delicate salt flowers decorating their surfaces in various densities. With ice shifting in every direction, the air was filled with a steady roar, punctuated by wild bangs, screeches, and deep moans. "This is one of the finest moments of my life," said Geoff as he sledded along with me. Then he commented, "With our luck, we're likely to find a perfect landing strip right at the Pole."

That was our next challenge, finding a spot for planes to land in this massive jumble. Within minutes we broke out onto a mile-long flat stretch. We just smiled at each other and continued on, knowing we had found our strip. I was completely mesmerized and could have traveled on forever. Fortunately, Richard and Brent were in a more rational frame of mind, and became concerned that we might go too far, that we might overshoot the Pole and spend the night in the Eastern Hemisphere. They came running up to Paul and me, insisting that we stop and take another set of readings. Good point, we thought. Paul pulled out the sextant while we set up tents. His reading placed us to the left of the Pole and a few miles from it. But he cautioned us that he couldn't be certain until he made a second confirming reading in the morning. At 4:00 A.M. we went to bed, fully expecting to spend the next day traveling again to fine-tune our position. Our "out time" was set for 10:00 A.M.

DAY 56

"THESE DOGS ARE AMAZING."

At 9:45 we had just finished our oatmeal and were sitting in our common bag, writing in our journals. Even with the stoves off, it was warm in the tent, so we knew it was well above zero outside. We could hear Paul tinkering with the sextant and Brent talking to his dogs as he prepared to harness them up. In my journal I was reflecting on the previous evening: "Last night, as I slipped Chester's harness off, he fell asleep in my arms. Yet he will pull another eighteen hours today if I need him to. These dogs are amazing. That is why they will—" My writing was interrupted by a loud explosion outside. As our hearing cleared, we heard Brent shouting, "We're at the Pole!" In celebration, he had left off a "bear scare," a large firecracker intended for driving bears from camp. I corrected my journal entry and finished the sentence, "That is why they *have* led us to the Pole, pulling our sleds behind them."

For the past few hours, Paul had been taking readings that showed the change in the sun's angle to remain constant. We had reached our goal. Oddly, in our tents there were no outbursts of hurrahs or handshakes. The overwhelming feeling was more one of great relief—no more long marches, no more agonizing obstacles, no more frozen fingers and chilled toes. We shifted our camp a few hundred yards back to the airstrip Geoff had spotted the night before, and then treated ourselves to the thing we wanted most, sleep.

That afternoon, Paul stretched the radio's antenna wires for the last time. Little did he know his resourcefulness was about to be tested one more time. Time and again for nearly an hour he called into the receiver, "Bradley 69, Steger expedition here. Do you copy?" The airwaves were absolutely silent. Not even static from satellite transmissions, which had interfered with all of his other radio messages, could be heard. What more could he do, he wondered. He was using his last set of fresh batteries, which he had saved for this moment and had warmed in a pan of hot water. We were now some 1,000 miles from our base camp, and the signal just wasn't spanning the distance. Somehow he would have to pump more power into the radio. We had long ago thrown away our headlamps, so the only additional fresh batteries we had were those in our satellite beacon. He carefully dismantled it to extract its two three-volt lithium cells. Then, with a bit of foil, he linked one of them in series with the radio battery pack, boosting its power from nine volts to twelve. It was a huge gamble. The extra voltage might blow a fuse, but it seemed his only chance for reaching Resolute. Nervously he clicked the radio on. Immediately, the Morse code–like beeping of satellite transmissions could be heard. Again he called the base. After several anxious tries, a voice responded. A Bradley pilot flying high over Ellesmere had intercepted his message and relayed it on to Resolute. The response he reported from our base camp was "Congratulations! Three planes are leaving now for Eureka to refuel and should arrive at the Pole by noon tomorrow."

EPILOGUE

We all slept soundly that night. It had not yet hit us that we had reached our destination. In Tent 2 the next morning, Brent and Paul stirred up a final pot of gruel, some pemmican scraps and oats. As they were about to dish it out, Paul looked up at Brent and groaned, "Oh, man, I just can't face another bowl of this shit, can you? Let's fast till we get out of here." They set the half-full pot outside, and to this day, the "Last Supper" remains freeze-dried in the bottom of it. The weather had been a bit hazy the night before, but Paul reported on his radio check that morning that it was a fine, clear day with "Hawaii" weather, nearly 15 degrees above zero. He also put in a special request for the cook at Eureka to stash the plane with a big order of his wonderful pastries—"especially the butter tarts"—when the plane stopped through on its way up.

Through the morning we busied ourselves with group photos. We posed for advertising photos with every item of equipment that remained. These photos of us smiling contentedly with a thermos and rifle and tent and a variety of other gear were soon to end up in the catalogs of many of our sponsors. With the film remaining in the movie camera, Ann shot quick interviews with each of us. Geoff took advantage of this opportunity to lay claim to a special feat. He skied around the world, cutting a mile-wide circle. We had but a few pounds of food left, hardly enough for a meal, but ironically, our fuel jug still contained a few gallons of the white gas that we had so often fretted about. The weather had warmed so much in the past several days that we had used only a little.

From time to time we'd stopped and looked about us, pondering the significance of this place, the point around which the planet spins. It has no identifying features. Surrounded by pans and ridges, it looked exactly like many other places we had seen along the way. There were no monuments, no brass plaques, no mementos from previous expeditions, because, of course, anything placed here would be carried along by the drifting ice. The Pole exists only as a mathematical concept, the point at which lines converge. It seemed somewhat disconcerting to be there. For so long, we had focused single-mindedly on the direction north. It permeated all of our waking hours and many of our dreams. And now we found ourselves at the one spot on our planet where the direction north does not exist. Nor does east or west. Every direction we faced was south.

As the morning drew on to midday, the scheduled arrival time for our charter flights, I took a walk to admire the pristine beauty of our surroundings. I said a silent prayer of thanks for being at the top of the world. The simple beauty of the ice and sky strengthened me for the complexities that were about to immerse us. In our radio message at 88 degrees, Jim had warned us that the media attention was snowballing. He put us on notice that if we made it, we would be deluged with interviews and appearances for the next several weeks.

Upon hearing the distant drone of a plane's engine, I sprinted back to camp. We had one more "dog and pony show" to perform. Jim had informed us that the television crews wanted aerial shots of us sledding at the Pole. The dogs were slipped into harnesses for one more brief ride, this time without loads. We wove among some big ridges while one of the planes maneuvered overhead. Soon all three planes—one loaded with barrels of fuel for the flight home—had glided to flawless landings on our smooth strip. A mob of reporters poured out onto the ice. Paul and I watched the commotion from a distance. It suddenly felt very good to be sitting peacefully in the middle of the Arctic Ocean, enjoying one last moment of reverie before dealing with the mayhem.

We returned our sleds to camp to join the throng. "How'd we do?" Paul asked one of the pilots, wondering how the reading on the planes' electronic navigation systems jived with his sextant fix. "Congratulations," the pilot replied. "Somewhere within a couple of hundred yards of here is the earth's hinge pin."

Meanwhile, the dogs were storming the reporters, knowing they had brought food. Before anyone could respond, one of my dogs, Tim, started chomping on a microphone. We posed for photographs with the flags of the various countries this expedition had represented, the United States, Canada, and New Zealand. Then we unfurled a light blue banner with the word PEACE emblazoned across it. With tears streaming down her cheeks, Ann read a statement Paul had drafted:

"It is a great day for us. We thank God we've arrived at the top of the world in good health and spirits. We are deeply indebted to the forty-nine huskies and Canadian Eskimo dogs who pulled so long and hard to bring us here. They are the real heroes of this journey. And at this special moment in our lives, we feel much gratitude to the governments, companies, organizations, and individuals who have been supporting us through their donations, volunteer assistance, thoughts, and prayers. We felt you standing by us every step of the way.

"The journey across the polar sea was filled with paradox. Surrounded by the gentle pastel beauty of the ice, snow, and low-lying sun, we endured the hardest work and most hostile conditions any of us have ever experienced. At times there were tears of despair when obstacle after obstacle seemed to spell defeat. At times we were overwhelmed by exhilaration as we made major breakthroughs.

"But most of the time we just worked hard, wrestling every mile of forward progress from the sea ice. We experienced pain, cold, hunger, and fatigue. For us, the significance of this is that we are able to better empathize with people all over the world for whom these are daily experiences much of their lives, and who deserve the world's attention more than we do.

"On a brighter note, this journey reaffirmed for us that hope springs eternal. In our moments of despair, we always found reason to persevere. As we, six adventurers from different parts of the world, stand here where the lines of longitude of all countries meet, we believe this journey stands for hope—hope that other seemingly impossible goals can be met by people everywhere. Our only regret is that two of our team members, Bob Mantell and Bob McKerrow, who gave everything they had for this journey before injury turned them back, are not here to share this moment with us. To them, we dedicate this day."

Then Paul ceremoniously pitched our "time capsule" over his shoulders and into a jumbled heap of ice. A one-foot chunk of wide plastic plumbing pipe capped tightly on both ends and painted blaze orange, it contained a scroll with an announcement of our journey and signatures of several hundred persons who had contributed to it, as well as various mementos contributed by team members during training: a Boy Scout scarf, a beaded

Indian belt, a letter to Santa Claus that Ann had received from a child just before the trip, and a small lace prayer circle. Jim had sealed the tube just before we left, and had now brought it with him from Resolute. Perhaps someday, after the ice has drifted beyond the polar sea and melted, it will wash up on some shore and be retrieved. Then we will find out where the ephemeral platform we stood on that day was destined. To add to the intrigue, our major sponsor, Du Pont Fiberfil, has since offered a $5,000 reward for return of the capsule. The money remains unclaimed.

The eternal vastness through which we had been moving in the past two months suddenly seemed crowded. Sixteen people shared the top of the world with us: four television and four newspaper journalists, three *National Geographic* staff members, four flight crew, and our base manager, Jim. They excitedly filled us in with news from the outside world, principally the explosion at the Chernobyl nuclear power plant, which had happened just the day before. They informed us of the radioactive gas cloud in the polar jet stream, which had passed directly overhead. How ironic, I thought, to be in so remote a place and yet face such risks. The polar sea was suddenly very small. Meanwhile, the press crew passed champagne among themselves, our champagne, the champagne we couldn't drink until a blood sample had been drawn from each of us. As part of a diet study for the University of Minnesota, we had agreed to ingest nothing before giving blood to ensure that the analysis reflected only our trail diet.

We harnessed up the dogs for the last time. They knew the planes meant rest and food, and raced toward them with our sleds bounding along behind. They vaulted into the bay doors with a surprising burst of power. Once airborne, Ann pulled out the Vacutainers to take blood samples from Geoff and Paul. They waited patiently for them to fill, but even after numerous attempts in different spots, nothing flowed. We joked about how anemic these guys were, but were perplexed. Then it suddenly dawned on us that the problem wasn't one of blood supply but altitude. As the plane gained altitude and the air pressure declined, the containers no longer had sufficient vacuum. "Tests will have to wait," shouted Paul gleefully as he tore into a suitcase Susan had sent up on the plane. It was filled with an endless variety of treats: M&Ms, oranges, chocolate-chip cookies, milk, beer, White Castle hamburgers, ham sandwiches, white chocolate bars, smoked oysters, and Zap brand sour drops, a hard candy whose name had no relation to our dog's. But it was big bright red apples that went first. "Oh, how good they tasted," Ann commented. Several of us had shared a craving for apples, something crisp, fresh, and juicy. We stuffed ourselves silly. Almost unconsciously, I began stuffing the pockets of my polar suits with cookies, loading up for later. Between bites, emotions unraveled. I sat pensively, chin in hand. Ann wrapped her arms around my shoulders. Paul fought back tears of joy, sadness, and relief. Richard commented in his journal on the way home, "I think of the journey as the most emotional time of my life. Way up when you're up, and way down when you're down. Everyone was so glad to get out, but already I am beginning to miss it a little. One readily forgets the hardships."

We stopped briefly in Eureka to refuel and then, eight hours after leaving the Pole, we landed in Resolute. A crowd of smiling faces circled the plane as we disembarked. The brightest among them belonged to Susan and Nala, Brent's wife. In the papoose-like hoods of their Eskimo parkas were Bria and Crystal, for whom the two sleds that reached the Pole had been named. The young fathers marveled at the changes their infant daughters had undergone in the past two months. Conspicuously parked on the runway was a huge, gleaming jet with a Minnesota flag painted on the side. We now learned that this jet, which belonged to Hubbard Broadcasting, the owner of the television station covering our journey, was there to whisk us home to Minneapolis the first thing in the morning. There would be no quiet time to wind down as a team in Resolute. We threw ourselves back into high gear. Most of us were torn between whether to hit the showers or the dining hall first. But not Geoff. He headed straight for the food line and ate straight through the night. "First I started with a salad, fried chicken, and several pork chops," he wrote in his journal. "Then when those items ran out I moved on to the pies—banana cream, lemon meringue, and pumpkin. After cleaning those up, I took a little break but shortly came back and sat down with a gallon of chocolate ice cream and a chocolate cake. By dawn I had finished those, and then, of course, it was time for breakfast. I ate two complete plates of pancakes, eggs, sausage, potatoes, fruit, etc. At that point I had hurt myself. It felt like something ripped in my stomach. So I quit."

In the morning we hugged Richard and Brent goodbye; they would be heading to their homes in Canada on a later flight. Then we climbed aboard the jet with our entourage of reporters, and plopped down in its padded swivel chairs. The flight was timed so that we would land precisely at the beginning of KSTP's 6:00 P.M. news broadcast in Minneapolis and St. Paul that evening. The station planned live coverage of our arrival, and said a small group of friends and family would be there to meet us. As the plane descended over St. Paul, the verdant spring landscape hit our senses. After looking at white for so long, it took a minute for us to adjust to vibrant greens. When the plane landed and the doors were opened, the sweltering, muggy heat of a 90-degree day swept over us, bathing us in temperatures some 160 degrees warmer than those we had experienced when we embarked on our journey two months before. Peering out the window, we were stunned by the site of a huge throng of cheering and waving well-wishers with banners and flags. Dazed, we pulled off our soggy mukluks and marched out the door. We sank our bare feet in the soft, hot asphalt of the tarmac as the crowd pressed in around us. Microphones were thrust into our faces as we answered a thousand questions at once. Dozens of children held up pens and paper for autographs in their tiny hands. "Imagine, a lowlife like me signing autographs," Geoff laughed. We were hoisted on a stage and, after accolades from various local dignitaries, each choked out a few words about how great it was to be home and how thankful we were to have been able to share this journey with so many faithful followers.

As the cheering throng milled about us, we found ourselves feeling very honored—and very overwhelmed. Why had our expedition caught the imagination of so many people? It was neither the first nor the longest polar journey, nor would it, surely, be the last. Over the days that followed, days filled with press conferences and countless interviews all over the country, we began to get a clue as we looked over newspapers for the period since mid-January: The world had been stunned by disasters—particularly the loss of the *Challenger* shuttle and the Soviet nuclear accident at Chernobyl. We realized that man's faith in technological wizardry had been badly shaken. In contrast, we six had pushed long and hard to meet our goal through sheer determination and the collective will of our dogs and ourselves. For many other people, as well as for us, our journey symbolized a reaffirmation of that will—the indomitable power of the human spirit.

APPENDICES

APPENDIX A

THE TEAM EIGHTEEN MONTHS LATER

The expedition "aftermath"—media tours, appearances, lectures, and writing—dominated the lives of many team members for nearly a year following the journey. The team, minus McKerrow, was reunited in August for a presentation at Vancouver's Expo '86. Will and Paul spent much of the first six months generating funds to retire the expedition debt and working with *National Geographic* on a magazine cover story that appeared in September 1986 and a documentary film, *North to the Pole,* that has aired periodically. Among the honors they received were the 1986 Outsiders of the Year award from *Outside* magazine and the Explorers Club's Citation of Merit.

The polar encounter with French explorer Jean-Louis Etienne proved fateful for Will. He and Jean-Louis are laying plans to accomplish the first dogsled traverse of Antarctica with a six-person international team (possibly including a Soviet) and forty-five dogs. Slated to begin in August 1989, the seven-month, 5,000-mile ski trek would take them across the South Pole in mid-December, the height of the Antarctic summer. Depots of supplies would be airdropped every 500 miles or so along the route in advance and marked with beacons. The main challenges are altitude—Antarctica is the highest continent on earth—and crevasses, deep and often snow-covered fissures in the overlying smooth glacial dome of ice that can snare the unwary traveler. To research these challenges, they plan to traverse Greenland, where similar conditions exist, in the spring of 1988. For more information write the International Transantarctica Expedition, Box 4097, St. Paul, Minnesota 55104.

Since the North Pole journey, Paul Schurke has been in steady demand by college and corporate audiences for his narrated slide presentation. He and his wife, Susan, are working with Wilderness Inquiry again, helping develop trip offerings overseas, and have become involved with a Soviet-American cultural exchange program with hopes of launching a joint-venture Arctic expedition as a demonstration of cooperation and goodwill between the two countries. They have also launched Wintergreen, a ski camping program, and Susan is marketing some winter apparel items based on her expedition designs.

Ann Bancroft, one of twelve recipients of *Ms.* magazine's 1986 Women of the Year award and many other honors, has also been in great demand for talks. She led canoe trips for Wilderness Inquiry this summer and has no immediate plans to return to her teaching position. Her many schemes and dreams include climbing Tanzania's Mount Kilimanjaro and starting an outdoor education program for disadvantaged youth.

Richard Weber, the Canadian national ski champion, was married in August 1986 and bought a house near Ottawa, Ontario, where he took a job as a mechanical engineer. He has traveled across Canada and the military bases in Europe to lecture about the expedition for the Association of Canadian Clubs. He is being considered as a member for a Soviet-American team that plans to traverse the Arctic Ocean on skis in the spring of 1988.

Brent Boddy returned to his outfitting business and hospital supplies job in Frobisher Bay, now known as Iqualuit after villagers voted to reestablish the town's original Inuit name. He and Richard have teamed up to plan another ambitious adventure by dogsled and kayak. Brent has applied for permission from the Soviet Union to retrace the migration of the early Inuit people from Siberia across the Bering Strait and North America to Greenland.

Geoff Carroll returned to Barrow, Alaska, the northernmost village in the U.S., where he administrates a study of bowhead and beluga whales, polar bears, and caribou. He has ridden on small rafts among whales the size of boxcars to implant radio transmitters that enable him to track them by airplane.

Robert McKerrow, who was evacuated from the polar journey with broken ribs, recuperated shortly after his return to Anikiwa, New Zealand, and resumed his duties as director of the New Zealand Outward Bound School. He is helping Will and Jean-Louis as a support staff member for the Transantarctica Expedition.

Bob Mantell didn't lose any of the frostbitten toes that forced him to retreat from the journey, but it took him a few months to recover after hobbling more than 100 miles on feet that had frozen. Undaunted, he led dogsled trips the next winter for the Voyageur Outward Bound School near Ely, Minnesota, and is now working as a carpenter.

APPENDIX B

DAILY LOG

TRIP DAY	DATE	AVERAGE DAY TEMP.	WIND	MILES NORTH*
1	3/8	−65°F.	calm	1.5
2	3/9	−70	calm	1
3	3/10	−65	calm	2.5
4	3/11	−45	SW, light	0
5	3/12	−45	SW, light	2
6	3/13	−45	SW, 10 knots	7
7	3/14	−40	SW, 8 knots	0
8	3/15	−40	SW, 15 knots	7
9	3/16	−38	SW, light	6
10	3/17	−40	calm	7
11	3/18	−40	W, 20 knots	8
12	3/19	−42	W, 20 knots	3
13	3/20	−38	NW, light	0
14	3/21	−30	SW, 8 knots	7
15	3/22	−34	calm	8
16	3/23	−30	SW, light	3
17	3/24	−15	SW, 50–80 knots	0
18	3/25	−22	SW, 20–50 knots	5
19	3/26	−35	SW, light	9
20	3/27	−40	SW, 8 knots	7
21	3/28	−44	calm	6
22	3/29	−40	calm	8
23	3/30	−42	calm	6
24	3/31	−42	calm	8
25	4/1	−32	calm	0
26	4/2	−44	calm	8
27	4/3	−44	calm	14
28	4/4	−44	calm	16
29	4/5	−43	calm	0
30	4/6	−40	SW, 25 knots	14
31	4/7	−43	SW, 35–55 knots	0
32	4/8	−30	SW, 30–50 knots	10

TRIP DAY	DATE	AVERAGE DAY TEMP.	WIND	MILES NORTH*
33	4/9	−30	SW, light	4
34	4/10	−30	SW, light	0
35	4/11	−28	NE, light	3
36	4/12	−25	NE, light	0
37	4/13	−22	S, light	16
38	4/14	−25	SW, light	8
39	4/15	−22	calm	24
40	4/16	−25	calm	12
41	4/17	−14	calm	16
42	4/18	−12	NW, light	18
43	4/19	−18	SW, light	15
44	4/20	−16	W, light	18
45	4/21	−25	SW, light	16
46	4/22	−25	W, light	18
47	4/23	−22	W, light	0
48	4/24	−25	SW, 10 knots	21
49	4/25	−18	S, 10 knots	26
50	4/26	−19	SW, 10 knots	32
51	4/27	− 1	SW, light	24
52	4/28	0	SW, light	18
53	4/29	+ 5	SW, 15 knots	0
54	4/30	−10	calm	25
55	5/1	+10	calm	0

*"Miles north" indicates our net gain toward the Pole each day, rather than total daily mileage. Owing to relays, detours, and ice drift, the total mileage we traveled was nearly twice the total of this column, 488 miles, the straight-line distance from Drep Camp to the Pole. Thus the "miles north" figures do not coincide with daily mileage figures reported in the text.

APPENDIX C

TYPICAL DAILY RATIONS

BREAKFAST

3 oz. Con Agra rolled oats
3 oz. Adam's Old Fashioned peanut butter
4 oz. Mid-America Farms unsalted butter
Celestial Seasonings herbal tea

LUNCH

One 6-oz. homemade energy bar consisting of:
3.5 oz. Bergin nut butter (cashew, almond, and sesame)
1 oz. finely ground Leona Farms fruit jerky
1.5 oz. dairy butter

DINNER

8 oz. Dawn Meats (New Zealand) pemmican (a 60/40
mix of finely ground dried beef and lard)
6 oz. Hershey's ribbon egg noodles
4 oz. Bongaard's white cheese
2 oz. Mid-America Farms butter oil (dehydrated butter)

OPTIONAL SUPPLEMENTS

Shaklee Vita-Lea vitamin and mineral supplements
Shaklee Slim Plan chicken soup mix
Shaklee Energy Bars
Carnation nonfat dry milk
Hershey's and Carnation cocoa

APPENDIX D

OUR DOGS—THE REAL HEROES OF THE JOURNEY

THE FORTY-NINE THAT BEGAN THE JOURNEY

Sled #1
(Indre)

Driver: Bob Mantell

Critter, lead dog
Captain
Piston
V.O.
Sequoia
Bandit
Carolyn
Spook
Dillon

Sled #2
(Gaile)

Driver: Geoff Carroll

Mitt Grabber, lead dog
Raven
Fang
Nimrod
Fuzzy
Scarnose
Cowpuck
Spot
Numpuck
Pucknum

Sled #3
(O'Donnell)

Driver: Paul Schurke

Chocolate, lead dog
Brutus
Worms
Ciarnuk
Rosebud
Zorro
Snickers
Hunto
Mugsy
Tarsalik

Sled #4
(Crystal)

Driver: Brent Boddy

Smarty, lead dog
Junior
Tip
Jake
Tigawak
Goofy
Pattimore 1
Pattimore 2
Scarface
Etuk

Sled #5
(Bria)

Driver: Will Steger

Chester, lead dog
Zap
Tim
Yeager
Leif
Choochi
Slidre
Mongo
Capone
Sam

THE TWENTY THAT REACHED THE POLE

Bria	*Crystal*
Chester	Tip
Tim	Junior
Yeager	Goofy
Leif	Jake
Sam	Mitt Grabber
Slidre	Raven
Mongo	Dillon
Capone	Rosebud
Chocolate	Spook
V.O.	Mugsy

APPENDIX E

EQUIPMENT USED ON THE EXPEDITION

The North Face "North Star" four-person tent (slightly modified)

Sierra Designs Quallofil-insulated sleeping bags (custom-made)

Karrimor backpacks

Epoke 900 skis

Berwyn Bindings

Swix Alulight Ski Poles

Swix Ski Wax

MSR Whisperlite and X-GK white gas stoves

Coleman Peak One lanterns

Gott steel vacuum bottle and plastic fuel jugs

Wenonah Kevlar canoe (custom-made)

REI carabiners

Remington .300 Magnum rifles

Spilsbury SBX-11A HF SSB radiotelephone

SGC SG 715 HF SSB radiotelephone

Eveready batteries

C. Plath sextant

Silva compass

Rolex watches

Nikon FM2 camera (winterized by *National Geographic*)

Olympus XA camera

Kodachrome 64 ASA film

Canon Super 8 sound camera

CLOTHING AND ACCESSORIES USED

The North Face Cordura/Gore-Tex wind shell jacket and pants
(custom-made)

The North Face "Brooks Range" Quallofil-insulated parka (slightly
modified)

Wilderness Experience Thermax/Thermolite/Thermoloft polar suits
(custom-made)

Sealskin wind pants

Demetre Thermax long underwear

Paris Gloves ski gloves and mitts

New Zealand wool wristlets

Beaver gauntlets

Caribou work mitts

Fox River Hollofil socks

Caribou socks

Sealskin socks

Surefoot Insolator Neoprene/Thermolite/Cambrelle insole

Moosehide mukluks

Sealskin kamiks

The Masque face mask

Bollé sunglasses

Aurora Warm Skin/Winter Guard Skin Protector

APPENDIX F

PSYCHOLOGICAL PROFILE OF THE STEGER TEAM*

Six men and one woman members of a successful North Pole Expedition team were studied through personality and coping pattern inventories, mood scale ratings completed while on the trek to the North Pole, and for some a post-expedition personal interview. The group demonstrated good psychological adjustment as manifested by low depression, anxiety, and stress reactivity, and relatively high scores on scales measuring achievement orientation, self-control, and feelings of well-being. The group as a whole did not exhibit sensation-seeking or risk-taking tendencies. The major coping patterns engaged in on the expedition were planful problem solving and positive reappraisal. The adaptive nature of the group's personality and coping characteristics for completing a successful expedition was discussed.

In interpreting the results of this study we need to refer to its aim. This was not a study in which hypotheses were posited and then empirically tested. Doing so with such a small number of subjects would have been meaningless. Nevertheless we felt that this was a unique group, well worth studying, and consequently our aim was to provide the best possible description of the group as a whole and of the individual differences within it in personality, mood, and coping patterns. Thus, our results are descriptive and should be interpreted and evaluated as such.

This investigation demonstrated that the North Pole expedition team members were a psychologically sound group of individuals. The members' attraction for participating in an expedition of this type seems most consonant with characteristics of high achievement orientation, feelings of well-being, high energy level, and low stress reactivity. The enticement

*Prepared by Dr. Gloria Leon, director of clinical psychology, Department of Psychology, University of Minnesota. Used by permission.

of the trek seems to have been in the adventure and challenge
rather than in the danger.

The test and interview data demonstrated a highly task-
oriented group who were mature, intellectual, and somewhat
extroverted in nature. They gave evidence of functioning well
in social situations, although some demonstrated greater social closeness and lower alienation characteristics than others. These individuals did not exhibit high stress reactivity,
but on the other hand, they generally were not high risk-
takers. Depression, anxiety, and somatic concerns were low,
while a moderate tendency to use denial as a defense mecha-
nism (as measured by the MMPI Hy score) was evident. The
use of denial may be adaptive over a short-term period since
minimization of stress may be an important means of reducing its psychological impact (Breznitz, 1983). The personality
data for the two who had to leave the expedition because of
injuries were consistent with the findings for the group as a
whole. There did not appear to be an obvious psychopatho-
logical explanation for the injuries incurred.

The personality data are also consistent with the findings
of Butcher and Ryan (1974) and those from an investigation
of the successful 1963 American Mount Everest Expedition
team (Lester, 1980). The Mount Everest group of eighteen
showed a characteristic described as "assertive individual-
ity," i.e., high in achievement, independence, and restlessness, exhibiting a desire for autonomy, a tendency to be dominant in personal relations, a dislike for routine, and a
disinterest in social interaction for its own sake. A striking
finding also comparable with the data from the North Pole
group was their high stress resistance as assessed by psychological, sociological, and physiological measures. The Mount
Everest team, however, was higher on introversion and im-
pulsiveness than the North Pole group.

The coping scale data demonstrated that the most characteristic means of coping with the exigencies and demands of
the North Pole expedition were planful problem solving, positive reappraisal, and self-control. These patterns of coping
are clearly important to the successful completion of an arduous and often unpredictable mission, and adaptive as well to
the group process. The expedition coping pattern data are
consistent with the report of Folkman, et al. (1986) of an
association between planful problem solving and positive
reappraisal in changeable encounters. The finding of an asso-

ciation between confrontive coping and vigor suggests that
direct action aimed at modifying a stressful situation is related to physical energy and a positive mood state. The low
level of consistency in primary coping patterns across stressful situations also seems adaptive, suggesting that the more
stressful the situation, the more necessary it is to engage in
coping patterns specific to that situation (Fleming, et al.,
1984).

Of interest is the finding that accepting responsibility as a
way of coping was an infrequently reported method. The
interview data confirm a general attitude of accepting fate
and destiny, with little evidence of self-blame or feelings of
responsibility as a way of dealing with unexpected or distress-
ing events. For example, although Subject 6 indicated strong
feelings of responsibility for the expedition's success because
of his role in navigating, he dealt with the situation of the
malfunctioning sextant by planful problem solving. Further,
the two team members who were forced to leave the expedition because of injuries reported positive reappraisal as the
most prominent method of coping. The absence of blaming
oneself or others and the ability to try to find something
positive in this highly disappointing situation is impressive.
The most extroverted of the group (Subject 4) also showed
an increase in using social support as a means of coping with
having to leave the expedition.

The team members tended to use the necessary heavy
physical labor as an outlet for their frustrations. This function of engaging in activity to reduce psychological distress
in challenging or threatening situations was described previously by Gal and Lazarus (1975). Thus, task-oriented activity
is highly adaptive not only in reducing distress due to various
dangerous or aversive situations, but in furthering the goals
of a particular mission.

The team members' interview data indicated a comfort in
being in the group situation which is consonant with the
relatively low MMPI Si scores of all members except one. A
highly introverted individual would most likely have a difficult time coping with a group situation requiring cooperation and close physical proximity, and would seem more
suited for some type of solo endeavor. On the other hand, one
should note that the social support and communication pro-
cesses of the group were described by a number of team
members as rather superficial or perhaps restrained. This lack

of personal sharing or emotional intimacy may actually have been adaptive and consonant with the goals of this group, since too much personal revelation and expression of vulnerabilities might have interfered with the task-oriented mission of the group. It appears from this investigation that effective social support in demanding situations does not necessarily involve a great deal of emotional intimacy.

These members of the North Pole Expedition Team formed a unique group in a unique situation. The assessment of their personality characteristics and coping styles in response to the demands of the expedition is informative. It highlights psychological patterns found adaptive under conditions characterized by sustained but relatively time limited physical stress, a high level of skill and preparation, and the fact that the participants shared extremely strong group objectives. The findings have relevance for enhancing the selection process for other groups that must function in highly challenging conditions necessitating close proximity of members and acceding to leader decisions. In task-oriented groups, planful problem solving is an important coping strategy, as is positive reappraisal in disappointing and unchangeable situations. Flexibility in employing a variety of coping strategies as the situation warrants may be highly adaptive to the accomplishment of a group mission and to maintaining a positive mood state.

APPENDIX G

MEDICAL PROFILE OF THE STEGER TEAM*

(CHANGES IN DIET, BODY COMPOSITION, AND BLOOD LIPID LEVELS OF MEMBERS OF THE STEGER INTERNATIONAL POLAR EXPEDITION)

The Steger International Polar Expedition presented a unique opportunity to study the effects on blood lipid levels of extreme physical activity, an extremely high-fat diet, and extreme environmental conditions. The daily rations planned for the expedition consisted of butter, pemmican, peanut butter, egg noodles, and oatmeal. Such a diet would be expected, under normal conditions, to increase blood cholesterol levels, particularly the low density lipoprotein (LDL) fraction, which increases the risk of heart disease. On the other hand, physical activity has been shown to moderately increase blood levels of high density lipoprotein (HDL) cholesterol, which is protective for heart disease.

Assessments of diet and blood lipid levels were made on members of the Expedition team two months and one week before the expedition, in Minnesota and in Frobisher Bay, Canada, respectively. Body weight and body composition were assessed pre-expedition only in Minnesota. Dietary records were maintained during the expedition. Body weight and composition and blood lipid levels were reassessed in Minnesota within one week following completion of the expedition. Complete data was available on six of the eight team members. Results of analysis on those six members (five male, one female) are reported.

Weight and body composition changes, pre- and post-expedition, were minimal (Table 1). Two male members of the team, on the pre-expedition evaluations, were overweight

*Prepared by Dr. Lawrence Kushi, Dr. Carl McNally, and Dr. Arthur Leon, Division of Epidemiology, University of Minnesota. Used by permission.

303

TABLE 1.

Mean Body Weight and Body Composition Profiles[1]

| | PRE-EXPEDITION | | POST-EXPEDITION | | |
	MEAN	(RANGE)	MEAN	(RANGE)	CHANGE
BODY WEIGHT (LBS.)	160.1	(125.5–198.25)	164.5	(130.25–197.0)	+4.4
PERCENT BODY FATNESS (FROM SUM 7 SKIN-FOLDS)	11.9	(6.3–20.4)	11.3	(5.1–19.9)	−0.6
BODY MASS INDEX	23.7	(20.8–28.4)	24.4	(21.2–28.3)	+0.7

TABLE 2.

Mean Serum Lipid Profiles[1]

| LIPID (MG/DL): | PRE-EXPEDITION[2] | | POST-EXPEDITION | | |
	MEAN	(RANGE)	MEAN	(RANGE)	CHANGE
TOTAL CHOLES-TEROL	175.9	(140.5–199.5)	191.3	(145.0–217.0)	+15.4
TRIGLYC-ERIDES	59.8	(34.5–95.5)	70.3	(41.0–128.0)	+10.5
HDL	80.0	(66.5–101.0)	93.3	(69.0–116.0)	+13.3
LDL	83.7	(52.5–112.5)	84.2	(67.0–107.0)	+0.5
VLDL	9.6	(8.0–11.5)	13.8	(5.0–25.0)	+1.3

1. Two team members with incomplete data were excluded from analysis.
2. Average of Minnesota and Frobisher Bay determinations

based on height-weight standards; however, only one of them was found to be slightly obese by skinfold measurements.

Three-day dietary records were completed by the team members before the expedition. During the expedition, predetermined rations were consumed. Individual team members' variations in these rations were noted in two expedition logbooks. Mean pre-expedition energy intake was 3,755 kilocalories (Kcals) per day, which is well above average for North Americans. This likely reflects the team's high pre-expedition physical training level. Their pre-expedition diet consisted of 15.8% of the total Kcals from protein, 49.0% from fat, and 32.1% from carbohydrate, and about 900 mg/day of cholesterol. Almost one-half of the team's total fat was from saturated fats. During the expedition, their mean energy intake increased to 7,812 Kcals/day, with 13.7% of the total Kcals from protein, 22.0% from carbohydrate, and 65.7% from fat (47.5% of fat was saturated fats). Dietary cholesterol intake increased to nearly 1,200 mg/day.

The team's high energy intake during the course of the expedition and stable body weight reflect the extremely high physical exertion experienced by the team. Table 2 shows the pre-expedition and post-expedition blood lipid levels. Baseline total cholesterol and triglyceride concentrations were low compared to average North Americans, with quite favorable levels of HDL. During the expedition, there was a significant increase in total cholesterol levels (+15.4 mg/dl), but this was primarily a result of an increase in HDL levels (+13.3 mg/dl).

It was anticipated from the high dietary intake of saturated fat and cholesterol that a sizable increase would occur in the LDL fraction. This was apparently aborted by the high level of physical exertion.

ABOUT THE AUTHORS

WILL STEGER has explored the North by kayak, ski, and dogsled on twelve major expeditions over the last twenty-five years. A former science teacher, he has established a business teaching winter camping skills and a reputation for superb outdoor photography. Steger lives near Ely, Minnesota, and is planning the first dogsled traverse of Antartica.

PAUL SCHURKE worked as a science writer while helping establish Wilderness Inquiry, an adventure program for disabled persons. He first teamed up with Steger in 1981 to offer dogsled trips for that program. Schurke and his wife, Susan Hendrickson, have one daughter, Bria, and operate Wintergreen, a ski-camping and winter-apparel business in Ely.